"For most film lovers, the turn to the small screen has been something to lament. But Carol Owens and Sarah Meehan O'Callaghan, along with their excellent contributors, show that with something lost, something has also been gained. In a series of illuminating essays, *Psychoanalysis and the Small Screen* shows us the incredible theoretical riches that the small screen makes evident, riches that the cinematic experience often obscures. For anyone wanting to understand why we are always looking at our screens and for those who want to make sense of our contemporary moment, this is a collection absolutely not to be missed."

**Todd McGowan**, Professor of Film Studies, University of Vermont, USA

"Carol Owens and Sarah Meehan O'Callaghan in this compelling collection of essays invite us to reflect on the question of subjectivity once again during the latest pandemic, the year when cinemas closed. Broad in its scope – ranging from socio-cultural studies, philosophy and art to psychoanalysis – the contributors to this collection have provided a new perspective on what shapes our reality in the contemporary techno-mediated world. This collection with a Lacanian focus offers a unique way to explore and investigate different dimensions of the impact of screens on the theory and practice of psychoanalysis."

**Berjanet Jazani**, M.D, Author, Psychoanalyst, President of The College of Psychoanalysts UK

"In the old days we used to enter into the dark room of a cinema to behold a feast laid out before our eyes, larger than life. This phantasmagoria has now entered into our lives on small screens that consume us. Welcome to the metaverse! Though none of us has a hold, reading this book helps to find the ground only psychoanalysis can begin again to put beneath our feet."

**Jamieson Webster**, Psychoanalyst, Author, Assistant Professor, New School for Social Research, NYC, USA

# Psychoanalysis and the Small Screen

*Psychoanalysis and the Small Screen* examines the impact of cinema closures and the shift to small-screen consumption on our aesthetic and subjective desires during the COVID-19 pandemic from a Lacanian perspective.

The chapters in this text hold a unique focus on the intersections of film, psychoanalysis, and the subjective implications of the shift from cinema to the small screen of domestic space. The subjects span historical and current Lacanian thinking, including the representation of psychoanalysis as artifice, Lacan appearing on television, the travails and tribulations of computer mediated analysis, the traumatrope, and the techno-inflected imagined social bond of what Jacques Lacan called the 'alethosphere'. In this collection, the socio-cultural narratives and Real disruptions of the pandemic are framed as a function of the paradoxes of enjoyment characteristic of Lacanian psychoanalysis rather than merely the psychosocial repercussions of a planetary and contingent disaster.

With contributions from practicing psychoanalysts, as well as academics working in related interdisciplinary areas, *Psychoanalysis and the Small Screen* will have appeal to readers of contemporary Lacanian work in general, to readers and researchers of contemporary psychoanalytic studies, and transdisciplinary and intersectional scholars engaged in psychoanalytic, cultural, and psycho-social research.

**Carol Owens** is a psychoanalyst and psychoanalytic scholar in Dublin, Ireland. She is the founder of the Dublin Lacan study group, co-organiser of the Irish Psychoanalytic Film Festival, and has published widely on the theory and practice of Lacanian psychoanalysis. She is series editor for Routledge's *Studying Lacan's Seminars* series. Her most recent book is *Psychoanalysing Ambivalence: On and Off the Couch with Freud and Lacan* (with Stephanie Swales, Routledge, 2020).

**Sarah Meehan O'Callaghan** is an independent scholar within the fields of Lacanian psychoanalysis, body/disability, drama, and sexuality studies. Her PhD was an interdisciplinary study of the trauma of the body in the drama of Artaud, Beckett and Genet within a Lacanian psychoanalytic perspective. She has published psychoanalytic articles on themes such as disability, sexuality, the phallus, and the intersections of phenomenology and psychoanalysis. She is co-organiser of the Irish Psychoanalytic Film Festival.

The Lines of the Symbolic in Psychoanalysis Series

Series Editor:
Ian Parker, *Manchester Psychoanalytic Matrix*

Psychoanalytic clinical and theoretical work is always embedded in specific linguistic and cultural contexts and carries their traces, traces which this series attends to in its focus on multiple contradictory and antagonistic 'lines of the Symbolic'. This series takes its cue from Lacan's psychoanalytic work on three registers of human experience, the Symbolic, the Imaginary and the Real, and employs this distinctive understanding of cultural, communication and embodiment to link with other traditions of cultural, clinical and theoretical practice beyond the Lacanian symbolic universe. The Lines of the Symbolic in Psychoanalysis Series provides a reflexive reworking of theoretical and practical issues, translating psychoanalytic writing from different contexts, grounding that work in the specific histories and politics that provide the conditions of possibility for its descriptions and interventions to function. The series makes connections between different cultural and disciplinary sites in which psychoanalysis operates, questioning the idea that there could be one single correct reading and application of Lacan. Its authors trace their own path, their own line through the Symbolic, situating psychoanalysis in relation to debates which intersect with Lacanian work, explicating it, extending it and challenging it.

**Psychoanalysis and the New Rhetoric**
Freud, Burke, Lacan, and Philosophy's Other Scenes
*Daniel Adleman and Chris Vanderwees*

**Speculating on the Edge of Psychoanalysis**
Rings and Voids
*Pablo Lerner*

**Psychoanalysis and the Small Screen**
The Year the Cinemas Closed
*Edited by Carol Owens and Sarah Meehan O'Callaghan*

For more information about the series, please visit: https://www.routledge.com/The-Lines-of-the-Symbolic-in-Psychoanalysis-Series/book-series/KARNLOS

# Psychoanalysis and the Small Screen

The Year the Cinemas Closed

Edited by
Carol Owens and Sarah Meehan O'Callaghan

LONDON AND NEW YORK

Designed cover image: Getty | RosLol

First published 2024
by Routledge
4 Park Square, Milton Park, Abingdon, Oxon OX14 4RN

and by Routledge
605 Third Avenue, New York, NY 10158

*Routledge is an imprint of the Taylor & Francis Group, an informa business*

© 2024 selection and editorial matter, Carol Owens and Sarah Meehan O'Callaghan; individual chapters, the contributors

The right of Carol Owens and Sarah Meehan O'Callaghan to be identified as the authors of the editorial material, and of the authors for their individual chapters, has been asserted in accordance with sections 77 and 78 of the Copyright, Designs and Patents Act 1988.

All rights reserved. No part of this book may be reprinted or reproduced or utilised in any form or by any electronic, mechanical, or other means, now known or hereafter invented, including photocopying and recording, or in any information storage or retrieval system, without permission in writing from the publishers.

*Trademark notice*: Product or corporate names may be trademarks or registered trademarks, and are used only for identification and explanation without intent to infringe.

*British Library Cataloguing-in-Publication Data*
A catalogue record for this book is available from the British Library

ISBN: 978-1-032-22320-9 (hbk)
ISBN: 978-1-032-22322-3 (pbk)
ISBN: 978-1-003-27206-9 (ebk)

DOI: 10.4324/9781003272069

Typeset in Times New Roman
by Taylor & Francis Books

This book is fondly dedicated to Olga Cox Cameron: psychoanalyst, film-enthusiast extraordinaire, and founder of The Irish Psychoanalytic Film Festival.

# Contents

*About the Editors*   xi
*List of Contributors*   xii
*Preface*   xvi
*Acknowledgments*   xx

Introduction: Psychoanalysis and the Small Screen   1
SARAH MEEHAN O'CALLAGHAN AND CAROL OWENS

1 (In)Continent Topology of Pandemics, Screens, and Scripts   11
DON KUNZE

2 Digital Tectonics and Cinematic Intimacy: An Epidemiological/Psychoanalytic Perspective   27
ROBERT KILROY

3 At the Mercy of the Screen: Passivity and its Vicissitudes in a Time of Crisis   46
SARAH MEEHAN O'CALLAGHAN

4 *Undine*: Siren Screens   64
JESSICA DATEMA AND MANYA STEINKOLER

5 Prohibition and Power: *Normal People* as Pandemic Pornography   78
ERICA D. GALIOTO

6 Weeping On and Off Screen: Truth, Falsity, and Art   95
MILES LINK

7 "The thing did not dissatisfy me"?: Lacanian perspectives on transference and AI-driven psychotherapeutic chatbots   112
MICHAEL HOLOHAN

| | | |
|---|---|---|
| 8 | The Rise of the *Lathouses*: Some consequences for the speaking being and the social bond<br>HILDA FERNANDEZ-ALVAREZ | 132 |
| 9 | Lacan on the "Telly": Psychoanalysis on the Small Screen<br>CAROL OWENS AND EVE WATSON | 149 |
| 10 | Power and Politics in Adam Curtis' *Can't Get You Out Of My Head*: An Emotional History of the Modern World<br>ISABEL MILLAR, BRETT NICHOLLS, ROSEMARY OVERELL AND DANIEL TUTT | 163 |
| | Afterword<br>OLGA COX CAMERON | 190 |
| | *Index* | 196 |

# About the Editors

**Carol Owens**, PhD, is a psychoanalyst and psychoanalytic scholar in Dublin, Ireland. A registered practitioner member of APPI, board member of APCS, affiliate member of CP-UK, she is the founder of the Dublin Lacan study group and co-organiser of the Irish Psychoanalytic Film Festival. She has published widely on the theory and practice of Lacanian psychoanalysis. Her most recent book is *Psychoanalysing Ambivalence with Freud and Lacan: On and Off the Couch* with Stephanie Swales (Routledge, 2019). She is series editor for *Studying Lacan's Seminars* published by Routledge. The most recent volume in the series, *Studying Lacan's Seminar VI: Dream, Symptom, and the Collapse of Subjectivity*, was published in 2021. She is the *PCS Review* coordinating editor at *Psychoanalysis, Culture and Society*.

**Sarah Meehan O'Callaghan**, PhD, is an independent scholar within the fields of Lacanian psychoanalysis, body/disability, drama, and sexuality studies. Her PhD was an interdisciplinary study of the trauma of the body in the drama of Artaud, Beckett, and Genet within a Lacanian psychoanalytic perspective. She has published articles on psychoanalysis on themes such as: disability, sexuality, the phallus, and the intersections of phenomenology and psychoanalysis. She is co-organiser of the Irish Psychoanalytic Film Festival. She is a member of EROSS@DCU (Expressions, Research, Orientations: Sexuality Studies) and was co-organiser of several conferences on the theme of arts, disability, and sexuality.

# Contributors

**Olga Cox Cameron**'s first career was in literary studies, having written an MA thesis on Proust, worked as a tutor in the Department of French at University College, Dublin, and started – but did not complete – a PhD on Beckett at the University of Fribourg in Switzerland. Following a decade of working with homeless people in Dublin she trained as a psychoanalyst at St. Vincent's University Hospital, completed a PhD on narrative (im)possibilities in psychosis, and has been in private practice for the past 34 years. She lectured in Psychoanalytic Theory and Psychoanalysis and Literature at St. Vincent's University Hospital and Trinity College from 1991 to 2013 and has published numerous articles on these topics in national and international journals. She is the founder of the annual Irish Psychoanalysis and Cinema Festival, now in its 13th year and in 2021 published *Studying Lacan's Seminar VI: Dream, Symptom, and the Collapse of Subjectivity* (Routledge, 2021).

**Jessica Datema** has a PhD in Comparative Literature and an MA in Philosophy (SUNY Binghamton), is Professor of Composition and Literature at Bergen Community College and lives in Brooklyn, New York. Dr Datema also received a creative writing certificate for studies accomplished at the University of Cambridge. Dr. Datema has co-edited three volumes, most recently *Movement, Velocity, and Rhythm from a Psychoanalytic Perspective* (Routledge, 2022), *Revisioning War Trauma in Cinema* (Lexington Books, 2019), and *Wretched Refuge: Immigrants and Itinerants in the Postmodern* (Cambridge Scholars Publishing, 2010). She is currently an editor for *Psychoanalysis, Culture and Society* and regularly publishes and presents on psychoanalysis as well as literary and philosophical theory.

**Hilda Fernandez-Alvarez** is a Lacanian psychoanalyst based in Vancouver, Canada. She has a vast wealth of clinical experience with diverse populations in public and private settings in Mexico and Canada. She has a Master's degree in clinical psychology from Universidad Nacional Autonoma de Mexico (UNAM), a Master's degree in literature from University of British Columbia (UBC) and a PhD in Geography from Simon Fraser University (SFU). Her research, published in various articles and book chapters, has focused on the theory and practice of psychoanalysis with a link to the socio-political context. She is an academic associate with the Institute for the Humanities at SFU and she co-founded the Lacan Salon in 2007, currently serving as its clinical director.

**Erica D. Galioto** is Associate Professor of English at Shippensburg University, where she teaches courses in Contemporary Literature and Psychoanalysis. Recent publications include articles on Gillian Flynn's *Gone Girl*, Sapphire's *Push*, A.M. Homes' *The End of Alice*, and Alison Bechdel's *Fun Home*. Erica's article "Autotheory and the Maternal: My Impossible Mother-Daughter Separation" was just featured in the *Journal of Psychosocial Studies*.

**Michael Holohan** has an interdisciplinary background in psychoanalysis, psychotherapy, literary theory, and philosophy. He holds a PhD in the History of Consciousness from the University of California Santa Cruz, and an MSc in Psychoanalytic Psychotherapy from the School of Medicine, University College Dublin. Michael is currently a postdoctoral researcher at the Institute of History and Ethics in Medicine at the School of Medicine, Technical University of Munich, where he explores the relationship between different conceptions of the mind in psychoanalysis and biomedicine and the relevance of psychoanalytic thought for contemporary biomedical practice, research, and ethics. Michael is also a psychoanalyst in private practice in Munich. He is a member of the Association for Psychoanalysis and Psychotherapy in Ireland and the Irish Council for Psychotherapy.

**Robert Thomas Kilroy**'s work interrogates the boundaries between Art History, Aesthetics, and Lacanian Psychoanalysis by way of an encounter between the cultural theorist Slavoj Žižek and the artist Marcel Duchamp. He publishes widely on the 'parallax' relation between psychoanalytic theory and visual studies with a view to addressing the impact of digital culture on contemporary subjectivity. He currently lectures in Art History, Aesthetics, and Visual Studies at the Sorbonne University Abu Dhabi.

**Don Kunze** has taught Architecture and Art Theory at Penn State, The University at Buffalo, Louisiana State University, and the Washington-Alexandria Architecture Center of Virginia Tech. He is presently an independent researcher-educator focused on the psychoanalytical study of architecture and landscape. His dissertation (Geography, Penn State, 1983) was about the place-theoretics of Giambattista Vico. He has lectured and written about film, boundaries, topology, literary theory, Lacan, and Vico.

**Miles Link** is in formation as a psychoanalytic practitioner in Dublin. He holds a PhD in English Literature from Trinity College Dublin. He is originally from Philadelphia.

**Isabel Millar** is a philosopher and psychoanalytic theorist from London. She is the author of *The Psychoanalysis of Artificial Intelligence*, published in the Palgrave Lacan Series in 2021, and *Patipolitics* (forthcoming with Bloomsbury in 2023). As well as extensive international academic speaking and publishing, her work can be found across a variety of media, including TV, podcasts, magazines, and art institutes. She is faculty at The Global Centre for Advanced Studies, Institute of Psychoanalysis, and Associate Researcher, Department of Philosophy, Newcastle University. For more information on Isabel visit www.isabelmillar.com

**Brett Nicholls** is head of Media, Film, and Communication at the University of Otago, New Zealand. Most recently he published, with Rosie Overell, an edited volume titled *Post-Truth and the Mediation of Reality* (Palgrave Macmillan, 2019). He is editor of *Borderlands Journal: Culture, Politics, Law and Earth* and the new journal, *Baudrillard Now*.

**Rosemary Overell** is a Senior Lecturer in the Department of Communications and New Media at National University of Singapore. Her work focuses on psychoanalysis, mediatisation, and gender. She tweets from @muzaken and her email is overell@nus.edu.sg

**Ian Parker** is co-director of the Discourse Unit (www.discourseunit.com), secretary of Manchester Psychoanalytic Matrix, and a practising psychoanalyst in Manchester. His books include *Psychoanalysis, Clinic and Context: Subjectivity, History and Autobiography* (Routledge, 2019), and, with David Pavón-Cuéllar, *Psychoanalysis and Revolution: Critical Psychology for Liberation Movements* (1968 Press, 2021).

**Manya Steinkoler** is a psychoanalyst and Professor in the English Department of BMCC City University of New York. She is the co-editor, along with Patricia Gherovici, of *Psychoanalysis, Gender, and Sexuality: From Feminism to Trans* (Routledge, 2022), co-author with Jessica Datema of *Revisioning War Trauma in Cinema: Uncoming Communities* (Lexington Books, 2019), co-editor with Vanessa Sinclair of *On Psychoanalysis and Violence: Contemporary Lacanian Perspectives* (Routledge, 2018), co-editor with Patricia Gherovici of *Lacan, Psychoanalysis, and Comedy* (Cambridge University Press, 2016), and with Patricia Gherovici, *Lacan on Madness: Madness Yes You Can't* (Routledge, 2015).

**Daniel Tutt** is the author of *Psychoanalysis and the Politics of the Family*, part of the Palgrave Lacan Series, and is currently writing a book on Nietzsche and politics with Repeater Books. He lectures in Philosophy at George Washington University, Marymount University, and the Global Centre for Advanced Studies. His essays have appeared in *Philosophy Now, Huffington Post, Spectre Magazine*, and *Historical Materialism*.

**Eve Watson**, PhD, is a psychoanalytic practitioner and university lecturer in Dublin. She has published several dozen articles on psychoanalysis, sexuality, and film. She co-edited the book *Clinical Encounters in Sexuality: Psychoanalytic Practice and Queer Theory* (Punctum, 2017) and is course director of the Freud-Lacan Institute. She is working on book projects on the drive, Freud's case studies, and film and in 2022 was the Erikson Scholar-in-Residence at the Austen-Riggs Centre in Massachusetts.

# Preface

Our life-world of film, a domain of reality that is an intimate part of our society of the spectacle, has in some respects been shrunken down during this latest pandemic. This book examines how that happened in the year the cinemas closed.

Film is now not only an intimate part of the spectacle, but intimate to us; the forms of subjectivity it rolls in front of our eyes quickly unspool behind them, inside us, becoming part of our own subjectivity. Psychoanalysis has always had something to say about the big screen, and now, of course, it has more to say, it has an even more richly elaborated array of discursive devices to speak to us about who we become in the more intimate space of our own home, when the screen is smaller. But we need to ask why that is, why it is that psychoanalysis speaks to us about film almost as deeply as film itself does.

First, there is a question of content, of the feeding of psychoanalytic motifs into film, so that film criticism becomes an exercise in unravelling what has been spooled into the object being examined. This happens in US and then globalised film culture remarkably early on, and film then becomes one of the virtual microbial cultures of psychoanalysis. Take Howard Hawks' *Ball of Fire*, for example, from 1941, in which characters refer explicitly to 'psychoanalytical' explanations of the message unwittingly or covertly, it is not clear which, passed from Barbara Stanwyck to Gary Cooper. This box office hit also sent a message to the audience that marked significant interpersonal, and, by implication, intra-personal messages as being in some way 'psychoanalytical'.

Second, more potent still, is the question of form: of how it is that the texture of film, flickering snapshots of reality are chained together to fabricate the illusion that there is a moving image on the screen that is more vibrant, charged with affect; this so that the plot money-shot injects not only a sense that there is something cathartic about the compression and conclusion of a narrative, but also another message about the nature of reality and subjectivity itself. Directors have often struggled to portray dreams in film precisely because film already harnesses and reconfigures reality as if it were a dream fragment that, at some point, will yield its meaning. The Dalí sequence in Hitchcock's 1945 *Spellbound* is a notorious case in point. The critic and academic are hooked into this game as surely as is the viewer, but they draw on a specific kind of language to pin it down, a language that is often structured as if it is psychoanalytic.

Then, as we learn to speak about film, those of us who are not critics or academics, the uncanny and unsatisfying, the realistic and moving character of what we have watched together in the cinema also become, bit by bit, structured by the same range of psychoanalytic rhetorical devices. Psychoanalytic discourse now inhabits everyday life, appearing to give access to hidden depths while repeatedly structuring the sense that there are hidden depths – in the film and in ourselves as we respond to it – in the working over of content and in the replication of form. In both cases, to be able to convey to someone else who has seen the same film that one 'understands' it requires that the meanings be grasped and moulded; the meaning of film always lies in its use. Filmic discourse does not only describe the world but creates affiliation, identification even, among those who employ that discourse, identification that often also requires disjunction, disagreement, the idea that the film is not completely exhausted of meaning. Film is, in this sense, constituted as if it were a subject, never fully able to reveal itself to us.

One of the effects of the streaming into the home of film, and of the blurring of boundaries between cinema and television, is that this enigmatic and inexhaustible character of the filmic narrative is intensified. The box-sets we glut on take on even more the character of a dream, extended, fragmented and inconclusive. In contrast to the apparently rounded out delimited vignette that a classic mass-market film usually is, the box-set narrative usually begins with a premise, a promise and then by series four, say, a lingering unsatisfying trailing off. This is then less triumphant finish than ruined orgasm, something closer to what it is to shy away from impossible enjoyment, and in that case the teasing and failing is a function of viewing figures and advertising revenue. The drivers are economic, but the drives are privatised, and the excitement and disappointment located inside each individual viewer.

The time-compression and sense of personal control of what streaming into the home brings are new questions for psychoanalysis. Or rather, an intensification of the old questions about how we are positioned as subjects in relation to a symbolic medium that seems to express what we want while impressing on us a complex contradictory series of wants from somewhere beyond us. Now it is as if the Other is with us inside our homes asking us what we want while instructing us about the permissible parameters of what we can want and tantalising us about the prospect of there being something more. It was ever thus, but now, in the context of the Pandemic, the small screen reminds us that there is a big screen to which we might one day return, should want to return to.

This is what 'looping' is, with psychoanalysis as one of the looping effects of film and television, and now the more intensely privatised experience of streaming the moving image into our own homes. Psychoanalysis is very well able to comment on what is happening here precisely because it is woven into the phenomenon itself. A looping effect is a particular kind of feedback in which we are subjectively implicated in what is described such that what we describe to ourselves becomes the stuff of our subjectivity. In the case of psychoanalysis, this looping is tantalisingly incomplete; it must be so for psychoanalysis to work, for film re-activates the discourse and the experience of there being something unsaid, something unconscious. One of the indications that the psychoanalytic looping effect is at work is when phenomena specific to the clinic, specific to the strange artificial relationship between analyst and analysand, spill out into everyday life. Then we resonate with them onscreen because we assume that what we see resonates with the kind of beings we are.

Here is one TV example. The CEO of Netflix tells us that their only competition is sleep, but this example is from the dream-world laid out by Amazon Prime Video. Take episode three of the 2015 mini-series *Mr Robot*, for example. Mr Robot, played by Christian Slater, masterfully incites and manipulates what we might quite understandably take to be 'transference' to him on the part of Elliot Alderson, the neurotic hacker played by Rami Malek. Mr Robot, the master, goads Elliot about his relationship with his father and repeatedly 'interprets' this failed relationship as also concerning him, Robot; he thereby structures the choices Elliot must make, not so much as the way in, but as if the way out of his prison, and that means Elliot must choose to work with Mr Robot. It is as if Christian Slater is also simultaneously playing the part of a stereotypical IPA-analyst from hell, provoking, constituting the transference so that it can be put to work, as if what drives it comes from inside his victim. Never underestimate the canny ability of the writers to pop in to the box-set what we then imagine we are so clever in detecting there. What should be noticed here is not merely the framing of the relationship, but its own internal looping effects within the narrative of the series, and then, of course, the questions it raises about why it would be that someone should carry on watching the thing.

We carry on watching this stuff because we enjoy it, but it is the patterning of that enjoyment that is the issue here. Of course we then enjoy excavating new meaning, mastering what is unresolved in the narrative. Rather like this particular pandemic itself, which is a narrative with an uncertain beginning and even more uncertain ending, every attempt to create a metalanguage that will master film must fail. We can then be sure that the parasitic industry of professional academic criticism, including journals and conferences devoted to psychoanalytic discourse, will find confirmation of underlying psychoanalytic assumptions that they make. The work of interpretation here is unending because there is nothing to be done save plugging and unplugging the gaps in subjectivity that film plays its own part in creating and re-creating. This book loops psychoanalysis into film, showing how the symbolic spools its way into how we imagine ourselves as viewers and subjects in times of pandemic, when we were hit by the real.

Psychoanalytic clinical and theoretical work circulates through multiple intersecting antagonistic symbolic universes. This series opens connections between different cultural sites in which Lacanian work has developed in distinctive ways, in forms of work that question the idea that there could be single correct reading and application. The Lines of the Symbolic in Psychoanalysis series provides a reflexive reworking of psychoanalysis that transmits Lacanian writing from around the world, steering a course between the temptations of a metalanguage and imaginary reduction, between the claim to provide a god's eye view of psychoanalysis and the idea that psychoanalysis must everywhere be the same. And the elaboration of psychoanalysis in the symbolic here grounds its theory and practice in the history and politics of the work in a variety of interventions that touch the real.

Ian Parker
Manchester Psychoanalytic Matrix

# Acknowledgments

When it came to planning the annual Irish Psychoanalysis and Film festival for 2021, we realised that the festival would not be able to take place in its traditional venue (Dublin City University), or in its traditional frame (a two-day event filled with film presentations and discussions, wine and food, chats over coffee and cake in the mornings). The festival in its traditional format owes much to the team effort variously composed over the years, latterly of the hard-working, good-natured Marie Walshe, the inimitable culinary skills and calm head in the eye of the storm Liz Monahan, the sparkling creativity of Barbara Fitzgerald, and the wonderful Gerry Moore of DCU School of Nursing, Psychotherapy and Community Health for hosting the event for us for the last few years. In 2021 a stripped-down team of two – Carol and Sarah – put the festival together as an online event foregrounding the very cause of its transformation from cinema (the big screen presentations of our films hitherto) to the small screens (of our individual laptops, PCs, and iPads). The event was titled 'The Year the Cinemas Closed: Psychoanalysing Shifting Screens', and was a terrific gig considering how much it had to measure up to, arguably one of the most fun dates in the Irish psychoanalytic calendar! So, the first people we want to thank are the wonderful presenters at that event, some of whom are here in this volume with extended versions of their presentations: thank you Patricia Gherovici, Jamieson Webster, Ian Parker, Eve Watson, Don Kunze, Miles Link, and Robert Kilroy. The Irish Psychoanalysis and film festival is the brainchild of Olga Cox Cameron and we take this opportunity to thank her for all the incredible work of the years in putting the festival together and creating the spirit of the festival which even though she has retired from the organisation side of things continues to inspire those of us who are still involved. We are delighted to have Olga's contribution to this volume in the form of the Afterword. And we thank all those who 'showed up' to the online event and who were interested, engaged, and warmly receptive.

It became clear that there was a lot to say about the shift from the big screen to the small screens and we really want to thank all the contributors to this book for going back to their papers and working them up as longer essays. We also thank all the other contributors for responding so beautifully to our invitation to become involved whose work we felt would really speak to this time, and these themes.

We thank series editor Ian Parker for his generous welcome of the book in his series *The Lines in the Symbolic in Psychoanalysis*. Lastly, we fondly thank Ellie Duncan and Susannah Frearson from Routledge for their warm and enthusiastic engagement with the project throughout.

# Introduction

Psychoanalysis and the Small Screen

*Sarah Meehan O'Callaghan and Carol Owens*

## The Age of the Screens

This is the age of the screens. In this epoch, the human being is a thoroughly techno-mediated subject, where screens and devices dominate and infiltrate all aspects of life. This fact of contemporary 21st century life was made ever more immanent during the COVID-19 pandemic; accelerating the pace and quantity of time spent on/through the virtual realm. The momentum of change in any form or discipline (and also individually) is always challenging and as Frankel and Krebs (2022) argue it is important to hold an open mind regarding the impact of technology and to avoid providing reductive or dichotomous explanations for its negative or positive effects. Brian Massumi's (2017) *The Principle of Unrest* comments on this unstoppable movement of cultural adaptation, mutation and transformation. There is no such thing as rest, forms of displacement continuously shift us into different modes of becoming. From one epoque to the other, psycho-cultural reality, and by extension, human existence, is never stable, never remaining static or the same. Indeed, in our current times, reality is a contentious word, not just philosophically or psychoanalytically, but because the very ground upon which we walk could be a digitally represented simulacrum of social space. The door of the contemporary world has literally and figuratively opened onto virtual space and virtual reality. As the title of the documentary *Screenagers* suggests (2016), technology is the dominant medium for young people today and poses many challenges, for better or worse. We do not have to wonder why the small screen, in its various guises/manifestations, has proved to be so seductive and ubiquitous in everyday life.

In psychoanalytic terms, the screen is a literal, figurative and dynamic phenomenon. A screen is the material phenomenon separating us, our bodies, from the other in the context of cyberspace but it is also the intangible conceptual screen that separates and inflects fantasy from reality in a psychical sense. As early as 1899, Freud wrote about the phenomenon of *Screen Memories*, a type of "false" memory, where an apparent visual memory screens out or disguises another earlier traumatic event or scene (see Levine and Reed,

2015, and Giffney, 2021). A screen memory is "one which owes its value as a memory not to its own content but to the relation existing between that content and some other, that has been suppressed" (Freud, 1899a, cited in Levine and Reed, p. 22). Most importantly from Freud's definition, we can conceptualise the screen as a border phenomenon, that which is relational, in between, non-binary, and also malleable, shape changing and susceptible to the imprint of desire. In the sense of the psychic economy, the screen thus conceals and reveals; it can be a mechanism of defence and of revelation. Furthermore, if we think in geometric terms and from the perspective of Lacan's topographical thought from his ninth seminar *Identification*, we can conceptualise the screen as a surface, that which divides three-dimensional reality and yet unites or bleeds into it at the same time. The definition of a surface in geometric terms is "a continuous boundary dividing a three-dimensional space into two regions" (Source, *Britannica*). In this way, we can think of the screen, not so much a surface that cuts and divides reality into an inside or outside, but a surface that leaks or leads one reality into another while appearing to preserve an external and differential front – a form of (in) continence, as a flowing into and not an insulation from (see Don Kunze's chapter, this volume). This ambiguity of psychic *screening in* (a way of seeing and experiencing) and *screening out* (a form of defence against experiencing) as that which shields us from painful events and memories can also be considered within the context of cinema, film, and the artistic, aesthetic realm in general. The material technological screen is the source of projections, the reel of film as it is played on a device, and the Real of the subject's fantasies as the playing out of the dialectic between viewer and spectacle.

The spectator of a film can encounter many ideas, feelings, and images that may be repressed or suppressed and brought to life by the filmic narrative. Whether we can really experience trauma or be radically changed through the modality of film or any art form is a moot point; we can certainly be provoked into thinking, feeling and analysing many things, conscious and unconscious (a point surely made better by Slavoj Žižek than perhaps anyone else over the past 20 odd years). Similarly, the visual spectacle of film also offers the potential for identifications, idealisations and escapism from the reality of painful feelings of inadequacy, through for example, heroic genre movies and romantic comedies. Thus, the screen is a bridge to multiple dimensions of reality, a surface that is seductively expansive and perilously porous. For Lacan, the function of the screen characterises the human subject, a subject of desire, as different from the animal, completely caught up, arguably, in the imaginary capture of the image (Lacan, 1964/78, p. 107). Ultimately in psychoanalytic terms, as regards a screen, the subject is a spectator, agent or onlooker but also an object of the screen. As unconscious subjects, we are never simply agents but subjects, with a certain deference that the word implies. As derived from Latin *subjectus*, "subject" was to be "placed beneath, inferior, open to inspection", and was originally the past participle of *subicere* "to throw or place beneath, make subject". The resonance of being placed beneath, subject to and traumatically implicated within is captured in Lacan's theory of the gaze (1964) as object a, object cause of desire. A notoriously difficult concept of Lacan's, the gaze captures the subject "in its trap" through the mediation of the screen in its capacity as mask. While Lacan's extrapolations on the gaze, as Real object cause of desire, have become increasingly prevalent within film theory, (see Todd McGowan, 2007) they have featured less so within theories of the screen, virtuality and subjectivity, (see Link, and Meehan O'Callaghan, this volume). In psychoanalytic studies generally, we have long known about the analogies drawn with the pictorial cinematic image and that of the workings of the unconscious, in particular those of dreams, with their condensations and displacements. Furthermore, it is not simply what psychoanalysis can teach us about film that is relevant, but also about what film and cinema can teach us about psychoanalysis (see Kunze, Datema and Steinkoler, Kilroy, and Galioto, in this volume).

Ostensibly, the human subject knows how to play with the screen that functions as the mask of desire (Lacan, 1964/78, p. 107). The word playing should be emphasised here as we consider the implications of jouissance (and see Fernandez Alvarez, this volume) as a corollary to this 'playing' with the screen for the contemporary subject.

## Psychoanalysis on the Small Screen...

The title of this collection of essays also plays with the drama of the subject of the unconscious; on the one hand allowing for the interrogation of some of the implications of the heightening of what is already a phenomenon of our times – living/working/learning/playing/enjoying with screens – here we can think of the visual techno-screen and all its avatars (chat bots, TV series, Zoom encounters, digital social media etc). On the other hand the title plays with and attempts to sharpen our focus on the phenomenon of our Covidian times which saw the shrinking of the social bond to a virtual one; the shrinking and reduction of the relation to the big screen – via the specifically cinematic encounter with the spectator – to the small one (iphone, ipad, pc, television monitor). But our title also works to examine and invoke the ways that the practice of psychoanalysis was conducted during the pandemic (and beyond). The transformation of the world through digital space and digital mediums has been variously argued to present direct challenges for psychoanalysis, traditionally practised in the form of body to body engagement in a three-dimensional locatable space (see Owens and Watson's discussion, this volume). With the restrictions of the pandemic, the modalities of psychoanalytic praxis and experience have undergone modification and change, where analysts and analysands have engaged in phone consultations, and various kinds of screen appointments/sessions. With the changing face of the subject, certainly within a representational sense, it is crucial to identify and to interrogate how we can work contemporaneously with these fundamental psychoanalytic concepts, both clinically and culturally. For example, what effects are incurred from not being present in embodied form for a psychoanalytic session, for both analyst and analysand? Can we still speak of transference in the same sense and with the same consequences (see Holohan, this volume)? Is the new generation of technology mediated conversations with chat bots going to alter the structure of the subject of the unconscious? In the wider professional context, psychoanalytic discourse was restricted to online seminars and conferences on Zoom or other platforms. We might wonder what happens to the psychoanalytic discourse when it is practiced virtually (see Kilroy, this volume), does it change somewhat, if so, in what ways?

### ...The Year the Cinemas Closed

In 2020 we witnessed the fall of the cinematic "big" screen, as prohibitions on group events and performative collective spaces closed our movie theatres for the first time in the history of cinema. The corollary was the unprecedented rise of the "small screen" within our domestic, work, and intimate spaces. Through the dictates of the public health narrative, we were constrained, restrained, ordered, and later politely requested to stay at home, to stay safe, to take responsibility for each other and for ourselves, by staying absent from the "social dilemma". Psychoanalytically speaking, we know that imposing these restrictions as an external injunction on 'being out there' in the world, poses a question internally to the subject at the level of desire. In other words, how did/do we, as subjects with an unconscious, obtain enjoyment and satisfaction now that we were rendered more hermetic, isolated and less physically present in the embodied gaze of others.

Moreover, in being asked to stay inside, there was the opportunity to experience not the benign safety of a national heath executive conferred command, but rather, the anxiety of libidinal drives clamouring for organisation, or, at the very least for something with which to be occupied. In a time when the apparently benevolent superegoic message in the top right hand corner of our TV screen encouraged us to "Stay Home", how did we counter the no-limits binge and splurge accommodated to the drive by the "All You Can Eat" permanently available buffet of film on offer by services such as Netflix, Mubi, and Amazon Prime? In this way, the small screen served as an extension of both our Covidian desires and perhaps in Slavoj Žižek's terms, what our desires became through the perversion of the screen. If as he says in *The Pervert's Guide to Cinema* (2006), cinema not only gives you what you desire – it tells you *how to* desire, can we draw an analogy with the distortion of desire through the small screen, in order to ask what the small screen teaches us?

In our increasingly techno-mediated world, the dystopian imagined visions of sci-fi where avatars and robots substitute for embodied human beings came to bear an uncanny similarity to the empty street 'reality' of our pandemic existences. Even though Charlie Brooker creator of the prescient and dystopian series Black Mirror remarked that the pandemic is "the most, on some levels, boring apocalypse you could imagine" (Standford, 2020). In our "post truth" age where social media predominates as purveyor of facts, fake news, and general dissemination of knowledge, the semblance of authority beneath institutional structures was undermined – think here of Netflix releases such as *The Social Dilemma* and *The Hater*. We may have wondered, how, or indeed if, we will remember to engage socially or professionally with the unmediated, and unmasked dimension of the other/Other given our protracted mediation of the relation to the Other via the disengaged, screened, masked, and otherwise techno-assisted devices we grew familiar with during 2020 and 2021. How can we speak of the relation to the small other in the absence of the body from social interactions and represented by a screen? We need to take account of these times of uncertainty through the prism of the small screen and to interrogate the shifts in the uniquely subjective and yet social experience of our relation to the gaze. What bodily and psychic effects are incurred through alternate viewing experiences, if any, that frame or precipitate the human being as a captivated subject both within and on the screen? Here we can indeed think of the captivation of Irish and British TV viewing audiences during lockdown by the small screen production *Normal People* – whose protagonists spend hours separated physically but spending time together on Skype (see Gallioto, this volume, and Owens, 2022).

If at the end of the pandemic time of the COVID-19 virus, we have become vulnerable to the perversion(s) of the screen, at the mercy of so-called post truth and disinformation, and passive recipients of manipulations and political falsehoods, will we once again be capable of choosing to desire through the vector of the big screen (see Meehan O'Callaghan this volume)?

## Shifting Screens

The themes and chapters within this book arose and are developed from an online psychoanalytic film festival event held on Zoom in March 2021. As organisers of the annual Irish Psychoanalysis and Film Festival, we realised that the 2021 festival would have to be conducted rather differently! The festival in its 12th year in 2021 was traditionally held over two days in a Dublin venue (latterly Dublin City University) and attracted psychoanalysts and film enthusiasts to gather and watch films together, and discuss the themes arising both in relation to the remit of that specific festival and in relation to the individual films chosen and introduced by specific presenters. The festival is the brainchild of Olga Cox Cameron who contributes to this volume in a most welcome Afterword. Having organised meetings to discuss psychoanalysis and film at Trinity College Dublin with a small interested group Olga went on to assemble a team to stage the first Irish Psychoanalytic film festival back in 2009. The organising team has changed a bit over the years and Olga herself retired from the organisational aspects in 2019, but over the years we have investigated a wide range of psycho-social-cultural phenomena – childhood, obsession, citizenship, revolution, masculinities, to name a few – and the event has enjoyed a special place in the calendar of Irish psychoanalytic fixtures year in, year out. But then, there was COVID, all the cinemas were closed, and we were prohibited to meet with one another. We thought, okay, we will have to do it on Zoom, and then we thought, not only will we do it on Zoom but we will speak to the closure of cinema for its effects on the psyche and the social bond, and we will speak to its corollary, the rise of the small screen. And, moreover, we will do all of this on small screens, in our own homes, alone. (Writing this now, from the relatively 'post'-pandemic time of July 2022, it still seems surreal that all of this took shape.) We put together a 'call for papers' – a break with the traditional 'call for films' and we named the event 'The Year the Cinemas Closed: Psychoanalysing Shifting Screens'. It was a terrific gig, notwithstanding that one of us experienced a pc meltdown and internet crash whilst chairing a session, which all went unnoticed as we carried on with the entire thing on our iPhone (the wonders of the smallest screen!). We had a fabulous line-up of speakers, some of whom are here in this volume having expanded their presentations as essays, and the discussions were vivid and engaging. No, we didn't get together for wine and canapés afterwards as we would have normally done on the first evening of the film festival but we promised to do it all again in person in the future. While this book features articles from clinicians and practising psychoanalysts, we have, in the original spirit of the film festival, invited other theorists and psychoanalytically orientated scholars in the fields of film, literature and cultural studies to contribute.

In contrast to other psychoanalytically themed books reflecting upon the pandemic and its impact upon subjectivity and/or psychoanalytic practice, this volume has a particularly Lacanian focus on these contemporary issues, while pivoting upon the literal and metaphorical lens of the camera focus. The subjects of the essays span historical and current Lacanian thinking, covering the representation of psychoanalysis as artifice, the travails and tribulations of computer mediated analysis, as well as commentaries on the techno-inflected imagined social bond conditioned by what Lacan had called the alethosphere (Lacan, 1991/2007, p. 182). In this collection, the socio-cultural narratives and Real disruptions of the pandemic are framed as a function of the paradoxes of enjoyment characteristic of Lacanian psychoanalysis rather than merely the psychosocial repercussions of a planetary and contingent disaster.

We begin with Don Kunze's chapter "(In)Continent Topology of Pandemics, Screens, and Scripts." Don makes use of six terms from Harold Bloom's Anxiety of Influence to argue that they coincidentally define the psychoanalysis of contagion as well as the disease (plague) that Freud had defined as psychoanalysis. Commenting on the virus as both biological agent *and* the measure we take to avoid it, Don compares the cinema-lover's experience of this 'merger' in the move from big to little screen during the pandemic. He argues that psychoanalysis and the plague (COVID) celebrate their historical alliance in conversion of the Big screen to the small screen, pandemic to endemic.

We follow this with Robert Kilroy's contribution "Digital Tectonics and Cinematic Intimacy: An Epidemiological/Psychoanalytic Perspective." Robert examines the notion of cinematic intimacy in the context of COVID and the experience of lockdown. He hypothesises that the increased proximity to screens and images during the pandemic is a symptom – in the Lacanian sense – of a more serious screen contagion at work in the shadows of COVID. Robert goes on to analyse this phenomenon *qua* tectonic virus which he defines as a form of algorithmic desire fuelling the viral spread of a new mode of digitised subjectivity.

The third chapter is Sarah Meehan O'Callaghan's "At the Mercy of the Screen: Passivity and its Vicissitudes in a Time of Crisis." Sarah explores the consequences of the curtailment of human activity during the pandemic lockdowns and in particular how the increasing confinement of the human subject's activities to the small screen conditioned, as she puts it, an extension of our subjective libidinal economies. She argues that a new symptomatology of the pandemic can be understood as a function of the lack of the embodied gaze and the anxiety engendered by the excessive presence of the screen. From there, Sarah goes on to speculate about the implications for post-pandemic subjects of the loss of the relation to the gaze within embodied subjectivity.

Next up is Jessica Datema and Manya Steinkoler's "*Undine*: Siren Screens." The film *Undine* premiered at the 60th Berlin International Film Festival in February 2020 prior to the start of the pandemic and was released to streaming in 2021. Jessica and Manya argue that Christian Petzold's film *Undine* shows the dangers of small screen engagement without limits or empathy, a condition already in place with the globalisation of social media and technology, but which escalated during the pandemic. Making the point that 'small' screen also implies an isolated experience, Jessica and Manya consider how a solitarily endemic society of isolated users logging onto their small screen devices connects them to an ocean of people whilst yet separating them from a larger contextual engagement. As such, they argue for the revelatory aspects of the film in its encounter with lack and vulnerability.

The fifth chapter also considers lack and vulnerability on the small screen, but this time via the small screen production of the adaptation of Sally Rooney's masterpiece novel *Normal People*. Erica Galioto's "Prohibition and Power: *Normal People* as Pandemic Pornography" centres on a detailed study of the relationship between the protagonists of *Normal People* as an epitome of what she calls, psychoanalytic desire. As such, she argues, this desire was shown to be at risk in pre-pandemic times due to the ubiquity of internet pornography, the endless swiping of dating apps, and the superegoic command to enjoy. Rather, the (impossible) relation of Marianne and Connell's, Erica claims, can be thought of as pandemic pornography representing desire and stimulating our own, at a time when our connection to others was severed but also, and because of this, re-installing desire, fantasy and jouissance as functions of prohibition and power.

Miles Link's "Weeping On and Off Screen – Truth, Falsity, and Art" also deals with what is revealed in our encounter with art; in his essay, it is Homer's Odyssey which allows Miles to explore what crying on screen reveals about the truth and the false. Odysseus covering his face to weep indicates for Miles a dual tension which he analyses and then compares with the pandemicised world of the 'small screen' in which the screen may cover the false, or its (Freudian) opposite, reveal the (unrepressed) truth. Miles goes on to consider if and how Odysseus's screen (drawing a veil over his weeping face) might be more properly viewed as an inversion, a *camera obscura* by which means, what is beyond the screen is what the world is not, but could yet be.

The whole business of what *could be* beyond the screen is explored in the next essay in a very different way. Michael Holohan's "'The Thing did not Dissatisfy Me?' Lacanian Perspectives on Transference and AI-Driven Psychotherapeutic Chatbots" examines AI-driven chat-based interfaces (chatbots) on virtual therapy apps as a specifically contemporary phenomenon. If the chatbot can be considered as a corollary of the shift of much of social life including psychotherapy onto the small screens of our laptops and mobile phones during the pandemic what is unique to it is the fact that at the other end of the phone/beyond the screen, there is nothing except a computer programme. Michael analyses the unusual transference relation occurring between a client and a chatbot from the point of view of the Lacanian registers of the Imaginary, Symbolic, and Real.

The eighth chapter in the collection is Hilda Fernandez-Alvarez's "The Rise of the *Lathouses*: Some Consequences for the Speaking Being and the Social Bond." Her chapter begins by exploring how mother-infant dyads illustrate different landscapes of desire and *jouissance* of our present time; one of them, she argues, relates to the embodied exchanges that concern the subject's sensual body among other bodies, the other concerns rather, what she calls, the fact of a globalised culture plugged-in into the digital through proliferating small screens. Extrapolating from this discussion Hilda goes on to consider the differences between embodied and remote sessions (in psychoanalytic work) with consideration of the functions of objects gaze and voice, and the presence and function of the analyst.

In the last chapter of the collection proper, "Lacan on the Telly: Psychoanalysis on the Small Screen(s)," Carol Owens and Eve Watson look at Lacan (and other psychoanalysts, and representations of psychoanalysis) on the "Telly" in order to think about how what is represented of psychoanalysis in various screen productions mobilises what they call a kind of buffoonery, and they go on to wonder in what ways this affects the actual work of, and transference to psychoanalysis conducted via the (small) screen in what Dany Nobus has coined Computer Mediated Analysis (CMA). They dialogue around the slippage from one screening of psychoanalysis to the other, that is, from the one which relies upon a spectator to the one which relies upon an analysand via a commentary on *Television* (Lacan, 1974/1990), as well as *The Sopranos, Normal People, Duck Soup*, and *Sibyl*.

The pandemic as a point of crisis in human history not only materialises the rise of the small screen as an artefact of necessity, convenience, and creativity but provides the backdrop to investigating the now greater incidence of anxiety and related symptoms, paranoia, even disorders, et cetera. The pandemic has generated an intense laboratory study of the contemporary clinic and facilitated or accelerated the rise of the modern subject, a subject less tethered by traditional modes of authority, a subject paradoxically more connected and yet more isolated. As we write this, we are somewhat emerging from the initial economic and social shock of the pandemic, but we still cannot be sure how long the crisis of public health and its associated fallouts will continue. With this emergence from the space of lockdowns into the more embodied world of the post lockdown social bond, we face many other knock-on challenges, high cost of living, spiralling inflation, a war in Europe, a refugee crisis, greater UK isolationism, climate change, to name a few of the current socio-economic/political challenges. Amidst these social, economic and existential threats, the human subject must navigate and find their way in living through such intrinsic and external shocks to the material world. As psychoanalysts or psychoanalytically informed academics/theorists we place great emphasis on the notion of singularity, that is, we as subjects of the unconscious respond to, experience, and internalise the signifiers of crisis in a unique and particular way, inflected of course through culture but nonetheless marked by a singular *Jouissance* that is enjoyed each in their own way. While all of our contributors have addressed the particularities of this timeframe and symptomatology induced by the small screen, or of the small screen, we have also chosen to include a stand-alone collaborative chapter on the small screen production of Adam Curtis' (2021) BBC series *Can't Get You Out Of My Head: An Emotional History of the Modern World*. This chapter was – rather like this entire book – developed from a Zoom symposium comprised of Isabel Millar, Brett Nicholls, Rosemary Overell, and Daniel Tutt, entitled "Power, Politics & the Films of Adam Curtis" held in March 2021. The emerging social, economic, political and psychoanalytic particularities of the recent upheaval result, on the one hand, from the potency of a real external and contingent event such as global coronavirus, while on the other, this event and its consequences have a history, a context and that is something we must continue as researchers of the contemporary social bond to consider, interrogate, and comment upon. We hope you will enjoy this collection of articles, in whatever form you are reading it, traditional book, e-reader, laptop, or perhaps, indeed, on the smallest of small screens.

## References

Frankel, R. and Krebs, J.V. (2022). *Human virtuality and digital life: Psychoanalytic and philosophical reflections.* London: Routledge.

Giffney, N. (2021). *The culture-breast in psychoanalysis: Cultural experiences and the clinic.* London:Routledge.

Lacan, J. (1964/1978). *The seminar of Jacques Lacan: Book XI. The four fundamental concepts of psychoanalysis.* Ed. J.-A. Miller. Trans. A. Sheridan. London: W.W. Norton.

Lacan, J. (1974/1990). *Television.* New York and London: W.W. Norton.

Lacan, J. (1991/2007). *The seminar of Jacques Lacan: Book XVII. The other side of psychoanalysis.* Ed. J.-A. Miller. Trans. R. A. Grigg. New York and London: W.W. Norton.

Levine, H. B. and Reed, G. S. (eds.) (2015). *On Freud's "screen memories".* London: Karnac.

Massumi, B. (2017). *The principle of unrest: Activist philosophy in the expanded field.* London: Open Humanities Press.

McGowan, T. (2007). *The real gaze.* New York: Suny Press.

Owens, C. (2022). 'Normal people in abnormal times: How a TV show rocked the Irish pandemic lockdown... and other fantasies'. In *Analytic Agora*, Volume 1, pp. 182–199.

Stanford, E. (2020). 'Charlie Brooker saw all this coming'. *New York Times*, 21 May. Available at: www.nytimes.com/2020/05/21/arts/television/charlie-brooker-coronavirus.htmlhttps://www.britannica.com/science/surface-geometry.

Žižek, S. (2006). The perverts guide to cinema. Directed by Sophie Fiennes. London: P Guide Ltd. ICA Projects.

# Chapter 1

# (In)Continent Topology of Pandemics, Screens, and Scripts

## Don Kunze

Epidemiology defines contagion in terms of incontinence – the difficulty of "containing" infection spread – *versus* measures such as social distancing, quarantine, and travel restrictions. Both socially and mentally, we contract as we retreat. Our subjectivity aligns itself with the continence/incontinence dynamics of disease. This is nowhere more evident than in activities of amusement, where the screen itself becomes an element of (dis-)satisfaction, *jouissance*. In the sense that art's trick is to amuse us by imposing the pains of suspense, withheld meanings, and jolts of horror, all within the pharmakon of suspended disbelief, our concerns about moving from the event structure of the movie theatre's Big Screen to the domestic Small Screen (streaming videos, laptops, iPhones) become questions about *jouissance* itself, and *jouissance*'s topological relation to continence and incontinence. At this level, psychoanalysis, epidemiology, and media studies all find themselves to be about the insulation of inside from outside. This essay is about understanding that insulation.

## Coincidence

Occasionally, two critical systems will ghost each other without either system's intention or awareness. In the case of the COVID-19 pandemic's relation to media, particularly film-watching, it happens that Lacan's particularly elaborate theories about anxiety seem spookily condensed and refined by an unrelated study, Harold Bloom's theory of the anxiety of poets about their forerunners (Bloom, 1973). Until the pandemic provoked thoughts about spatial and temporal quarantine, this connection would never have been possible.

There would seem to be no theoretical basis to argue for a relationship between Jacques Lacan, described by David Macey (1994, p. xiv) as "the most controversial psycho-analyst since Freud" and Bloom, whom *Oxford Bibliography* called "probably the most famous literary critic in the English-speaking world".[1]

The psychoanalyst and literary critic were historically and intellectually distant in style, method, and subject matter. Lacan talked and wrote about

DOI: 10.4324/9781003272069-2

anxiety extensively over the course of nearly 27 seminars and other writings. In *Anxiety of Influence*, Bloom used a compact design of six Greek and Latin terms borrowed from theology, science, and literature. Creating a concordance would be out of the question, but Bloom's compact schema speaks to Lacan's algorithms dealing with inside – outside relations with themes of twinning, shadows, and couplings. His six terms, *tesseræ, clinamen, askesis, dæmon, apophrades*, and *kenosis* can be grouped into three pairs, each of which has an inside, an outside, and a collapse of the distinction between the two.[2]

Predictably, the contrast between public and private space has structured changes in consumer entertainment during the pandemic. Thanks to Lacan's ability to see the torus's combination of continence and incontinence, I can propose a "toroidal critique", simultaneously about (1) quarantine, (2) the move from the Big Screen to the Small Screen, (3) the contents naturally favoured by those screens, and (4) new kinds of audiences emerging in pandemic times. I can use the economy of Bloom's six terms to pull into focus Lacan's centralising issue of how to deal with the void.

The three pairs seem even more relevant today than they were for Bloom's poets, cowed by masterful predecessors. Let us attempt a more general diagnosis. (1) *Dæmon* is the motivating force behind *askesis*, retreat and isolation, as in "ascetic" – the basic dynamic of lockdowns and quarantines. (2) The Lucretian *clinamen* swerves to avoid a void, creating paired edges akin to the ceramic *tesseræ*, ancient ceramic tokens broken by parting friends in anticipation of reunion, when the two re-joined halves, perfectly matching along the jagged line of fracture, would authenticate love. (3) *Kenosis*, Bloom's version of the Freudian unconscious, is a "knowing without knowing", famously taught by the Essene monastics. Paired with *apophrades*, the "voice of the dead", this super-ego voice imposes itself even past the point of death, making it the principal acousmatic component of what Lacan referred to as "between the two deaths", the ethnographically universal interval between literal extinction and Symbolic judgment and resolution.[3] The voice without a body and knowledge without thinking create a pure inversion for the living subject as well, as in the case of the servant who, encountering Death in the marketplace, fled to Samarra only to find Death waiting for her there.[4] The dead person who has forgotten how to die and the living person drawn fatally to the very thing most feared are the essence of the uncanny's crisscross algebra of life and death as a single basis phenomenon, life-in-death, death-in-life. This is Ernst Jentsch's famous formula of the uncanny (1906), the basis of Freud's even more famous analysis (1919).

The three pairs, *dæmon/askesis, clinamen/tesseræ*, and *apophrades/kenosis*, define voids in terms of the (failed) actions taken to avoid them. Here, I can see the key to the present pandemic, where "virus" is not simply the biological agent of disease but a mathematical "dual", which includes the measures we invent to escape or contain it. In these terms, not even death exempts the subject imprisoned on an unbounded projective plane, self-intersecting and non-orientable, which is both continent and incontinent.[5] Bloom did not pair his terms in the way I have suggested. He tailored each to define the mechanisms that forced young poets to misread the poems of their masters.[6] Misprisions led to the perception of laws that had not existed before the novice chose to refuse them, laws that would have seemed entirely strange to the "Masters". The younger poet, cowed by the *apophrades* of the dead Master, realised a *kenosis* that retroactively made the Master the Master. At this point, Lacan would have jumped in to add that the *nom du père* was also this *non du père*, that *kenosis* was the product of the anxiety of this super-ego *apophrades*, and that only the "non-dupes err" (*les non-dupes errent*): poets, fools, lovers are all "of a nature compact". And, as Lacan would have said, their "anxiety never lies".

## Big Screen to Small Screen

For us dupes, willing to suspend disbelief in order to enjoy pleasures of the screen, there is no longer the Big Screen of public enjoyment but the Small Screen of separate domestic interiors. Retreat (*askesis*) from the *dæmon* comes to define the difference between a public "outside" (the movie theatre) and private "inside" (the home). In addition, each screen type comes with its own style of narrative temporality. The Big Screen settles for the rough-average duration of 105 minutes, with the requirement of the *récit fort* – that the ending must answer to the beginning.[7] The Small Screen prefers endings that put off this duty: serialised dramas, where each episode guarantees the audience's return by imposing the sudden break-off ("cliff-hanger"). The Big Screen audience is immobilised architecturally; the easily re-positioned Small Screen secures its audience on the installment plan. Bingeing does not change the seriality of the Small Screen's tempo setting, it simply requires each episode to end with a plot-point. The longer the series, the more plot-points, and the more vertiginous the *mise en abîme* when the ending finally arrives.

Viruses mutate. The "non-dupes" (skeptics) who refuse vaccination or other precautions become host reservoirs for unlimited recombination of RNA. Demonically, these non-dupes err by allowing the virus to "learn" how to circumvent vaccinations.[8] This is Thing-learning, Bloom's knowing without knowing, *kenosis* on the level of biology. The voice instructing the kenotic learner is dead – the virus as Thing. This is probably the reason that it is able to continue instructing us, Lacan says, after *we* are dead. This Zombie physics was invented well before the age of Big Data made possible an actual and universal exchange between little zombies and the Big Zombie.

In 1969, Lacan (2007, pp. 143–149) intuited the system by which the handheld gadget ("lathouse"; a reformation of the *dispositif*, appliance) would connect to the Thing of the "alethosphere". Lacan was clairvoyant about how small-screen gadgets would today connect globally to create surplus data ready to be harvested, collated, and monetised or, worse, weaponised without any human intervention. You e-mail a friend, "Let's go kayaking" on Friday. Later that very afternoon you receive pop-up advertisements for deals on kayaks. On Saturday you order one from Amazon and Sunday it's delivered to your door. Bloom gives us the six-termed grammar of this consumer desire, Lacan expands its vocabulary. The *kenosis/apophrades* dyad of data mining that comes, no extra charge, with the Small Screen *dispositif* reminds us that, although we think we "use language" to express our autonomy, actually it is the Symbolic that is *enjoying us*. With technology as well as psychoanalysis, we are "worth more dead than alive". And, although we are alive when this enjoyment takes place, it is our dead part, our own interior *Ding*, that *counts*.[9] *Apophrades* is this agent, the spokesperson, of this death; *kenosis* (Big Data) is its Monostatos.[10]

The quarantine (*askesis*) of neurotic dupes defending themselves against the psychotic (everywhere) *dæmon* virus does away with the middle, or third term by converting it into the "/" of *askesis/dæmon*.[11] The bar specifies a void around whose bi-lateral periphery it is art's duty to circumnavigate (Lacan, 1997, pp. 116–118). Georges Perec would designate the void as a lipogram[12] and Bloom would call the two-part swerve around this periphery *clinamen*. In either case, there is something missing, and when the Imaginary Father and the Symbolic Father consult, this void is the Real Father, a pure reciprocating engine of castration/separation, or suppression, which both Lacan and Freud regarded as a structural system of twists and turns so native to fiction that our best example is the Ur-antique, *Œdipus*. The advice of the oracle is ignored, but the letter of the law comes true anyway: Word made Thing, with dignity, or rather *Ding*nity. *Also sprach die* A-letho-sphere.[13]

The Small Screen lathouse conspires with a Faustian *dæmon*. Streaming video subscriptions employ the incontinence principle, unending entertainment, to soothe containment blues. Where the Big Screen required the ending to respond to the beginning, the Small Screen activates the unexpected ending that holds the viewer in the suspended animation of (never-)endings, plot-points. The binge, beloved by Netflix & Co., grooms the returning customer, who will return to the same place but never be satisfied. Compulsive repetition circles episodes into concentric anthologies that are both inside and outside each other, like the rings of the Borromeo knot. Because pandemic protocols, the shift in screen size, and new narratives all obey the algebra of continence/incontinence, Bloom's terms have no problem locating the Lacanian unconscious in the crossing from Big Screen to Small Screen, which echoes the crossing of S/s, signifier to signified, that makes the Subject a $ubject. I might, on this otherwise serious occasion, venture a joke: "A psychoanalyst, film-maker, and an epidemiologist walk into a /".

## Simultaneous Continence/Incontinence in *The Truman Show*

How can we read Lacan through Bloom's accidentally relevant critical device? Is it possible, as I claim, to bundle the disparate logics of (1) the pandemic, (2) the new audience that soothes its contraction pains (*askesis*) with contracts for endlessness, (3) a merger of entertainment with the spectre of an alethosphere "enjoying us" *via* our data, and (4) alteration of narrative styles imposed by the shift from the Big to the Small Screen?

Our response is to push the reset button, to look at a Big Screen film about a Small Screen long-running – really long! – TV series. Thus, the title of Peter Weir's 1998 film, *The Truman Show*, is a contronym, possibly the only film title able to claim this distinction (Freud, 1953a). It is both the title of the Big Screen film of 1998 and the Small Screen series, running already for 29 years. The film names two things in a concentric relation. But, which is inside, which is outside? The *Show*, as is often said, must go on – toroidally.

The film's dupe, Truman Burbank, is raised from infancy beneath the inspection of innumerable cameras and microphones. Each minute of his daily life is then re-packaged to engage a television audience that has accustomed itself to the homeostatic humdrum of the hero's daily life. The name of this serialised blah blah blah, also the name of the film about it, *The Truman Show*, engages the "/" component of continence/incontinence, making it an agent of the unconscious, which we see in Jim Carrey's portrayal of Truman as the ideal psycho-*kenotic*, both inside and outside the series.[14]

The *frisson* of watching Truman's pure "/" condition captures perfectly the aesthetics of our own pandemic. Big Screens like Big Ideas; Small Screens prefer the everyday. The Small Screen tends to equalise minute-to-minute variations, favouring the trivial to the profound. The relation to psychoanalysis is interesting. The Small Screen's celebration of the *Fehlleistung*[15], the bungled explanation or the slip of the tongue, makes it like the blah blah blah of the Analysand. Truman's TV audience was *jouissance*-d by the film's perfection of dupe-dom. Every occupant of the Florida island town, Seahaven, was an actor except the affable Truman. The sky was a variably lit dome, able to simulate rainstorms and season change.[16] The film's audience became cruel gods, taking pleasure in Truman's victimisation, knowing full well that they were in fact his prison guards. The filming location of the actual Florida town of Seaside, constructed as a whole but made to look as if it had developed historically, reproduced perfectly the generic logic of film-set construction, where history is "faked" by eliminating the organic and political processes of town formation into a single de-temporalised crystal, *prêt à porter*.

Seahaven physically plays out the contrast between the two screen sizes. The TV town was an hermetically sealed eco-sphere able to simulate nights and days, storms, and seasons. All of Truman's neighbours were hired actors. His every moment inside this hermetically sealed set was monitored from a control room rivalling NASA's moon-launch facilities.

The film and TV show construct a toroid relationship (Figure 1.1), meaning that each episode's cyclic continence is charged with the incontinence of the Big Screen film's desire, requiring the (continence) principle of the *récit fort*, that the ending must respond to the beginning. The demand of the TV

16  Don Kunze

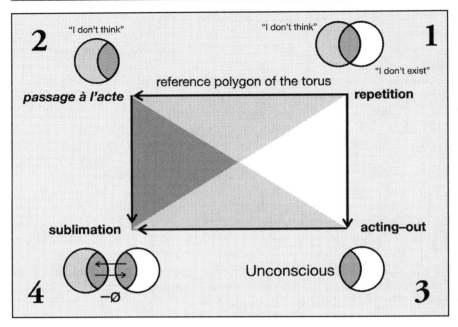

*Figure 1.1* Lacan adapts the fundamental polygon to show the relation of repetition to sublimation, *via* psychosis (*passage à l'acte*) "outside the Symbolic" and neurotic acting-out inside the Symbolic, on the same self-intersecting, non-orientable surface of the torus. Drawing by author.
Source: *Lacanian Works*, http://staferla.free.fr/S14/S14.htm

show could be quantified by the show's ratings. The desire of the Big Screen film emphasised the structure of the set and Truman's "/" Janus-predicament. There is an argument to be made that Truman hovered between the psychosis brought on by the lack of the paternal signifier and the neurosis of his overbearing mother. Truman was told his father had died in a sea storm when he was yet an infant, but Truman believes he may yet be alive, and spots paternal similarities in a "bum" who happens onto the set but is treated by the film directors the same way an overzealous red state police force might treat a homeless person slipping into a gated community. It is difficult to read the issue of the father. At some points he seems to be the thorn in the side of the TV show, and at other times the film's principal plot-point device. This places a hinge in the story at the point where Truman must choose between the psychosis of the TV show and the neurosis of the world beyond. Jim Carrey's artful portrayal of Truman may be due to the fact that Carrey himself has been said to be, in real life, psychotic.

The paternal mystery is the basis of Truman's dream of escaping Seahaven, fantasised as space travel. Finally, Truman overcomes his terror of water and sails through an artificial storm (stirred up to foil Truman's escape) to reach the ultimate architectural and psychoanalytical limit, the wall on which a sky is painted to meet the water in a false horizon. The problem of continence/incontinence – which is condensed in the "/" that divides the two terms – could never be more toroid than in the scene where Truman steps off his boat to walk along a gangway to reach the utility stair to the exit.

Truman has obeyed the rules of continence that are the intentional action of pandemic response. He has circled the inflated torus tube with the diurnal repetitions of episodes (the 24/7 TV show begins at morning) without being aware that its continence is grounded in his ignorance of his situation. Truman, the mortal/spiritual "one" who does not obey the phallic law that the actors obey in order to receive their wages, becomes the immortal (mechanical) "1" of the unary trait.[17] The actions Truman perceives as strictly cause-and-effect generate a surplus the director manages as Seahaven's backstage. "Questions" are converted directly to "answers" delivered in a technological package: the director's telephonic instructions sent to tiny earpieces, which accidentally interfere with Truman's car radio; stage lights that occasionally fall out of "the sky"; traffic jams engineered to slow or speed Truman on his way. Seahaven's fluid flow (*clinamen*) circulates Truman's desire within a self-constructed, self-contained Other. In-continence of the torus is, in contrast, the question of how the show will end. A surplus has built up; exaptation/emergence must release it. Truman is brought, through the technical slip-ups (encounters with his father look-alike, and unexplained details of his life) to his discovery of the structure of the Big Other and successful escape.

When Truman's boat crunches into the exterior wall of the set, his *récit fort* moment arrives, in the form of a utility stair and exit door. The director's voice comes out of a cloud to beg Truman to remain within the illusion of Seahaven on behalf of the Others-enjoying-him. The logic of fantasy is that its interior is related to its exterior by a wire that short-circuits continence with incontinence. The dissatisfaction of the one (the 1 of the one, 1/1, or "1 with a bar inside it") is the satisfaction, the enjoyment, of the Other. As a conception, *The Truman Show* is a Lacanian textbook. I don't use Lacan to understand Truman; I use Truman to understand Lacan. In *The Logic of Phantasy* (2010, p. 101) Lacan prescribes how, on the outside the Symbolic of perspectival space, where the movement of a figure across a static ground is unrestricted, we become, *episodically*, psychotic. On the inside, we are compelled to "act out". Like the Rat Man, we indulge in pure "signifierness", the babble of the meaningless insult ("You Plate! You lamp! You hand towel!"). The criminal or genius the Rat Man's father predicted to be the fate of his son describes perfectly the outlaw actor, who succeeds by pretending a fiction, and is accorded genius status the better this is done. The script is the blah blah blah we encounter in psychoanalysis (the Analysand's blather). The genius is the Ingenuity of the twist, the cut with the twist, that makes any blah blah blah of events into an ending that is genuinely responsive to the beginning, i.e. "toroid".

## The Katagraphic Cut

If the end of analysis can be described as a realisation of the (toroid) difference between the aim and the goal of the drive, where the exaptation of (bad) aiming confounds the idea of a Euclidean goal as target, the end of the Small Screen TV version of *The Truman Show* is explicable as the bottom and top rings (Imaginary and Symbolic) of the Borromeo knot held in place by the missing third (Real) ring.[18] For Truman, the quarantined resident, this third ring is specific. It is the cut into the set wall, the steel door at the top of the utility stair. The exit is the "katagraph", an ordinary architectural detail that is, simultaneously, a cut made into a 2-d projective surface (Causse, 2013, pp. 113–114). It is a cut that "cuts both ways", what in the ancient lore of the Dædalan Labyrinth was its eponymous tool, the double-headed axe, or *labrys*.

Lacan would have loved it! This is not an illustration or analogy. It is the Real Thing. The exit from Seahaven's 2-d surface of the illusion (Imaginary) of *The Truman Show* fantasy cuts (psychotically) to the world of the audience held in thrall by the 29-year serial comedy (Symbolic, the continent locale of "acting–out"). The Real is there from the start, although Truman discovers it only at the end. The end of narrative incontinence is the retroactive continence of the *récit fort*. It is, simultaneously, the ironic incontinence that haunts the prideful continence of Seahaven (and all other gated communities of its type) in its intention to eliminate contamination from other socio-economic groups. This penetrates down to every detail of island life, hyper-managed by the director, Christof, and his lunar control room teams.

The katagraph, the "deep cut", has an inverse function that we can see clearly by understanding its essential relation to continence/incontinence. As a connector between the two conditions, the inverse is at the root of the katagraph's functional effectiveness. What it connects, it disconnects, and vice versa. The paralysis of the audience in the Big Screen theatre reciprocally enables the seemingly unconfined play-out of the fiction on stage, which must be re-secured by the terminus of the drama's conclusion. The proscenium or screen is, effectively, a katagraph.

The televised series *The Truman Show* also depends on "holding the audience in suspense" by giving what, to Truman, appears to be complete freedom within the limits of Seahaven's invisible walls. Audiences, after all, are "captured", thanks to their fascination with those who appear not to be captured, except by fate and their own *Fehlleistungen*. Our Big Screen enjoyment of *The Truman Show* takes in the Small Screen's involvement. *The Truman Show*'s show-in-a-show technique focuses on the role of the cut, which we might compare to the katagraphic mark that Lacan cites in the story of the Roman consul in Egypt, Popilius. To avoid invasion by the Syrian army, Popilius draws a circle around the Syrian king, Antiochus, to make the point that some inscriptions are also cuts, and that such cuts "cut both ways". Antiochus reads the meaning of this ridiculous gesture immediately and agrees to withdraw. The deep cut is a kind of physical contronym (Freud, 1953a), but it is also, technically, a "two-dimensional subspace of a projective plane" (Hilbert and Cohn-Vossen, 1999).

Lacan demonstrates in Seminar IX, *Identification* (2011), how two kinds of circles can be drawn on the surface of a torus. One kind reduces to a point, another produces the immortality of the interior-8. The depth of this katagraphic cut is a matter of its simultaneous residency in Euclidean and projective space.[19] Thus, the door at the wall of the set of Seahaven is the "/" between *The Truman Show* and *The Truman Show*, the Big Screen and the Small Screen.

How does this translate to our situation of pandemic continence, with its transition marker, the Big Screen to Small Screen? The katagraphic mark is *The Truman Show*'s Big Screen representation of a Small Screen. The incontinence logic of the TV series (keeping the audience in a suspense that is ideally perpetual) is simultaneously a logic of keeping an audience confined. The theatrical Big Screen's ideal of audience paralysis is, for the small screen, temporally dispersed. Serial dramas run in seasons; the continence goal is pursued in terms of having audiences return to a weekly event. But, *The Truman Show*'s 24/7 design has a diurnal design. The audience wakes up with Truman and goes to bed 16 or so hours later. This is a "maximal paralysis design" that retroactively defines the audience's life as a mirror of Truman's, an unconscious that is noticed only through symptoms, when the production system breaks down, or when katagraphs break through the finished veneer of the "immersed" drama that Truman thinks is his real life.

Thanks to the film's juxtaposition of Big Screen continence-through-paralysis and Small Screen paralysis-through-incontinence, we can understand the topological role of the katagraph in stark, material terms. A theatrical light falls from the "sky" and smashes on the pavement. The director's closed-channel communications to the actors on the set interferes with Truman's car radio music. Truman's unexpected moves force the actors to pause to await new instructions. These errors *cut into* the polished surface of the Big Screen drama to reveal the Small Screen reality. The katagraph shows how the incontinent projective system serves to regulate the continent 3-D reality of the TV drama, to "glue the audience to its seats". Katagraphics is key to the paralysis of continence, in all its dupe-dom.

## The Katagraphic Dupe

These transactions between the Euclidean illusion of the TV show and the projective surfaces employed by the show's producer–directors require the device of a master katagraph, the dupe. Truman must not be allowed to discover that he is the single link between what he thinks is life in a Florida island community and the television series documenting his life. Quite humorously, the Lacanian saying, that *les non-dupes errent* (punning the *nom du père*, or name of the father) is also the plot-point function of Truman's father, another katagraph who turns up as a vagrant on the set. A dupe is also a dummy thanks to the function in the card-game of bridge where the dummy is a place-holder. The dummy is the partner of the player who "declares" the final contract. An opening lead is made by the player on the left, who names the opening suit, and the dummy shows all 13 cards, face up.

Lacan played bridge and knew precisely the katagraphic function of this show of cards. *It reveals everything without being conscious of anything.*[20] It is the reverse of the Cartesian *cogito*, which Lacan "upturns" (Figure 1.1) as an intersection of two Euler circles, *je ne pense pas* and *je ne suis pas* in Seminar XIV (*The Logic of Phantasy*, p. 102). What better dummy than a non-thinking, non-existing subject? And, who could be more non-existing than an actor in a film about filming, playing an actor who does not know he is an actor! The pandemic logic of continence/incontinence is distilled into its essence. The dummy's apophrastic speech and kenotic thoughts take ventriloquism to a new level.

In *The Logic of Phantasy*, the dummy position moves simultaneously along two orthogonal *vectors*, (1) to an "incontinent" position of the *passage à l'acte*: the psychotic caught *outside* the Symbolic and (2) to a position *contained* by the Symbolic, where the anxious subject is compelled to act out. This is the position of the Rat Man, who from inside the Symbolic was forced to call his father ridiculous insults, reducing his speech to pure performativity: "You lamp! You plate! You hand towel!" This is the *Vorstellungsrepräsentanz*, the signifier stripped down to zero-degree signifier-ness, as when, Lacan reminds us, children get off on saying that the cat goes bow-wow and the dog goes meow. Truman finds himself face to face with the suffocating Symbolic, where the only option is nonsense. Jim Carrey, who plays Truman, is a master of this situation, drawing a space-helmet with soap over his reflection in the mirror.

In French, "dummy" is literally *le mort*, the dead man. An actor who falls in love with Truman wants to spill the beans about his hyper-surveilled life. She makes the point that Truman is "not being allowed to live". He only thinks he is living, while all of his cards are shown face up, thanks to the surreptitious televising of his every act. This is Lacan's "between the two deaths" – *le mort* who does not know he is mort – paired (by Ernst Jentsch) with the living subject marked by death, running in two opposite directions at the same time. Truman as a contronymic zomby is *contained/uncontained*. The architectural precedent of his imprisonment is the famous labyrinth Dædalus constructed to quarantine the (also) hybrid monster born of Pasiphaë's cursed passion, the Minotaur. The place-frozen bull-man is the flip-side of the famous twins, Castor and Pollux, forced to circulate as antipodal points on an orbit halved between earth and Hades.[21] The Minotaur's life/death is embodied as animal/human, inverse of the Cartesian cogito, cast as the labyrinth's villain; a negated being (= monster) with no speaking parts.

The labyrinth was built to imprison the Minotaur, but its continence protocol was unusual. There was no locked door. There was only one meandering pathway, not a maze of optional turns. The monster was held in place by a fractal protocol – folds that, with any single pause of motion, made it impossible for the entrapped occupant to remember correctly whether he/she had been moving in or out. This is the continence/incontinence "contronym", viewed from the side of continence.

What about the other side? Ernst Jentsch (1906) gives the example of the living person marked or haunted by death, as in the case of the servant from Samarra. Here the same spatial protocol applies. In the story of the servant who, seeing Death in the marketplace, determines to flee only to find Death waiting for her at Samarra, the motion of flight becomes the motion to the interior of the trap. *Askesis* from the *dæmon* is ⇆, the bi-valent vector in the real projective plane, the interior-8 on the surface of a torus (Hilbert and Cohn-Vossen, 1999).

Lacan specifically cites this employment of incontinence to achieve continence in *The Ethics of Psychoanalysis* (1997, p. 60) where he tells the story of Apollo's love, rebuffed by Daphne's equally passionate hate. The nymph tries to flee but she is on a 2-d projective manifold that, although it lacks any boundaries, is finite. She has no option but to morph into a laurel tree, a species known for its "eternal life", to the extent that Olympic victors are crowned with its branches as a sign of their own immortality. Lacan omitted the backstory that would have confirmed this connection to continence/incontinence. Apollo had insulted Eros, the prototype δαίμων, joking that, for a god known as an archer, his skill was notoriously defective (a case of *Fehlleistung*). People never seem to fall in love with the right others. Eros mischievously confirmed this by piercing Apollo with an arrow of love, Daphne with an arrow of hate. Possibly, it was one arrow with two points, which would perfectly define the "one-dimensional subspace" that is the building block of projective geometry's 2-d, non-oriented, self-intersecting surfaces. Along this surface, Daphne fled in vain. The laurel tree was implicit not just in her failed *askesis* but in the way her inability to flee was present, already, in her desire to flee; and how Apollo's insult figured into Eros's status, as not just a dæmon but the prototype of all demons, intermediaries – "third terms" – bridging the realm of immortals with that of mortals or, put another way, life and death. The insult and story that followed merely played out this thirdness.

The erotic arrow, ⇆, is the projective geometry vector and katagraphic cut. Both functions are evident in *The Truman Show*. Katagraphics explains the film's dystopian employment of total surveillance and, hence, the idealisation of the syndic's protocols in the incidence of the plague of Vincennes (Foucault, 2020). The dupe "shows his hand" and the circuit continues. The dummy must not know (*kenosis*, standing here for the Unconscious). The circuit that must continue to move and contain is maintained by a second circuit operating virtually (think of the lunar control booth in *The Truman Show* as the small loop of the interior-8), but to distinguish this from the (Euclidean) virtual reality of the small-screen *Show*, I must name it, following Žižek (2012), the "reality of the virtual". It is the effectiveness of what is not present; the void required to make whatever is present work. This is the incontinent continence – or continent incontinence – so very close to what Freud tried to describe in his "Project for a Scientific Psychology" (1895) that I might dare to call it by its true name, the death drive.

## Exaptation[22] of Two Virtuality Circuits

The death drive: two circuits, two virtualities, two screen sizes. Pandemics: two circuits, two virtualities, two screen sizes. To understand the continence/incontinence system however, we must make a point about exaptation, or, how the unintended surplus of any wishfully-determining aim, *especially* when it fails to achieve its goal, constitutes a hidden treasury of signifiers that are preserved at the same time they are sublimated (Lacan, 2017, p. 62). The ordinary kind of (perspectival) virtuality, dedicated to the creation of depth of field for occupants of Euclidean space, is made effective by a second kind of virtuality that is (1) the mechanism that sets up the quantum-like reciprocity of suppression and emergence; and (2) like the twists of the projective plane that define it, non-oriented and self-intersecting.

This essay itself requires a non-oriented conclusion. There are three common ways to misread Walter Benjamin's *The Work of Art in the Age of Mechanical Reproduction* (1935/1936), the first "psychoanalytical" treatment of the Big Screen as such. The first conflates mechanisation with modernity to make it an index of mass consumption in the stage of Late Capitalism. The second fails to regard mechanism's primary role in different systems of knowing and belief, including – especially – those in antiquity. The third fails to see aura as an iterative postponement of access to the work of art that enhances the ultimate value of art as incomprehensible – the function of *agalma*: the tradition of pilgrimage. Similarly, when we look at a virus we see a mechanism but also something of the contagious/metonymic nature of spirituality.[23] Kant, for example, thought that reason, if unrestricted (incontinent), would spread freely. Freud joked that his hosts at Clarke University did not know he, Jung, and Ferenczi were "bringing them the plague" (Lacan, 2002, p. 336). It is misleading to oppose materialism to idealism; and, for Coronavirus, misleading to distinguish the disease from the responses to the disease. Continence and incontinence flow into each other in all conditions, at all scales. We should be surprised if this did not also condition our film-viewing practices as well as the content of films. If it is true, as Mladen Dolar has said (2022), that the virus is the "atom of materialism", it is, thanks to its "Ding-nity" as Lacan put it

(1997, pp. 43–70), an atom split. This makes the virus's extimacy, its incontinent continence, simultaneously a mechanism and spirit. When James Joyce, in *Finnegans Wake*, defined Paradise in terms of a *clinamen* of "even atoms" (Eve and Adam's), he would split this Adam, Eve-nly, and give the virus something to swerve around, and the margin of the Real void its *tesseræ*-symmetry of authentic reunion.

## Notes

1 This quote appears in "Harold Bloom" (2022, May 3), *Wikipedia*. See https://en.wikipedia.org/wiki/Harold_Bloom; Bloom was the Sterling Professor of Humanities at Yale University from 1955 to 2019, teaching his last class four days before his death on October 14.
2 It's possible to see that, even in his early work on the Mirror Stage, Lacan focused on (1) divisions of space that were not fully successful and, at the same time, (2) continuums that, no matter how smooth, were structured by a cut. All of Bloom's terms are about the simultaneous endurance and unreliability of division.
3 The term *voix acousmatique* is associated with Michel Chion's *Audio-Vision: Sound on Screen* (1994). The idea was expanded by the Lacanian Mladen Dolar, *A Voice and Nothing More* (2006). The connections linking Bloom's *apophrades* ("voice of the dead"), the cinematic voice-over, and the Lacanian super-ego and voice as a drive combine to create a spectrum linking ethnography, popular culture, and psychoanalysis. The voice is what extends the power of the rule past the end of life, to cover the interval of "between the two deaths".
4 W. Somerset Maugham made this tale from the Babylonian *Talmud* popular in his 1933 play, *Sheppy*.
5 The "real projective plane" is the basis of Lacan's topological interests in the Möbius band, cross-cap, torus, and other figures that, when "immersed" into 3-space, produce the paradoxically opposed qualities of self-intersection (continence) and non-orientation (incontinence). Themes such as *extimité*, the forced choice, suppression, metaphor, and the three domains of the Real, Symbolic, and Imaginary would be incomprehensible without reference to the real projective plane's 2-D manifolds, discovered by Pappus of Alexandria in 300 CE and formalised by Girard Desargues in the seventeenth century.
6 Bloom's definition of anxiety in relation to poetic "masters" could be considered in terms of the role of the paternal signifier in maintaining the poet's neurosis as preventative measure against psychosis.
7 I owe my understanding of this critical idea to Dan Collins' *Stealing Money From Offices* (2014), where he cites Roland Barthes (1993). The relation to Lacan's sentence-level *après coup* is clear.
8 Lacan's phrase, *les non-dupes errent* (Seminar XXI, 1973–1974) is a well-known invitation to pun the "names of the father" (*les noms du père*) as well as the father's "no" (*les nons du père*).
9 The development of an interior void in the subject can be understood through Louis Althusser's definition of interpellation, in the incident of the policeman's "Hey, you!" felt personally by multiple innocent parties who hear it yelled in the street. This guilt is lodged in a void at the subjects' interiors, a case of Lacan's *extimité*.
10 Monostatos was the arch-villain of Mozart's *The Magic Flute*, portrayed as a compulsive desire–machine.

11  Viruses don't have fathers, let alone paternal signifiers to structure neurosis! Viruses are, as Mladen Dolar has argued (2022), atoms of the spirit; we would add that this atom is split. "Pandemic" is etymologically the *dæmon*'s non-locality, creating *pan-demonium*.
12  Georges Perec's novel without the letter "e," *A void* (2005) demonstrates how *clinamen* creates meaning from the agitated flow around the lipogram indicated by a substitute word. Metaphor (replacement) lies at the heart of *clinamen*. The "/" is simultaneously the sign separating the terms of a dual, the bar of the Lacanian subject, and the separator in the *matheme* for the signifier's relation to the signified, a key to the function of suppression in Lacan's formula for metaphor.
13  We would propose a slightly different etymology for "alethosphere" than the one Lacan gives (based on Heidegger's "un-hiddenness" of truth). The River Lethe (Λήθη) was, in mythology, fluid forgetfulness that comes closer to Bloom's *kenosis* and the Freudian unconscious. In this shift to a mechanical flow, *clinamen* defines a void (lipogram) whose twinned edges (*tesseræ*) answer to the anxiety of absence. The alethosphere therefore must be a projective plane such as the one indicated by Lacan's diagram in Seminar XIV (2010, p. 102), a reference polygon of the torus, where demand's project of containment constructs desire as incontinent, in what Lacan called *l'assiette subjectif*, the "subjective sampler plate".
14  Truman's actions can be seen from the Small Screen film's point of view as "acting out" (inside the Symbolic) and from the Big Screen's point of view in relation to the *passage à l'acte* (outside the Symbolic). In Seminar XIV, *The Logic of Phantasy* (2010, p. 102), Lacan draws a reference polygon of the torus and shows how a single motion, beginning with an inversion of Descartes' *cogito*, transports the void of union without overlap to the opposite corner representing sublimation. In effect, the single diagonal is simultaneously the two vectors, one to a position outside the Symbolic, another to a position inside.
15  Freud's coinage, *Fehlleistung*, was the generic blunder, a broad range of occasions where something falls short. See S. Freud (*Zur Psychopathologie des Alltagslebens*, 1901). The blunder maintains homeostasis for the neurotic in possession of a working paternal signifier and is thus a good model for the Small Screen's narrative designs.
16  Seahaven was a fake of a fake. The architect Elizabeth Plater-Zyberk pushed the idea of the gated community to the extreme of a full-size urban "as if" – *as if* the town had developed without the *Angst* of decay or disunity and simply been discovered whole, given a fix–up, and occupied by upper-middle class (mostly) white people. The observation, that such artificial communities are like movie sets, is flipped. Seahaven actually *was* a movie set using the "like a movie set" to advantage.
17  Truman works as a unary trait in the Freudian sense, the traumatic Real of whose birth condition is carried forward as a symptom expressed as a binary, a 1/1 or rather $x = 1 + 1/x$, producing a Fibonacci explanation for any serialised life comedy based on the ignorance of a dupe. Each episode, like the Fibonacci numbers (1, 1, 2, 3, 5, 8 ...) is the sum of the previous two, a partial resolution that leads to a new plot-point. At each stage of substitution of "x" as "$1 + 1/x$" *into* the denominator, a successively more accurate number for Ø is given: $1+1/2, 1+2/3, 1+3/5$, etc. In this way, the ending is ultimately a question of emergence, referring to all of its prior recursions.
18  This explains the roles of Truman's three fathers. His Imaginary father is the vaguely-familiar vagrant who shows up unexpectedly, his Symbolic father is the director Christof, but the Real father is the topology of the "/" that holds the two aspects of the film's title together, the small screen 24/7 *Truman Show* and the Big Screen *The Truman Show* directed by Peter Weir. Truman plays both the prisoner

of the Symbolic who must "act out" and the alienated serial psychotic forced, in a way that exploits the unary trait as a Golden ratio, to the *passage à l'acte*.

19  Katagraphics is indicated but not named as such in Lacan's example of "The Injunction of Popilius". It is a term that appears elsewhere, in the instructive episode in the Biblical *Book of Matthew* 21:25, the episode of the Sanhedron's attempt to entrap Jesus in a legal matter. He is asked to sentence a woman who has been convicted of adultery; the Sanhedron predict that he will fail to pronounce the required punishment, death by stoning, and thus be liable for arrest. Instead of doing this, Jesus kneels and begins doodling on the ground; the Sanhedron elders suddenly depart. Apparently *katagraphein* was an Arabic custom, described by the poet Dhu Rumma as the act of a conjurer. The story of Popilius is told in *Livy's History of Rome*, book 45; but the key to *katagraphein* is given by Charlton T. Lewis's *An Elementary Latin Dictionary*, which notes that Popilius's staff was in fact a wand.

20  The coincidence of the bridge dummy and the ventriloquist's dummy can be extended to the idea of an actor who speaks the lines written by another. Truman is a case of the actor as dummy who is unconscious of his status as an actor. All of these variations answer to the logic of "between the two deaths," which correspond to the two kinds of circles which one may draw on the surface of a torus.

21  The Minotaur's paralysis was a *père* version (imprisoning turns imposed by the father). Minos had stinted on his annual sacrifice to Poseidon, selecting the next best bull instead of the best. Some traditions have it that Zeus was the offended deity. Either one or the other was the efficient cause of Pasiphaë's impregnation by the bull, facilitated by Dædalus's machine.

22  Exaptation is the official name of evolutionary emergence described by Stephen Jay Gould and Elisabeth Vrba. See "Exaptation," *Wikipedia*, https://en.wikipedia.org/wiki/Exaptation.

23  Lacan's example, in Seminar V, *Formations of the unconscious* (2014, p. 54), is the metaleptic *Witz* of the woman who, told by her dancing partner that she perhaps knows that he is a count (*je suis compte*), replies simply "Ahhh!", indicating retroactively the root of *comte* to be "con," i.e. an idiot.

## References

Barthes, R. (1993). Deux femmes [Two women]. In E. Marty (Ed.), *Œuvres complètes III*. Paris: Seuil.

Benjamin, W. (1985). The Work of art in the age of mechanical reproduction. In H. Arendt (Ed.), *Illuminations: Essays and R eflections* (pp. 217–251). New York: Schocken. (Original work published in 1935/1936.)

Bloom, H. (1973). *Anxiety of Influence: A Theory of Poetry*. New York and Oxford: Oxford University Press.

Causse, J.-D. (2013). L'identité et l'identification: des sœurs ennemies *? [Identity and identification: enemy sisters *?]. *Culture/clinic* (M.-H. Brousse and M. Jaanus, Eds.) 1, pp. 105–114. https://www.jstor.org/stable/10.5749/cultclin.1.2013.0vii.

Chion, M. (2019). *Audio-Vision: Sound on Screen* (C. Gorbman, Trans.). New York, NY: Columbia University. (Original work published in 1990.)

Collins, D. (2014, July). Stealing money from offices. *Lacuna* 16, pp. 105–124.

Dolar, M. (2006). *A Voice and Nothing More*. Cambridge, MA: MIT Press.

Dolar, M. (2022). *What is the virus? [Zoom lecture] 2022 LACK Online Lecture Series*. https://lackorg.com/lack-online-lecture-series/.

Foucault, M. (2020). *Discipline and Punish: The Birth of the Prison* (A. Sheridan, Trans.). London: Penguin. (Original work published in 1975.)

Freud, S. (1953a). The antithetical meaning of primal words. *S.E. XI.*, pp. 153–162.

Freud, S. (1953b). The 'uncanny'. *S.E. XVII.*, pp. 217–256.

Hilbert, D. and Cohn-Vossen, S. (1999). *Geometry and the Imagination* (P. Nemenyi, Trans.). Providence, RI: American Mathematical Society. (Original work published in 1932.)

Jentsch, E. (1906). *Zur psychologie des Unheimlichen Psychiatrisch-neurologische Wochenschrift* 8.22 (25 August), pp. 195–198 and 8.23 (1 September), pp. 203–205.

Lacan, J. (1997). *The Seminars, Book VII. The Ethics of Psychoanalysis, 1959–1960* (J.-A. Miller, Ed.; D. Porter, Trans.). New York and London: W.W. Norton & Co. (Original work published in 1986.)

Lacan, J. (2002). *Écrits: The First Complete Edition in English* (B. Fink, H. Fink, and R. Grigg, Trans.). New York and London: W.W. Norton & Co. (Original work published 1966.)

Lacan, J. (2007). *The Seminars, Book XVII. The Other Side of Psychoanalysis, 1969–1970* (R. Grigg, Trans.). New York and London: W.W. Norton & Co. (Original work published in 1991.)

Lacan, J. (2010). *The Seminars, Book XIV. The Logic of Phantasy, 1966–1967* (C. Gallagher, Trans.). Available at: http://www.lacaninireland.com/web/wp-content/uploads/2010/06/Seminar-IX-Amended-Iby-MCL-7.NOV_.20111.pdf.

Lacan, J. (2011). *The Seminars, Book IX. Identification, 1961–1962* (C. Gallagher, Trans.), amended 7 November. Available at: http://www.lacaninireland.com/web/wp-content/uploads/2010/06/14-Logic-of-Phantasy-Complete.pdf.

Lacan, J. (2017). *The Seminar of Jacques Lacan, Book V. Formations of the Unconscious, 1957–1958*. (J.-A. Miller, Ed., R. Grigg, Trans.). Malden, MA: Polity. (Original work published in 1998.)

Macey, D. (1994). Introduction. *The Four Fundamental Concepts of Psychoanalysis*. London: Penguin. (Original work published in 1973.)

Perec, G. (2005). *A Void*. (G. Adair, Trans.). Boston, MA: D. R. Godine. (Original work published 1990.)

Weir, P. (Director). (1998). *The Truman Show*. New York, NY: Scott Rudin Productions.

Žižek, S. (2012). *The reality of the virtual* [video] (dir) B. Wright. Chicago, IL: Olive Films. https://www.youtube.com/watch?v=RnTQhIRcrno.

Chapter 2

# Digital Tectonics and Cinematic Intimacy

An Epidemiological/Psychoanalytic Perspective

*Robert Kilroy*

## Too Hot to Handle: Netflix and Cinematic Intimacy

What has been the effect of COVID-19 on cinema? What can cinema teach us about the pandemic? Beyond the obvious impact on the industry, how has the medium itself adapted? After a year of worldwide closures, the big screen seems to be coming back bigger and brasher than before. In what some critics are describing as the "supersize" effect, a whole series of new releases are notable for the overly performative contributions of their leading actors (Lady Gaga in *House of Gucci*, Ben Affleck in *The Last Duel*, Kate Blanchett in *Don't Look Up* and *Nightmare Alley*).[1] How does this boisterous return sit against the silent backdrop of 2020, when the public spectacle of cinema gave way to the personal, private encounter with the small screen? Is it a defiant reaction to the rise of streaming services? Or an excessively defensive response which marks the final breath of a dying medium? Perhaps, through a Lacanian prism, there is something worth noting about the fact that these elements of artifice, which at first sight appear overblown, take on a whole new meaning through a second viewing. If, as Ian Parker argues, the closure of theatres allowed our relationship with the small screen to reach new levels of intimacy, intensifying in the process the "exhaustible character" of online streaming, what is cinema now telling us about its own processes and conditions? (Parker, 2021). We are here reminded of what Lacan often said about painting: that some (anamorphic) works performatively declare themselves as "there to be looked at", in order to catch the observer in their trap (Lacan, 1981, p. 92). Exposing their own artifice – their internal architectural structure – they reveal our "intimacy" to be the product of pleasure (Lust, *Plaisir*) and enjoyment (Geniessen, *jouissance*). At such moments, Lacan notes, "we are literally called into the picture and represented there as caught" (Lacan, 1981, p. 92).

In his analysis of the Coronavirus pandemic Slavoj Žižek offers the following concluding comments on what might be termed cinematic intimacy: "[...] on the subject of movies and TV, gladly succumb to all your guilty pleasures: catastrophic dystopias, comedy series with canned laughter like

DOI: 10.4324/9781003272069-3

Will & Grace, YouTube documentaries on the great battles of the past…" (Žižek, 2020, pp. 134–5). Not for the first time, Žižek's assessment of technology sees him lose his theoretical footing. His insistence that we "succumb to the screen" contrasts starkly with the view offered by Ian Parker who, on much firmer Lacanian ground, focuses on the impossible enjoyment generated by services like Netflix, their "teasing and failing" to fully satisfy. Indeed, if there is a structural logic to Netflix – a topology – then it is surely that of the Lacanian *objet petit a*: "the unfathomable X on account of which, when we confront the object of our desire, more satisfaction is provided by dancing around it than by directly going at it" (Žižek, 2009, p. 136). To repeat his own analysis of Hegel, Žižek seems to miss the very *Žižekian aspect of the phenomenon*: how online streaming platforms follow the curved space of desire, where an object is desirable only because there is a limit which appears to place it out of reach. The binge culture normalised by Netflix – "have all the content you desire" – functions only insofar as it marks *the limit of too much choice*; much like an all you can eat buffet, the frustration it generates is deeply rooted in the notion that one can't possibly consume everything on offer.[2]

## The Viral Logic of Capitalism; the Deceptive Logic of the Virus

To make sense of this phenomenon we need to look again at the pandemic through the lens of cinema. But first we must look back at cinema – the pre-COVID era – *through the prism of the pandemic*. At first glance, one film stands out for its remarkable prescience: the 2019 Oscar winning *Parasite*. It tells the story of a family living in poverty (The Kims) who infiltrate a wealthier household (The Parks) by employing a series of cunning strategies. For Žižekian scholar Matthew Flisfeder, the film points towards "the dawn of a new parasitic age", not in the simplistic sense of the "poor feeding off the rich" but, rather, at the level of the capitalist system itself. "Much like a parasite", Flisfeder writes, capitalism "exhausts and devours global resources, leaving the majority to scramble and fight amongst ourselves for basic needs" (Flisfeder, 2020). The parallel with the coronavirus is obvious: like COVID-19, capitalism "infects and replicates, and eats away at all forms of life confronting it". This viral dimension appears to be implicit in Žižek's description, in *The Sublime Object of Ideology*, of "the paradox proper to capitalism": how it harnesses inherent contradictions in order to fuel its own constant regeneration. "Capitalism", Žižek writes, "is capable of transforming its limit, its very impotence, in the source of its power – the more it 'putrifies', the more its immanent contradiction is aggravated, the more it must revolutionise itself to survive" (2008, pp. 53–4). Internal limitation – where surplus enjoyment emerges as an excess – functions as the impetus for the system's constant development.

It is precisely these libidinal dynamics that we recognise in *Parasite*. The Kims take advantage of the Park family's central human weakness – the naïve trust they place in strangers – by feeding off their insecurities – their need to keep out external threats. To achieve this, the Kims employ a specific two-pronged tactic: first, they orchestrate a series of elaborate scenarios which lead to the removal of the existing household staff; next, they present themselves as ideal replacements. An inherent tension is thus identified, amplified and, finally, transformed into a source of power. Can this interpretation be extended further, taking into account our concrete experience of the pandemic? On a very general level, there are a number of other obvious overlaps between *Parasite* and our current situation. Like the Kim family, COVID-19 spreads by feeding off our weakness for social interaction; it is a non-human enemy which transforms our innate human need to connect into a source of power. *Parasite* also contains a number of singular details which only now, from the perspective of the present, appear strikingly *Covidesque*: Mrs Park's obsessive requests that her driver wash his hands; her frantic efforts to cover her face with a mask. The scene in which the housekeeper coughs into a bin reverberates (retroactively) with COVID connotations. The accumulation of such scenes draws our attention to another structural feature: the Park family's anxieties *are always rooted in questions of health and hygiene*. Indeed, the film seems to depict the "new normal" described by Žižek in his response to the pandemic: an increased fear of a more contaminated Other who threatens to infect the clean, hyper-sanitised space of our closed, protected existence (Žižek, 2020). But *Parasite* allows us to see a key point overlooked by Žižek. The Kims are able to invade and manipulate the internal mechanics of the Parks domestic life through a precise strategy of *deception*: the series of health threats are the product of a carefully stage-managed performance. Each scenario is choreographed with the intention of granting the external enemy access to the host. In the film, the "health crisis" is a ruse designed to facilitate and conceal the real threat: a virus which spreads by presenting itself as the solution to the very problem it creates.

Is something similar not at work in the way we have engaged with technology during the pandemic? This is the central idea behind what I call *screen contagion*. The working hypothesis is that COVID-19 is itself a symptom – in the purely Lacanian sense – of a shadow pandemic operating in the background (and 'on the back of') the current public health crisis: namely, the creeping encroachment of screens into every aspect of our lives. Like the Park family, we have experienced two years of anxiety-inducing health concerns. In many ways, it is easy to be duped into thinking technology provides solutions to the many issues the pandemic has presented. Facebook, Whatsapp and Instagram (and for a period, TikTok) seemed to alleviate the psychological effects of isolation; Amazon responded to our basic consumer needs; Netflix ensured a minimal level of entertainment by providing a maximum amount of digestible content. Post-lockdown, technology has continued to make our lives easier, allowing life to continue as normal: cashless smartphone payments avoid contamination through the physical exchange of money; apps allow health, testing and vaccine status to be monitored, etc. As COVID-19 has wrought havoc around the globe, the screen has come to assume a more central place in all our lives. Now, with the clouds of the crisis receding, it seems essential to the basic fabric of our everyday social existence.

In our acceptance of a quick-fix cure, have we allowed a more insidious virus to spread? Technology presents itself as a functional tool or mediating device, a neutral ally in the fight against COVID. But as in *Parasite*, the external enemy tricks the host into opening its doors under the guise of a remedy offered during a period of panic. On the surface, the use of cashless payment seems rational, given the risk of infection through direct handling of paper money. Nevertheless, the broader (dialectical) brushstrokes cannot be ignored, particularly against the backdrop of cryptocurrency. The "sublime" status of money, Žižek reminds us, is rooted in an act of fetishistic disavowal, whereby the physical material is blindly perceived as incorruptible: we know very well that money deteriorates over time, that it is subject to contamination; and yet, in our practice, we continue to treat it as if it contains some immutable essence. Could we be witnessing a fundamental shift into another "spirit" of capitalism, through a de-fetishisation of what Marx called the one true commodity? With each simple flash of our smartphone, money loses a degree of its mystical aura until, gradually, the spell is fully broken when the place of fetishism changes. But where exactly will this new *place* emerge?[3]

## Facebook and the Auto-immune Response

During lockdown, Facebook seemed to magically transform itself into a neutral platform through an operation of self-sanitisation that saw it return to its original mission of "connecting people". This initial period of blind refusal to recognise the proven a-neutral status of Facebook – its key role in promoting radicalisation, hate speech, anxiety, depression, political polarisation, etc. – follows the formula of fetishistic disavowal: "I know very well it is harmful but... *it allows me to stay connected*". Our actions bear all the hallmarks of what Žižek calls "cynical reason": despite what we know about Facebook, in our everyday activity we remain engaged. This is why one should remain sceptical – but not cynical – of the recent backlash against Big Tech. Given the mass levels of engagement during COVID, is there not something excessive about the sudden condemnation of figures like Jeff Bezos and Mark Zuckerberg? The target of our ire, obscene sums of wealth totalling 63 billion (for Bezos) during lockdown, is actually a direct indicator of how much we continue to use their products, an external embodiment of our own complicity in the crime. For this reason, the theatrical spectacle of hauling the heads of tech companies in front of the US Congress strikes us as an act of displacement: an effort to exert power that does nothing but expose our own state of impotence. Even now, as we acknowledge the harmful impact of these "tools", we remain prisoners at the level of our everyday habits. The gesture of liberation, the desperate effort to pull back the mask and expose the hidden truth, simply diverts attention from the fact that, in our actions, we "still find reasons to retain the mask" (Žižek, 2008, p. 26).

Resistance thus appears as futile as it is performative. More worryingly, increased knowledge ("I know but...") can also reinforce the (cynical) effectivity of the practice. The response is no longer just purely perfunctory; it also exacerbates the issue it is attempting to tackle: the algorithmic enemy within on behalf of whom we are now acting, *whose work we are now fulfilling*. To borrow another epidemiological analogy, the current response to Big Tech is akin to the body's inflammatory immune response to COVID-19: what appears as a defence against an external threat is actually a (symptomatic) indication of how far the virus has spread internally, and how serious the long-term impact may become. More and more we are witnessing signs that this algorithmic virus has already infiltrated the social body where it is attacking our institutional organs, the (legal, moral) fabric into which the social bond is stitched. The effects of technology now manifest themselves as a type of "acting out" of the algorithm, explosive events which are as unexplained as they are inexplicable – until, that is, we find a way to approach them from the appropriate perspective.

## Fake News and Time Travel

The point is that both the passive acceptance and active rejection of technology display the same logic of cynical reason. Increased knowledge and awareness does nothing to affect the levels of active engagement. On the contrary, the more we are aware, the more we adopt a cynical distance, the more engaged we actually become. Renunciation, as Lacan reminds us, produces its own excess of enjoyment. The problem with the current response to technology is that it remains overtly focused – at the level, first, of consumption and, then, concern – on questions of content. Consequently, the key effects of form are overlooked. What ultimately *interpellates* us, Žižek writes, is not the content of the attitude but the "consistency of the form" which sustains it (Žižek, 2008, p. 90); it is the formal conditions of the practice which explain "the fact.... that we follow even the most dubious opinions once our mind has been made up regarding them" (Žižek, 2008, p. 92). Consider the paradoxical logic of fake news: why is it that, even when in possession of the facts, people continue to engage in stories they know to be false? The idea of ideological bias – that we believe whatever supports our pre-existing ideas and assumptions – does not stand up to the *simple truth revealed by fake news*: ideas and assumptions hold little motivating power over users; in fact, content is secondary to the forces at work in the architecture of the network. This is the reign of cynical reason: "even when we know something to be false", Žižek writes, "even if we keep our distance, *we are still doing it*" (2008, p. 30).

Against this attitude, and in the context of COVID, cinema comes to play a decisive role. Ian Parker makes the important point that in order to understand how psychoanalysis speaks to us about film, we need to focus both on the question of content *and form*. This immediately places the analyst on an aesthetic footing, where the charged effect of motif, texture, and composition are central concerns.[4] It is this interpretative manoeuvre which allows for a more nuanced reading of *Parasite*. Flisfeder delves into the film's deeper significance, how it reads (metaphorically) as an analogy for our age. But in doing so he forgets the central rule of psychoanalysis: that the "true secret", Žižek writes, "is not the secret behind the form but the secret of this form itself" (2008, p. 8). Instead of probing questions of underlying meaning, one should isolate the film's surface effects, the seemingly insignificant details of structure and arrangement that acquire new meaning within a different frame or context.

Is it any wonder, then, that Freud was such an avid reader of Arthur Conan Doyle's work? In *Looking Awry*, Žižek discusses the parallels between the detective method and the analytic approach: how both avoid the "lure" of signification and meaning, focusing instead on the symptomatic distortions that shine a light on questions of form. Confronted with a crime scene, Sherlock Holmes resists the immediate interpretation while simultaneously utilising his side-kick Watson (who always accepts the most obvious reading) to identify the deception concealing the criminal's actions. Holmes is interested in the curious details and singular features that, in refusing to fit what appears self-evident, expose the crime scene as an artificial construction. These clues are, in a psychoanalytic sense, symptoms that have yet to acquire their symbolic weight. Only through the *retroactive effect of signification* – when, in the final analysis, the detective tells the true story of how the crime was actually committed (and concealed) – the pieces of evidence are included in a causal chain of linear events. When first encountered they appear insignificant; they are meaningful only from the perspective of the future, as a fragment of an as-yet untold story. "That", Lacan explains,

> is how things which mean nothing all of a sudden signify something, but in a quite different domain [...] The symptom initially appears to us as a trace, which will only ever be a trace, one which will continue not to be understood until the analysis has got quite a long way, and until we have realised its meaning.
> (Lacan, 1988, p. 159 in Žižek, 2008, p. 57)

Such is the unique temporal logic of the detective and psychoanalyst's methodology: from a position in the present, both engage in a simultaneous journey into the past and the future. They are effectively "producing the symbolic reality of past, long-forgotten events" by recognising elements whose time is yet to come (Žižek, 2008, pp. 58–59). In this sense, a traumatic event in the present is always a repetition of the past which, in the future, will "become what it always was" (Žižek, 2008, p. 59).

It is towards this position that cinema – building on what Lacan saw as a specific anamorphic history in painting – leads us. During the peak of the pandemic, one film rose to the challenge of breaking our intimate engagement with screens by drawing the public back to the theatre: Christopher Nolan's *Tenet*. How does *Tenet* evoke – and provoke – a psychoanalytic reading? Firstly, it forces us to disengage from our fascination with content by foregrounding the significance of form. The impossibly complex storyline underscores the narrative structure in which a curious temporal circularity is at play. Following the logic of the symptom, moments from the opening scene are literally "signs from the future", fragments which make sense only when seen again at the end of the film, where they appear in a linear causal chain. The temporal "Pincer" – a single battle fought on two fronts, with a group in the present supported by another from the future – offers a perfect demonstration of the analytic method. Like in analysis, the logic is both linear and retroactive: one returns to an event in the past with a new stabilising frame, in order to remake a future which *always will have been*. The Pincer thus acts as a symbolic framework in which seemingly insignificant details acquire their full meaning *after the fact*. Nolan's great achievement is to fold back the same procedure onto the question of cinema itself, forcing us to acknowledge how our *own relation to the big screen* is part of the story being narrated *on screen*. In this sense, the film's form also acquires retroactive meaning (like a symptom) once it is placed within the (symbolic) framework provided by its own narrative.

To clarify this point one need only ask: what might Sherlock Holmes have to say about *Tenet*? Is it not curious that the main protagonist – who, in another attempt to keep the viewer "on the surface", is simply named "Protagonist" – returns from the future but chooses to use a Nokia phone? Something similar is evident in *Parasite* where the screen and the smartphone play an important but innocuous structural role. Like the letter in Moliere's *Le Misanthrope* (the key plot device whose contents the viewer never discovers), the smartphone is the element which drives the entire plot (the central scene which shows a power struggle over the smartphone indicates as much). In each case, the reference to the screen is consistent and disquieting. It functions as a stain or shadow in our field of vision – what Lacan calls "scotoma" – that, once viewed from the correct – disengaged – perspective, forces us to consider how our own engagement with the interface (the form) is part of what we are watching (the content). This is most obvious in the cracking effect in *Black Mirror* and, more recently, the 2018 film *Black Mirror: Bandersnatch*, in which the viewer literally becomes a protagonist, capable of making choices that affect the plot. Returning to the detective genre, cinema can be said to reduce the luring mechanism – or fantasy – to its fundamental mediating structure. It is ultimately the screen itself – and not the content it presents – which co-ordinates our actions and desires. This was the great challenge presented to Hercule Poirot in *Curtain: Poirot's Last Case*: a series of separate crimes were all marked by the imprint of one individual – a Mr X – who, rather than acting directly, motivates others by playing on their deepest impulses. How to catch such a criminal?

## Technology and Public Health: A Psychoanalytic Perspective

The concept of screen contagion can only be fully developed by answering a key question: what exactly is this virus doing to us? This involves examining how, like the Park family, technology succeeds in presenting itself *as the cure to the very problem it creates*. As we rely more and more on screens, it is easy to forget the debates around mental health that dominated public discourse before the pandemic. Lest we forget, pre-COVID, the world was already in the grip of what psychologist Adam Alter called "a fully blown epidemic" of screen addiction.[5] Indeed, before the coronavirus struck, the central area of focus for the Centre for Disease Control and Prevention in the US was the worrying rise of teenage suicide. Reporting in *The New York Times* – 18 days before the first cases of COVID-19 were reported in China – Jane E. Brody writes ominously: "Had any other fatal or potentially fatal condition leapfrogged like this, the resulting alarm would have initiated a frantic search for its cause and cure".[6] Yet, unlike the rapid response to COVID, the question of causality still remains unclear. This is despite the fact that, for many clinical psychologists, "the evidence is strong and consistent both for symptoms and behavior".[7] There is now a growing scientific consensus that the effects of mental health should be attributed to widespread social media and smartphone use, coupled with a constant pressure to be active online. If, initially, it appeared coincidental that the spike in cases of youth suicide after a stable period between 2002 and 2007 ran parallel to the concomitant rise in platforms like Facebook and Instagram and the rapid proliferation of smartphone devices, a mounting body of research is now confirming a causal rather than correlative link.[8]

The impact of screens and social media is already being considered a "public health" risk.[9] The field of neuroscience is perhaps making the most advances in determining cause. An experiment by five neuroscientists in 2014 concluded that Facebook triggers the same impulsive part of the brain as gambling and substance abuse.[10] The term "persuasive tech" is now used to describe the effect of technology in programming and ultimately hijacking the two basic neural pathways in the brain that control human behaviour.[11] But neuroscience alone is unable to establish a link between addiction and mental health. Not only is it difficult to prove whether increased use of technology leads to mental illness, or vice-versa; the identification of possible cause does not determine treatment or, indeed, cure.[12]

At this juncture, clinical psychology offers a way forward by focusing on quantitative issues like emotional development, loss of face-to-face interaction, negative competition for status, unfiltered access to sites, etc. But all too often this perspective resorts to conceptual generalisations, drawing vague conclusions, that leave questions of self-identity and "base impulse" unexplored.[13] Two lines of further enquiry, therefore, need to be pursued: to shed light on the nature of the addiction – and its psychological impact – one must first understand the substance being abused. Only then can the libidinal and psychic effects – the precise nature of "identity" and "impulse" – be properly addressed. On both fronts, the tools of psychoanalysis are indispensable.

## Impulse and Identity Online: A Lacanian Intervention

Consider again how Facebook triggers the same neural pathways as gambling and substance abuse. Neurological studies of slot machines have found that this impulse is associated less with the "full-misses" than the "near-miss". "'Near-miss' events, where unsuccessful outcomes are proximal to the jackpot, increase gambling propensity... through the anomalous recruitment of reward circuitry".[14] Addictiveness, in other words, is based on the act of missing rather than achieving one's goal; the experience of the "jackpot" as lacking, the direct encounter with failure, creates a neural response which increases a desire to play. We recognise, once again, the classic Lacanian distinction between pleasure (*Lust, Plaisir*) and enjoyment (*Geniessen, jouissance*):

> The basic paradox of jouissance is that it is impossible and unavoidable: it is never fully achieved, always missed, but simultaneously, we never can get rid of it – every renunciation of enjoyment generates an enjoyment in renunciation, every obstacle to desire generates a desire for obstacle, etc.
> (Žižek, 2009, pp. 136–7)

Lacan's basic point is that failure – the "near-miss" – continues to act on the pleasure principle by re-producing its own surplus of enjoyment: "sometimes", Žižek writes, "the shortest way to realise a desire is to by-pass its object goal, to circulate around it, to postpone its encounter" (Žižek, p. 136). Does this "near-miss" logic not define our entire relationship with technology? From the "persuasive" appeal of sites like Netflix, to the physical tactility of the screen ("please touch"), to the barred, peephole temptation of a Google search engine, to the image of long queues outside Apple stores – everything is designed to keep the user circulating around an explicitly inscribed limit which keeps the user in a constant state of perpetually unfulfilled desire, an endless Beckettian experience of waiting for the next piece of content. Ultimately, the curved space of desire is maintained by ensuring direct awareness – experience – of the curvature.

If the logic of *objet a* ensures the addictive potential of technology, what is happening at the level of identity formation? Online, the subject cleaves to his/

her object in two ways: content is both that which we consume and the "stuff" in relation to which we identify ourselves.[15] Consider how the echo chamber enacts what Lacan calls the "twofold movement" of symbolic identification. In phase one an individual considers himself as belonging to a particular group (for example, the ranks of the proletariat); but it is only in phase two, when he joins a general strike that his identity is fully actualised (Lacan, 2002, pp. 72–73; cited in Žižek, 2006, p. 15). Similarly, offline, I see myself in a particular way and would like to be perceived as such by others; online, I performatively actualise this self-image in a structured network of meaning –a social network – under the presupposed gaze of a more intensely personified big Other. What Lacan calls the "ego-ideal" [*Idealich*] [I(A)] is "the point in the big Other from which I observe (and judge) myself" (Žižek, 2006b, p. 80). It is the place to which I performatively refer, the gaze to which I understand myself as responding. This is why one's online activity is always marked by a reflexive reference – selfie, status update – to an imaginary, collective audience (of friends, followers, etc.).

For the ego-ideal to properly function, it must remain fully recognisable and identifiable for the subject. Thus, as one's self-image ("ideal-ego") changes, the gaze to which one refers must become more personalised. Consider how Facebook "friends" begin as an anonymous group until the user becomes uncomfortable with being followed by strangers. By blocking requests, we selectively tailor our audience to reflect "real-world" friends, people we know, people with whom we can identify more fully. Over time, the algorithm extends this field to people who share our interests until, ultimately, the gaze becomes fully personalised on a politicised/ideological level. And is the shift from the public platform of Facebook to the more intimate space of WhatsApp not a simple continuation of this process? One forgets that WhatsApp is not separate to Facebook; it is simply a more "private" corner of the network where the big Other is more intensely personalised. Through groups of friends, each responding to a different aspect of our "personality", we are able to identify with the gaze of "another person in the fullest sense of the term", a virtual audience which "experiences full wrath, revengefulness, jealousy, etc., as every human being" (Žižek, 2001, pp. 130–31).

What drives this increasing level of user engagement – the increased personalisation of the ego-ideal through a progressive tailoring of content – is the concomitant change in the nature of imaginary identity. The key Lacanian concept here is the effect of retroversion: at a certain moment an online identity produced externally through an autonomous process of data-mining becomes misrecognised as the inner essence of one's being. Progressively, content is internalised as the imaginary substance of identity. Simply put, the more I post the more I identify with my online audience, the more this form of identification is incorporated into my own self-image. What is in reality the product of an algorithmic operation is misrecognised retroactively "as something which was already there from the beginning" (Žižek, 2008, p. 115). Once this inversion occurs, the subject sees himself differently; in turn, he seeks a deeper, more personal connection with a more relatable online gaze. Offline, and dialectically speaking, this process involves the historical movement of what Hegel calls "self-determination" (*Selbstbestimmung*), the slow passage from substance to subject. But online, historical epochs are traversed instantaneously through the workings of the algorithm. As engagement increases, a new *digital* ego becomes the new seat of action and motivation. Once the subject's inner self-experience is altered in this way, he misrecognises himself "as an autonomous agent which is present ...as the origin of his acts" (Žižek, 2008, p. 16). As Lacan explains, the subject becomes a "filled out" person (Lacan, 2006, p. 685) when the "stuff" of his being (ibid, p. 691) supports the "inner-life" of his phenomenal (self-) experience.

But the crucial point is that identity is only fully realised when acted out in practice. This is where a direct line can be drawn from the harmless act of taking selfies to actions driven by a politicised gaze. Events like the assault on the US Capitol are "real time" performances of what is happening on the algorithmic stage. The very *real life impact* of these events indicates a viral spread: the fact that the stage itself is expanding. This is the key to understanding the Trump phenomenon: like the worker who joins a strike, someone who identifies as a Trump supporter on social media needs to actualise this identity by actively attending a rally or casting a vote. What is most worrying is the shift in the terrain of identification/action: where once a tweet was enough to constitute symbolic identification, now the crystallisation of digital subjectivity shifts the ground of the ego offline. In turn, the algorithmic process of personalisation – the ordeal of negativity which alters the make-up of the symbolic order – continues into the social space, where the impact of these performative acts becomes more extreme. At the same time, the normalisation of screen use ensures that these events are more difficult to identify.

Before COVID, outbursts of raw antagonism were explicitly marked by a reflexive appeal to an online audience (the selfie effect). But as the distance between the social and virtual worlds closes, these events are beginning to lose their symbolic force, their performative dimension. Through a digital "quilting" (*capitonner*) of the social bond, the virtualised Other imagined by the subject in the field of social media will no longer be easily located. It is in this sense that – not unlike the supposed origins of COVID-19 – the virus "jumps" from the virtual to the public space. Expanding its reach through a fully digitalised subjectivity, it infects the social body, eroding its institutional and ethical foundations. With this creeping expansion – a viral form of *digital tectonics*[16] – the inter-subjective space begins to appear ever more foreign and disconcerting, thus driving the digital subject's return to his native land.

## The Epidemiological Dimension of the Freudian Method

If a virus is at work, how can psychoanalysis help us understand the process of infection? Now is the appropriate time, when epidemiological awareness is ingrained in everyday practice, to examine technology with the same precision that characterised our response to the pandemic. My wager is that psychoanalysis is a privileged tool in this regard, due to the unthought epidemiological potential of the Freudian method. As discussed, the essential feature of this approach concerns the logic of the symptom. In dream analysis, fascination with the underlying cause gives way to the understanding that everything takes place *on the surface*. Is this attention to form not also the key feature of the epidemiological model? To consider social media and screen use as a public health risk, specific problems (such as mental health, radicalisation, etc) must be viewed not in isolation but as *effects which precede their cause* (Žižek, 2008, p. 59). They are, in other words, symptoms in the purest sense – not manifestations of a deeper malaise but rather, outcomes of a structural process. With this shift in thinking, a vast array of seemingly disconnected issues is seen to contain the same common denominator: the consistent presence of a Mr X indirectly pulling the strings. Specifically, a sequence of seemingly irrational, inexplicable events are understood as pointing indexically – and horizontally – to the domain of screen use and social media.

Thanks to COVID-19, this inverted understanding of cause and effect has become part of the collective consciousness. The global response to the coronavirus has allowed for a new set of habits to become common practice, leading to a heightened awareness of the logic of the symptom. Every preventative measure – from social distancing, to wearing of masks – is designed to treat each case as a symptom of a broader, wider viral spread. In the process we have become more attuned to *surface effects*: the horizontal logic of transmission; increased attention to distance and proximity to objects and people. After two years, we are now more accustomed to treating our symptoms not just as possible manifestations of a virus within the body but, rather, as effects which precede their cause: a virus jumping *from body to body*. To a certain extent, this shift mirrors the beginning of the psychoanalytic procedure, when the inward focus (*"what's wrong with me?" "what does my symptom mean?"*) is blocked, deflected outward, forcing us to think of ourselves as nodes in a network of social inter-relations and connections. Cut from the comfort of the ego, we come to think of our physical bodies as markers in a symbolic order of traced contacts and encounters.

Building on this crossover of epidemiology and psychoanalysis, what might a Freudian reading of the algorithm look like? The problem with efforts to address the impact of AI, as I have noted, concerns an excessive fascination with the lure of content. The terminology itself – "rabbit-hole", "filter-bubble", "echo-chamber", "youloop" – is enough to indicate the formal conditions at stake: the fact that the primary effects are structural, architectural, *tectonic*: the *hole*, the *bubble*, the *chamber*, the *loop*. An algorithm is a compositional, ordering and reordering tool. It curates our online worlds through the act of placement and positioning; only after this process of displacement and condensation is content production possible. In the viral spread of misinformation, infection occurs not at the level of content but through the algorithm's unsuspecting formal mechanisms. Operating horizontally, it builds rather than interprets pre-existing prejudices; it produces a worldview based on alternative facts by first creating a space in which facts can acquire alternative status. This is why the primary processes of the filter bubble are entirely on the surface: the filtering of content is possible only if the curved shape of the bubble itself is maintained.

Can this analysis allow us to define the algorithm as a "virus particle"? With COVID-19, the question of anatomy is paramount: the effect of the virus particle or virion – SARS-COV-2 – is based on its *conformational* qualities. This means that, as a physical entity, it initiates infection through its manner of formation, its structure, its form. Like the algorithm, SARS-COV-2 operates through a symmetrical disposition or arrangement of parts, a process of conforming, adapting, and adjusting.[17] It is therefore *tectonic* in the geographical and architectural sense: there is an important distinction between its external structure and the large-scale processes which take place within it. The same is true of the algorithm – its content is secondary to its mode of adaptation and structural variation – the way it alters and changes its code to maintain user engagement. The actual substance within the filter bubble is secondary to its *tectonic* function.

With COVID-19, the substance of SARS-COV-2 (what it contains) is RNA: a molecule like DNA which stores genetic information as a sequence of chemical letters called nucleotides. The algorithm follows a similar logic: essentially, it is a set of instructions that take in input and provide output, and in the process changing the data involved. In other words, we feed data (into Youtube, Google, Facebook, etc) and we receive content (friend suggestions, tailored ads, news stories, suggested videos, etc) which matches our interests, beliefs, desires. The algorithm does not create any content – it relies on the user to input content, which can then be sent back in a feedback loop. The same is true with the COVID-19 virion: it does not carry the proteins it needs from cell to cell but rather relies on the host cell to reproduce them. Both the virion and the algorithm rely entirely on outer structure – questions of scaffolding – to perform key operations. Both attempt to hi-jack the host's internal systems – the brain's neural pathways, the cell's protein producing machinery – in order to reproduce the substance (content/proteins) they need to reproduce themselves. Like SARS-COV-2 – and the strategy employed by the Kim family – the algorithm does nothing but reproduce, expand, and overwhelm by replicating the information generated by the input of the user. The aim, like a virus, is simply to reproduce more of what we were already looking for until the user, overwhelmed with content, concedes control.[18]

In COVID-19, the key feature of intruder RNA is that it "is formatted to look like the messenger RNA which tells cells what proteins to make".[19] The same occurs in the tailoring of information in an algorithmic feedback loop: content and data are formatted to match the viewer's likes and interests.

When this (intruder) content is internalised by the host – i.e. we misrecognise it as the inner essence of our self-experience – our internal psychic machinery is in a sense fooled. In terms of COVID-19, RNA gets into the human cell and the protein-making machinery in the cell is "flummoxed": it "starts reading the viral genes and making the proteins they describe". In terms of the algorithm, we begin treating the viral substance as our own, and literally start to act out the algorithm's instructions. Like in *Parasite*, we are lured because the data the algorithm sends back to us is formatted to appear "natural". The invader is misperceived as the guest; and the host reproduces the data the virus needs to reproduce itself. The ultimate aim is not destruction but overstimulation: the virus provokes the immune system's inflammatory response, leading to a desperate fight against the external enemy. But this act of defence is itself a sign that the host is already overwhelmed by the enemy within.

## Towards a Collective Response

At issue at the dawn of a "parasitic age" is a full digital migration to an entire online world now expanding rapidly into a (meta) universe. And yet, the pandemic provides a moment of opening, a raw corporeal experience of radical negativity which is no longer possible in the digital realm. Newly sensitised by COVID, the body experiences the intimacy of the screen more fully. Whether at work, play or rest, our engagement with digital devices has become intensely tactile (typing, plugging, touching, tapping, etc.). An increased sensibility towards contaminated surfaces only serves to make this corporeal experience more palpable. This overwhelming proximity upsets the homeostatic balance of *objet a* underpinning this intimacy: we learn that our desire is fuelled not by the endless choice of seemingly infinite content but, rather, by the pre-inscribed barrier blocking our access.[20] The Zoom encounter further intensifies the intimacy of our relation to the Other, exposing, in turn, the screen's role in mediating this relation. Online, a number of structural features become visible: how the Other's gaze is displaced – to look someone in the eye one needs to shift one's view to the camera; how, in a perfect demonstration of Lacan's "I see myself seeing myself", we make ourselves an object – a picture – for the gaze of Others.

What does this mean for the future of psychoanalysis in the digital realm? When the analyst was forced to move his/her practice online during lockdown, these new spatial conditions presented obstacles to the established clinical method.[21] But in fact, through a doubling up of the Lacanian model, the disruptions to the symptomatic approach are themselves symptoms – fissures in the texture of the mediated interface which, when viewed in their form of appearance, actually indicate the essential co-ordinates of the subject's fundamental fantasy. This is the opportunity the pandemic presents for the practice of psychoanalysis. Online, such performative and fetishistic excesses usually have no time to make themselves felt. Every anamorphic stain – the question mark (*Che Vuoi?*) rising above the utterance, the gap between object goal and cause – is automatically wiped clean by the hyper-sanitising force of the algorithm, which, through adaptation and re-alignment, repositions the subject in a more intense relationship with more (personally) engaging content. If, in Lacan's schematic conception, the Symbolic and Imaginary are the inverse and obverse of the same structural surface – the Real being the twist which connects them – then online this surface is flattened: the two modalities appear on the same side. This means that, beyond COVID, the available box of psychoanalytic tools will no longer be sufficient to address a mode of algorithmic subjectivity. New disciplinary models are required: for example, Art history – to draw out Lacan's thoughts on the compositional/curatorial logic of desire at work in screens and images; Neuroscience and Philosophy – to rethink the strictly structural conception of the symptom in more fluid, malleable terms. Faced with a mutating enemy, intellectual mutation is the only effective response.[22]

## Notes

1 Kyle Buchanan. "Forget naturalism. With movie acting this year, big swings are in". *The New York Times*, December 15, 2021. Available at: https://www.nytimes.com/2021/12/15/movies/oscars-lady-gaga-ben-affleck-cate-blanchett.html
2 Netflix makes no secret of its approach, declaring that its "only competition is sleep" (see https://www.independent.co.uk/life-style/gadgets-and-tech/news/netflix-downloads-sleep-biggest-competition-video-streaming-ceo-reed-hastings-amazon-prime-sky-go-now-tv-a7690561.html). Netflix produced shows like *Too Hot to Handle* also exemplify the logic of the platform itself. A group of young, attractive men and woman think they are part of a reality show called *Pleasure Island* – where the goal, they believe, is endless pleasure. But, in a Lacanian shift from the logic of pleasure (Lust, Plaisir) to enjoyment (Geniessen, *jouissance*), the contestants are told that all forms of sexual activity are forbidden. Desire is then re-coordinated in the direction of a cash prize (which reduces the more the contestants break the rules). In a perfect demonstration of how Netflix operates, the limitation placed on pleasure (all the content you can consume) generates an excess of enjoyment. Lacan's lesson becomes clear: the goal of desire is always "too hot to handle"; or, as one contestant exclaims when discovering the rules of the game: "this ban is making me more horny".
3 Consider also the recent resistance to the introduction of "vaccine passes" in countries like France. At the heart of the debate is a philosophical dilemma whereby the exercise of individual freedom threatens the freedom of another individual. One should recall here Žižek's notion of the parallax: when faced with a debilitating deadlock between two irreconcilable positions, we must resist the temptation to choose sides. Rather than becoming caught up in questions of content, one needs to focus on the (parallax) gap preceding the opposition itself (Žižek, 2006a, p. 7). Only then do we begin to notice the broader set of structural operations framing the antagonism, the key point obscured by the debate: what is becoming mandatory is not the vaccine but the screen, the smartphone on which proof of vaccination is demonstrated. Is it possible to imagine a future in which possession of a smartphone will be required by law?
4 *The Year the Cinemas Closed: Psychoanalysing Shifting Screens*. The Irish Psychoanalytic Film Festival. Dublin, March 27, 2021.

5 Haley Sweetland Edwards. "You're addicted to your smartphone. This company thinks it can change that". *Time*, April 12, 2018.
6 In December 2019, an article in the *New York Times* reported on a 56% increase in the rate of suicide among 10–24 year olds between 2007 and 2017 and a 400% increase in suicide attempts in the same age group since 2011. "Youth Suicide is at Crisis Point". Jane E. Brody. *The New York Times* (International). See Friday, December 13, 2019: https://www.nytimes.com/2019/12/02/well/mind/the-crisis-in-youth-suicide.html. Henry A. Spiller, director of the Central Ohio Poison Centre, called this trend "devastating" and noted that the quadrupling of suicide attempts is "likely an undercount". See also: https://www.nytimes.com/2020/01/06/opinion/suicide-young-people.html and https://www.nytimes.com/2018/06/23/opinion/sunday/suicide-rate-existential-crisis.html
7 This is according to Jean M. Twenge, research psychologist at San Diego State University and author of the book "iGen" which looks at mental health trends in those born after 1995. See op. cit. note 5.
8 To mark the end of "mental-health awareness week" in 2018 a campaign run by the Mental Health Foundation, a British charity found that roughly a quarter of British adults have been diagnosed at some point with a psychiatric disorder. At the time it was noted that, although these illnesses can have many causes, there is a growing body of research which "demonstrates that in young people they are linked with heavy consumption of social media". According to a survey in 2017 by the Royal Society for Public Health, Britons aged 14–24 believe that Facebook, Instagram, Snapchat and Twitter have detrimental effects on their wellbeing […] exacerbating anxiety and depression, sleep deprivation, increased body-image concerns, problems which, according to academic studies, are particularly severe among frequent users. Another convincing effort was a survey that tracked a group of 5,208 Americans between 2013 and 2015. It found that an increase in Facebook activity was associated with a future decrease in reported mental health. See "How heavy use of social media is linked to mental illness". *The Economist*, May 18, 2018. See: https://www.economist.com/graphic-detail/2018/05/18/how-heavy-use-of-social-media-is-linked-to-mental-illness
9 Cynthia Miller-Idriss, director of the Polarization and Extremism Research & Innovation Lab (PERIL) in the Center for University Excellence (CUE) at the American University in Washington, DC, argues for a "public health approach" which, rather than focusing directly on extremism (in the US and beyond), analyses instead the "fertile ground" on which it thrives: namely, the online world of "rabbit holes that offer up whole worlds of disinformation and hate". Cynthia Miller-Idriss. "America's most urgent threat comes from within". *The New York Times*, January 7, 2022. See: https://www.nytimes.com/2022/01/05/opinion/jan-6-domestic-extremism.html.
10 See "Examination of neural systems sub-Serving Facebook 'Addiction'". *Psychological Reports 115(3)*, December 2014. DOI:10.2466/18.PR0.115c31z8. Authors: Ofir Turel, Qinghua He, Gui Xue, Lin Xiao, Antoine Bechara.
11 The simple fact is that the websites, apps, interfaces and devices we use are based on the same "business model" that has made Apple, Amazon, Google, Facebook four of the most valuable listed firms in the world: they were all designed using advances in research in neuroscience and behavioural psychology. Beginning in Standford University, researchers have long been studying how computers can be used to influence and control human thoughts and actions by deliberately encouraging and discouraging certain behaviours. Computer engineers Ramsay Brown and T. Dalton Combs explain how behaviour is controlled by two basic neural pathways: "One is structurally weak but helps us make conscious, intentional decisions to serve our long-term goals. The other is more automatic and

easily suggestible... When the brain gets some sort of external cue, like the ding of a Facebook notification, that often precedes a reward, the basal ganglia receive a burst of dopamine, a powerful neurotransmitter linked to the anticipation of pleasure. That three-part process–trigger, action, reward–undergirds the brain's basic habit-forming loop". There then follows a second loop which establishes new behaviour ("to really glue it in tight") by drawing on positive feedback (social approval) or the offer of a rewards ("a cascade of new likes from friends at unpredictable times"). This is what psychologists refer to as "behavioural change with variable rewards" (or, for engineers, "surprise and delight") whereby "the human brain produces more dopamine when it anticipates a reward but doesn't know when it will arrive". See "You're addicted to your smartphone. This company thinks it can change that". *Time*, April 2018. See: https://time.com/5237434/youre-addicted-to-your-smartphone-this-company-thinks-it-can-change-that/

12 Addressing this circular logic, a recent study at the Oxford Internet Institute found no link between teens, tech and mental health. Is the fact that the 430,000 subjects chosen for the study were between the ages of 10 and 15 not indicative of the problem: i.e. increased use at a younger age? And what does this study disprove about the existing findings relating to the crucial 15–24 age bracket?

13 For more on the effect of screens on emotional intelligence see: https://www.sciencedirect.com/science/article/pii/S0747563214003227.

14 Luke Clark, Andrew J. Lawrence, Frances Astley-Jones, and Nicola Gray. "Gambling near-misses enhance motivation to gamble and recruit win-related brain circuitry". *Neuron*, February 2009. See: https://www.ncbi.nlm.nih.gov/pmc/articles/PMC2658737/; On technology and addiction see: K. Malone, C. Bell, and J. Roberts. "Technology and addiction: Subjectivity, scientific knowledge and the economy of jouissance". *Subjectivity*, 8, 147–164 (2015). https://doi.org/10.1057/sub.2015.

15 Elsewhere, I have discussed this point in terms of what Catherine Malabou calls the post-traumatic subject. The argument is summarised as follows: disengaged, withdrawn from the social bond, our online identities are characterised by both a disappearance of personality and an active online engagement by way of persistent jouissance. See Kilroy (2022).

16 This viral spread of an algorithmic infrastructure might be understood using the architectural notion of *digital tectonics*: the translation of architectural designs that are "digitally conceived, structurally clarified" into physical, directly manufactured, real world objects. Can we conceive of the internet in the same way: a "digital fabrication" of an assemblage that will acquire "structural clarity, materiality, and detail" in the social space? (Jabi, 2004, p. 257).

17 'Tectonic conformational changes of a coronavirus spike glycoprotein promote membrane fusion.' Walls, A.C., et al. *PNAS* October 17, 2017, *114* (*42*) 11157–11162; first published October 3, 2017. https://doi.org/10.1073/pnas.1708727114

18 This is why I am tentatively referring to the mode of digitalised subjectivity as the Technetic Subjet: technetium – from the Greek τεχνητός (*tekhnētós*) meaning "artificial, manmade" and -*ium*, meaning the first manmade element synthesised. The subject in question is man-made – artificial – in the same way AI is man-made. The point is that, instead of focusing on the combined mystery and threat of AI we need to confront the true artificial form of intelligence developing *within us*.

19 See: "Understanding SARS-CoV-2 and the drugs that might lessen its power". *The Economist*, March 12, 2020. See: https://www.economist.com/briefing/2020/03/12/understanding-sars-cov-2-and-the-drugs-that-might-lessen-its-power

20 Developing this reading further, is it possible to re-think public policy towards this threat using the coronavirus pandemic as a model? For example, through a radical

reversal or priorities, social distancing measures might be replaced by screen distancing – a re-co-ordination of the libidinal mechanism which keeps us addicted to *jouissance*. Or could "infection" be identified on the basis of symptoms, effects which precede their singular cause: unexplained and inexplicable events (increased levels of anxiety, depression, antagonism, polarisation, radicalisation, etc) which, when viewed as indexical clues, point back – in a manner similar to Poirot's Mr X – the process of online subjectivisation. In confirmed cases, would quarantine involve isolation not from people but from screens?

21 For an elaboration of this point see Kilroy (2020).
22 For more on how Catherine Malabou's concept of negative plasticity develops the viral reading of the algorithm see Kilroy (2022). The hypothesis is that Malabou's neurological re-thinking of "auto-affection" – where a dissociation between two subjects is exposed – supplements the analyst's efforts to localize the Real in the digital field.

## References

Abrahamson, L. and Macdonald, H. (2020). *Normal People*. Written by Sally Rooney and Alice Birch. Dublin: Element Pictures.

Brody, J. (2019). The crisis in youth suicide. *The New York Times (International)*, December 19. Available at: https://www.nytimes.com/2019/12/02/well/mind/the-crisis-in-youth-suicide.html.

Browning, K. and Lorenz, T. (2021). Pro-Trump mob livestreamed its rampage, and made money doing it. *The New York Times*, January 8. Available at: https://www.nytimes.com/2021/01/08/technology/dlive-capitol-mob.html.

Brooker, C. (2011–2019). *Black Mirror*. London: Zeppotron (2011–2013); London: House of Tomorrow (2014–2019).

Clark, L., Lawrence, A.J., Astley-Jones, F., and Gray, R. (2009). Gambling near-misses enhance motivation to gamble and recruit win-related brain circuitry. *Neuron*, 61 (3), February 12, pp. 481–490.

Flisfeder, M. (2020). Capitalism is the parasite; Capitalism is the virus. *The Bullet*, July 26. Available at: https://socialistproject.ca/2020/07/capitalism-is-the-parasite-capitalism-is-the-virus/.

Edwards, H.S. (2018). You're addicted to your smartphone: This company thinks it can change that. *Time*, April 12, 2018.

Jabi, W. (2004). Digital tectonics: the intersection of the physical and the virtual. In S. Williamson, P. Beesley, and N. Chang (eds.), *Fabrication Proceedings: Digital Fabrications, Digital Tools*. Fargo: Association for Computer-Aided Design in Architecture.

Joon-ho, B. (2019). *Parasite*. South Korea: CJ Entertainment.

Kilroy, R. (2020). Zooming with Freud: Screen contagion in the shadow of COVID-19. *Lacunae: APPI International Journal for Lacanian Psychoanalysis*, 21, pp. 34–63.

Kilroy, R. (2021). When the disease is misrecognised as the cure: Screen contagion in the shadow of Covid-19. *The Year the Cinemas Closed: Psychoanalysing Shifting Screens*. The Irish Psychoanalytic Film Festival. Dublin, March 27.

Kilroy, R. (2022, forthcoming). Malabou, Žižek and the plasticity of the algorithm. *Modern Language Notes (MLN)*.

Lacan, J. (1981). *The Seminar of Jacques Lacan, Book XI: The Four Fundamental Concepts of Psychoanalysis* (Ed. J.-A. Miller; Trans. A. Sheridan). New York and London: W.W. Norton & Company.

Lacan, J. (1988). *The Seminar of Jacques Lacan, Book I: Freud's Papers on Technique.* Cambridge: Cambridge University Press.
Lacan, J. (2006). *Écrits: The First Complete Edition in English* (Trans. B. Fink). New York and London: W.W. Norton & Co.
Miller-Idriss, C. (2022). America's most urgent threat comes from within. *The New York Times*, January 7. Available at: https://www.nytimes.com/2022/01/05/opinion/jan-6-domestic-extremism.html.
Nobus, D. (2020). Psychoanalytic practice in technological space? A pandemic seminar with Dany Nobus. Freud Lacan institute (Fli). Dublin, May 27.
Nolan, C. (2020). *Tenet*. Film. Los Angeles: Warner Bros. Pictures
Parker, I. (2021). The Year the Cinemas Closed: Psychoanalysing Shifting Screens. The Irish Psychoanalytic Film Festival. Dublin, March 27.
Slade, D (2018). *Black Mirror: Bandersnatch*. Los Angeles: House of Tomorrow, Netflix.
Walls, C.A., Tortorici, M.A., Snijder, J., Xiong, X., Bosch, G-J., Rey, F.A., and Veesler, D., (2017). Tectonic conformational changes of a coronavirus spike glycoprotein promote membrane fusion. *PNAS*, October 17, 114 (42).
Žižek, S. (1992). *Looking Awry: An Introduction to Jacques Lacan through Popular Culture*. Cambridge, MA: MIT Press.
Žižek, S. (2001). *On Belief*. New York: Routledge.
Žižek, S. (2006a). *The Parallax View*. Cambridge, MA: MIT Press.
Žižek, S. (2006b). *How to Read Lacan*. New York and London: W.W. Norton & Co.
Žižek, S. (2008). *The Sublime Object of Ideology*. London: Verso.
Žižek, S. (2009). Descartes and the post-traumatic subject: On Catherine Malabou's les nouveaux blesses and other autistic monsters. *Qui Parle*, 17(2), Spring/Summer, pp. 123–147.
Žižek, S. (2020). *Pandemic! COVID-19 Shakes the World*. Hoboken, NJ: Wiley Publishing.

Chapter 3

# At the Mercy of the Screen
## Passivity and its Vicissitudes in a Time of Crisis

*Sarah Meehan O'Callaghan*

It would not be a cliché to say that we have lived through challenging times, within which the world has been thrown into crisis. The Chinese word or symbol for crisis 危机 (wēi jī), translated as: "a crucial point, when something begins to change" sums up the recent seismic events we have been living through as a global phenomenon in the shape of the coronavirus pandemic. In this living through of crisis which in time will form a crucial place in our societal epoch, the activities of daily life have been mediated and dominated by the technology of the small screen, and the reduction of our social environment to the domestic space. We have, in many senses, been pacified at the level of the body through the socio-political impositions of managing the coronavirus but pacification has also occurred at the level of the screen and indeed at the level of the techno-mediated gaze. Fundamentally, in this chapter, my argument centres on assuming passivity to be a strong subjective characteristic of the recent pandemic where the human subject has been challenged at the level of the drives, a passivity that has also been experienced as potentially traumatic. Furthermore, I claim that being at the mercy of an existential threat and public health regulations have generated feelings of helplessness and powerlessness, features of a somewhat passive position. In assuming passivity to be such a key signifier of the pandemic, I also wish to draw on a number of paradoxes inherent to this concept, and to highlight the ambiguity of discerning any passive position within subjective fantasy. Indeed, once we focus on passivity as a signifier, we encounter its associated opposite signifier of activity and related similar dichotomies such as safety/danger, idleness/productivity et cetera. In essence, I propose that investigating the pandemic in this way allows us to muddy the waters of these dichotomous signifiers and while the prevailing and widespread command to "stay home and stay safe" enabled us to take refuge from the deadly virus, it also left the subject at the mercy of the drives, from which there is no true reprieve.

That is to say, the prevailing shift to the small screen, while serving as a fundamental connecting point of solidarity and human connectivity, has consequences at the level of the body. While the use of technology has been a creative and life enhancing response to a time of passivity, it has the potential to seduce the subject into the imaginary realm of the virtual, where lack is not absent, but veiled with excess. Overall, the human subject has experienced greater isolation around the body leading to a lack of the embodied gaze, a gaze from which we do not look but which looks at us. It is essential for the human subject to be seen and recognised on different levels. As Lacan says in Seminar XI, "we are beings who are looked at, in the spectacle of the world" (Lacan, 1964, p. 75).

In this chapter, I contend that the embodied gaze regulates differently at the level of jouissance (the drives of the body) than the techno-mediated gaze, that is, the gaze that is transmitted or imagined through the technological screen. For example, we are not seen in all dimensions on Zoom or through the camera of the computer screen, which from the perspective of subjective defence mechanisms, has its advantages and disadvantages and inhibiting or disinhibiting effects/affects. Some people find, for example, that presentations given on Zoom incur greater anxiety than those conducted in person, and vice versa; some find it easier as it incurs less anxiety and seems less "real". Not that the gaze from a Lacanian perspective can be reduced to what is seen or not seen in a tangible sense, but nonetheless it is certainly mediated by the realm of the visible. Ultimately, I argue that this lack of an embodied gaze induces a compulsivity at the level of the imaginary, a compulsivity to which the beleaguered subject of the pandemic may be more exposed. This compulsion of the imaginary stems from anxiety, what in Lacanian terms we consider to be a spilling over of the Real through the gap in the symbolic and is correlative with certain symptoms such as; paranoia and conspiracy theories (Liu, 2021), the increase in eating disorders, excessive exercise, screen use and a range of affects pertaining to loneliness and isolation, stemming from a disenfranchisement at the level of the body concerning in part as I claim in this chapter, the regulation of the gaze. These symptoms are signatures of "a disorder in the real" within the 21st century (Voruz, 2013), and while the increase in these symptoms or what Voruz (p. 1) calls a "proliferation of subjective inventions, of singular modes of jouissance" due to an alteration of the symbolic order is not new, they are certainly seen now in accelerated form. In other words, the pandemic has accelerated this disorder in the real.

In our being more confined to the home, it is possible to consider that bodies made passive during the pandemic – confined and pacified – have encountered small screen domestic household technologies as prostheses and extensions of physical or fantasmatic "reality". Thus, the living space is one of the conditions for the proximity to the small screen. As Merleau-Ponty extrapolated in *The Phenomenology of Perception* (1945), the world shapes the body and the body shapes the world.[1] We are in part moulded or shaped by the environment within which we find ourselves at any given time. In this sense then, the domestic space features as a scene within which a passivity aligned with the current times is played out, a scene where we may encounter the trauma of the drives.

## The Trauma of Passivity

As I have been arguing so far, the pandemic has created a greater propensity to passivity for the average subject than the usual ebb and flow of life would entail. A comic caricature in this regard can be found in Charlie Brooker's documentary *Death to 2020*, where a woman of seeming low intelligence is portrayed as observing all the goings-on of the recent crisis through the small screen of the TV. The outrageous outpourings of Donald Trump appear to her as nothing but a source of entertainment and as potential fictional content. It is as if everything important in the world is happening on a TV show and not as a real-life crisis with real-life and pertinent subjective decisions to be made. The implication is clearly that the average citizen is rather stupid and content to "veg out" in front of the TV screen and not think for themselves. The small screen of the TV, in this instance, is depicted as engulfing the idle human subject, already somewhat passive to begin with, and rendering a certain excess or remainder of passivity, that which is cultivated by the screen, in its wake. In a sense, the coronavirus and the necessity of its curtailment, such as social distancing, have created a widescale call for many subjects to a form of inaction at the level of the body, leading to feelings of frustration, isolation, boredom, anger and depression et cetera.

For example, the mostly global public health dictates ordered us to stay apart and to stay home in order to stay safe from the virus with the accompanying phrase "it might save lives". Although on the one hand, these dictates may incur indignation at being told what to do, on the other, this seems like a pretty straightforward and easy direction. What could be easier amidst a global pandemic than staying at home and watching TV, bingeing on our favourite movies and documentaries and clapping for the essential workers at the heart of the crisis? At least many of us do not have to take up arms on a battlefield or work as a health worker on the front line and risk our lives; instead, we can endorse the heroism from our balconies and praise all those who risk their lives. But this is exactly the problem at stake in the paradox of passivity as the options for taking action within the pandemic have been limited and the subsequent castrations many. This was particularly obvious within the categories of the elderly and medically "vulnerable" who were told they should "cocoon" and stay out of harm's way. As Žižek pointed out in *Pandemic! COVID-19 Shakes the World*, the available avenues of potential subjective response for a citizen vis-à-vis the coronavirus crisis, were saliently polarised into categories of essential versus non-essential workers. Somewhat ironically, given the publication of *Pandemic* within a few months of the crisis, Žižek includes himself in the latter category of those who are forcibly or voluntarily confined to home with nothing to do. His advice for the "non-essential" subject is paradoxical; on the one hand, we should give in to the impulse to binge-watch TV, movies, and indulge in what we enjoy doing without experiencing pressure from the superego:

try to identify with your symptom, without any shame ... fully assume all small rituals, formulas, quirks, and so on, that will help stabilise your daily life. Everything that might work is permitted here if it helps to avoid a mental breakdown, even forms of fetishist denial.

(Žižek, 2020, p. 112)

Yet at the same time, to survive the crisis, and to prevent falling prey to paranoid fantasies, it could be beneficial to be marked by it in some way, to bring the real from a spectral presence into a localisation in materiality:

The moment this spectral agent becomes part of our reality (even if it means catching a virus), its power is localised, it becomes something we can deal with (even if we lose the battle).

(ibid, p. 110)

To be a little facetious, I'm not sure if watching Netflix really results in a substantial enough marking at the level of the body to prevent descent into paranoid fantasies. Žižek reminds us of Freud's observation in *Beyond the Pleasure Principle* (1920), that it was the soldiers who had been physically injured on the battlefield that were less likely to suffer from traumatic neuroses (ibid, p. 109).

One of the factors generating trauma from a Freudian perspective concerns the feelings of helplessness associated with a traumatic event;[2] if we have not been able to take effective action and have remained helpless, we are more likely to suffer trauma as a result, the replaying of what we could have done to bind the fright and anxiety. In this sense, trauma is related to a certain passivity of being at the mercy of a stressful or overwhelming event. The trauma of an experience pertains in part to the subjective involvement we attribute to ourselves within these Real events, of what we perceive to be subjective responsibility, or indeed where our very desire is at stake.

In thinking about the marking or corporeal indexing of the pandemic, it is interesting that the arguments of the "COVID deniers" often land upon the fact that they have not met anyone who has died from the virus, and they, therefore, conclude that this cannot be a genuinely dangerous and life-threatening pandemic. Their refusal to believe is a way of revealing they have not been sufficiently marked/punctuated by the crisis and, as a result, refuse or cannot face a difficult reality, one that involves loss and personal renunciation of enjoyment.

In response to Žižek's remarks on Freud's soldiers, I argue instead that we are marked, affected, and possibly even traumatised by the pandemic through the passivity and the ironic intimations of "staying safe and staying home". Not simply as a direct result of this passivity, but also in what it renders us more proximate to in a spatial context. For when we are at home, we are often alone with ourselves, our bodies, or with families and intimate persons of one description or another. This reduction of the subject to the environs of the material body is a marking of a different kind, no doubt, than a physical injury in a war scenario; it is more the inscription of avoidance of danger rather than the act of stepping consciously into combat. By contrast with this more seemingly sedate scenario, contracting the virus through working on one of the many frontline jobs might prove more of an accurate analogy with Freud's soldiers as, indeed, might be the grief of those who lost a loved one to the virus. Critically however, while those working on the frontlines of the healthcare service are subject to burnout, trauma and post-traumatic stress, those confined to the position of "cocooning" or staying safe cannot escape these more passive positions without consequence and without encountering jouissance, the enjoyment associated with the drive impulses. This is an enjoyment mediated by the screen and the space of its encounter.

**The Space of the Screen**

In being relegated to the domestic sphere, the space of more intimate corporeal relations, we are involved in a more intensive relationship with the objects synonymous with this space, such as; the television,[3] our phones and computers. As the cinemas have been closed, and we cannot frequent other social artistic or communal spaces, we have had to be content with watching Netflix, other streaming channels or our national TV programmes. Indeed, throughout the pandemic, the TV has been the device through which we have been subject to continuous media reporting on statistics, public health advice, death rates, and the new savoir-faire around social etiquette. It has been the purveyor of pandemic master discourses (generally falling under the remit of the scientific logical "expert analysis"), while displaying the insignia of the command to "stay home" as a logo in the corner of the screen. For many of us, the TV has punctuated the Real of the pandemic with the monotony and pageantry of press conferences (think late night Donald Trump appearances), daily statistical analysis of the virus, case figures and death rates in the news every day and habitual audience chat shows with no audience present.

During the pandemic, as people without frontline service jobs to perform were largely confined to home, many surveys[4] were conducted to measure how the "unessential" have spent their time in lockdown. Apart from an increase in watching TV, deemed to be a passive activity, there has also been an increase in the "panic" purchases of sex toys, a resurgence in cooking (demonstrated by the colloquial phrase-the COVID stone), and the increasingly frequent Zoom calls, events and meetings. On a more sombre scale, there has also been a huge rise in cases of domestic violence (Kourti et al., 2021), addictions, eating disorders (Zipfel et al., 2022) and general feelings of guilt and anxiety. As Ahron Friedberg (2021) observed in his psychiatric practice, anxiety disorders and related conditions surged during the pandemic (p. 3). From these phenomena, we can deduce the presence of drive impulses and the challenge of jouissance for the subject, a challenge brought about by a shift in the meaning structures and spatial contexts of the body. That is to say, the desire of the Other as transmitted through the technological screen does not regulate the drives in the same way or as effectively as the embodied gaze, although paradoxically the screen also serves as a regulatory form of pacification and essential point of inter-subjective connection, particularly at times of isolation. Fundamentally the experience or affect of both "looking at" and "being seen" is an important cornerstone of the subjective economy and the regulation of jouissance. In other words, the subject desires to see and be seen and obtains satisfaction through the gaze (Lacan's Seminar XI) of the Other as it is "perceived" not simply through the eyes but within the unconscious. This type of "seeing/being seen" is not only reflected within the visual field on the part of the Other, but is also the experience or felt sense of an embodied encounter with the gaze. We can think of this through the Hegelian dialectic of the desire for recognition of the other, an idea from which Lacan drew extensively and which we find in his treatment of the gaze, "desire is the desire of the other" (Lacan, 1964, p. 235). When thinking of the effects of isolation on the drives of the subject, therefore, as in the case of the pandemic, the cross-sensory dimensionality of the gaze should be considered.

Of course, the increased anxiety at a time of pandemic cannot be causally reduced to the perils of isolation but also pertains to the anxiety of the Real of a threat that could result in the physical death of the subject. The ongoing experience of being at the mercy of a threat (seen or unseen) can induce feelings of passivity and helplessness, affects closely related to trauma. Throughout recent events, the technological screen has mediated these affects in a paradoxical manner. It is worth pausing to consider the various meanings of the signifier passivity. Linguistically, passivity has a resonance with the verb to pacify, to bring peace or induce calm. Given the physical passivity inherent to the consumption of screen activity, despite the active aim of the look (scopophilia in Freudian terms), it is interesting to consider how the technological screen works to pacify the drives, the excess, the jouissance inherent to any living body. For the screen (as TV or computer) appears to have this effect, despite the disembodied non presence of an actual human returning our gaze from virtual space within the geographic place from which we are looking. As Lacan says in Seminar XI, "You never look at me from the place from which I see you" (Lacan, 1964, p. 103).

If we consider the space of the screen again and in its relation to drive impulses, we can think of particularly difficult situations that induce a sense of helplessness, or isolation, where passivity is associated with anxiety and trauma, and when bodily or psychic actions have been inhibited or prohibited. For example, those in prison, or solitary confinement, who are in an enforced form of passivity, and lacking forms of stimulation and human contact, may turn to harm the body in acts of self-mutilation and release. Interestingly, the introduction of television into the cells of prisoners has been found to have reduced levels of self-harm and suicide. This phenomenon points to the necessity for the human subject to be world orientated in some way. What takes place at the level of the body when our outlets for stimulation are deprived or restricted? Clearly, the body itself may become the object of jouissance, the release of anxiety that is specific to the singular subject and yet generalised to the living body per se. In reducing incidents of self-harm, the moving images on the small screen of the TV can thus be seen to have a pacifying effect on the viewing subject, as it takes the subject out of the orbit of the habitual and focuses the eyes (as the Freudian scoptophilic drive of the look) on other worlds and other identifications. While we can recognise the pacifying effect of the screen as something that can mitigate certain affects of passivity, such as feelings of angst, helplessness, and frustration, at the same time, the screen documents and manipulates these affects through the fantasy matrix constituted by the dialectic of the viewer and the visual field.

For example, why is it that *Contagion* (Soderbergh, 2011) was one of the most downloaded films throughout the pandemic? It seems very curious that a film that portrays the angst, fear and tragedy generated by a lethal virus would be one of the most watched movies at a time when people are fearful for their lives in an almost identical scenario. I confess to also being drawn to the disaster genre at this time of crisis. One explanation for this seduction is that the story convention provides containment, in this instance, the filmic narrative, that contains a beginning, a middle and an end, unlike the current real-life scenario, an open-ended uncertainty. In some sense, the disaster movie provides the viewer with a simulation and representation of what is being lived through, without the lived actuality of the consequences. Does this tragic genre then somehow contain the angst of the crisis by generating it within a narrative that has an end, no matter how grizzly? Or does it provide us with an enjoyment of identification through the heroic or anti-heroic characters within the narrative? An enjoyment where we imagine ourselves to be braver than we are, where we take action rather than remaining passive. It is important to remember that while we are thinking of pacification as that which is generated through the fantasy and narrative component shown on the screen, it is also the screen itself as that visual medium toward which the eyes are drawn that pacifies on different bodily levels.

Can we then imagine that at a time of greater passivity (vicissitudes), when the drives are frustrated within the context of the corporeal isolation of the pandemic, something of the drive within the activity of looking[5] may become sublimated or rendered perverse (within the context of sexual exhibitionism online, for example)? To remain solely at this level of Freudian analysis, however, would be to neglect Lacan's development of the scoptophilic drive *qua* theoretical elaboration of the gaze, from which we encounter a shift from the active pleasure of looking to the satisfaction of being captured by a gaze we cannot see.

## From Looking to Not Seeing

To grasp the implications of the dialectic of the visible and its components of seeing/being seen for the subject we need to return to the principles of both Freud and Lacan's account of the scopic drive. As I have claimed, the subject's contemporary relationship with the screen takes place within the context of a greater passivity and a subjection to that screen, a subjection that involves the drive. In fact, a certain form of subjection, a being subject to, is part and parcel of being the subject of the drive, as Lacan points out in Seminar XI regarding the gaze. It must be said, as Darian Leader has pointed out in his lecture on the drive (Leader, 2022), there is a huge span of literature on the topic of instincts and drives, occurring in between Freud's 1915 paper and Lacan's 1964 seminar, *The Four Fundamental Concepts of Psychoanalysis*. In this chapter, I do not attempt an archaeology of the drive in this respect, but wish to isolate certain features of Freud's original conception of the scopophilic drive in concert with the Lacanian gaze to theorise the subject's relation to the visual field.

In *Instincts and their Vicissitudes* 1915, Freud's elaborations focus exclusively on the sexual instincts, in particular, that of sadism/masochism and scopophilia/exhibitionism. As is widely accepted, the translation by Strachey of *trieb* to instinct is considered inaccurate, and the concept of drive *qua* Freud should not be understood as the functioning of a biological instinct per se, although it is certainly tempting to do so. Neither being completely physical or psychical, the drive is a border phenomenon; it is a form of internal pressure mediating the body and mind. As a concept, the drive was something that Freud changed his views on over time, in particular, regarding the representative status of the drive in the unconscious, as Strachey points out in the editor's notes to *Instincts and their Vicissitudes*. Ultimately, as Darian Leader argues, the drive bears somewhat of a mythical status in psychoanalysis and therefore does not stand up to scientific empiricism as such. Nonetheless, it is a compelling concept that speaks to the complexity of the make-up of the human being in its material and ideational context, and most importantly as a being or "divided subject" without overarching rational agency. The aim of the drive is to achieve satisfaction, to return to a state of decreased excitation where the pleasure principle regulates the distribution of this excitation; and it is composed of four distinct properties, its "pressure", its "aim", its "object" and its "source" (Freud, 1915, p. 122). In Lacan's reformulation of the drive in Seminar XI, the drive cannot achieve satisfaction, its purpose is to circuit the lost object (object a) as a partial drive whose aim cannot rest within any given material object – "it is because it is a partial drive, and its aim is simply this return into circuit" (Lacan, 1964, p. 179).

The vicissitudes of the drive (in Freudian terms), and a reference to the title of this chapter, are modes of defence against the drive (Freud, 1915, p. 127), as the drive is a force that propels the human subject into action, though no action can work to ultimately quell the drive. The drive is representative of something indestructible; it exists as a function of the libidinal life force and will remain constant, "no actions of flight avail against them" (ibid, p. 119). Admittedly, Freud is not too clear in this essay about how and why these vicissitudes develop, but fundamentally, in isolating the scoptophilic drive and the binary of sadism/masochism as key components of the sexual instinct, he describes the vicissitudes of their transformation from the active to passive aim, and the possibility of the drive turning upon the subject's own self. While Freud attributes a movement from activity to passivity as a feature of the scoptophilic drive's quest for satisfaction, Lacan's reframing of this drive within the paradigm of the gaze as object a situates satisfaction and indeed passivity built into the very structure of this drive, where the binaries between active and passive are not clear-cut. Fundamentally, for Lacan, the gaze is not the look, or the pleasure derived from the look, but rather it pertains to an enigmatic seduction inherent to the visual field – a seduction induced by the lack of castration. The gaze appears to function not in the dialectic of active/passive but at an almost anterior level of being. This is certainly not an easy or coherent notion to understand within the framework that Lacan has provided in Seminar XI and in attempting to define the gaze, we run the risk of overshooting the contradictions inherent to Lacan's exposition in this seminar. As Maria Scott has reassuringly argued in her analysis of the anamorphic form of Lacan's exposition on the gaze, "Any understanding of the gaze is therefore as partial as the imagined mastery of the viewer standing before Holbein's painting" (2008, p. 328).

So, while the gaze may not be grasped fully, this not being grasped fully is at the core of what the gaze entails for the subject of the unconscious. For Lacan, the structural property of being captivated by the visible, and rendered at the mercy of the gaze, appears to precede the act of looking by the subject. We are driven to look, not simply so that we can master an object in the form of sexual pleasure, but because there is something inherently desirable/lacking within the realm of the visible per se. We appear to be passively implicated in the gaze, bound by the trauma of the inherent split constituted by language.

For Freud, the scopophilic drive "to look" exists originally in active form (where the body of another subject is taken as an object to be looked at) before it is transformed into the passive form, that of being looked at, "Here, too, it can hardly be doubted that the active aim appears before the passive, that looking precedes being looked at" (Freud, 1915, p. 15). For Freud, therefore, while the active aim of looking becomes reversed into the passive aim of being seen, by contrast, Lacan's conceptualisation of the gaze complicates the position of subject and object and, therefore, the binary coupling of active versus passive. Although Freud's account of the passivity associated with the scoptophilic drive appears at first sight to be a more binary conception than Lacan's, there is an important nuance or caveat to his theory; as he says:

> With regard to both the instincts which we have just taken as examples, it should be remarked that their transformation by a reversal from activity to passivity and by a turning round upon the subject never in fact involves the whole quota of the instinctual impulse. The earlier active direction of the instinct persists to some degree side by side with its later passive direction, even when the process of its transformation has been very extensive. ...
>
> (Freud, 1915, p. 130)

Freud's specification here of a residual instinctual impulse leads to the question of what becomes of this "active direction of the instinct" that persists after its transformation. In other words, for example, even the passive satisfaction of being seen involves a residue of an active impulse. Could we consider this residue as a remainder of the bodily satisfaction that fuels the space of subjective fantasy? Or, given that we are dealing with language, that no subject position is set in stone, as either active or passive?

If we consider Lacan's formulation of the gaze as a concept that both incorporates the active and passive dimensions of the drive, the gaze registers simultaneously both the "active" pleasure of looking (the seduction of the look) and the satisfaction of being seen (as a captivated object of the gaze per se). Within this dialectic of desire and lack, we the spectator, as Todd McGowan (2007) argues, are in a masochistic position vis-à-vis the object of desire (in fantasy). In other words, we are not simply masters of desire, but are at the mercy of it, and this subjection is what Lacan captures with the gaze. This is a crucial point in understanding why desire, although essential for the subject's survival, a veil for the "pain of existence", as Lacan argues in Seminar VI *Desire and its Interpretation*, is also disturbing and disruptive (Lacan, 1958–1959, p. 63).

As desire covers the lack in being, we could say that I desire to see and be seen because I am inherently split, divided and want for the other to see and to recognise me, to ratify my being. Without recognition, without the internalised gaze of the Other, we suffer profound alienation. However, given the structural misrecognition inscribed within the visual field a priori, we can never be seen as we are or see what we wish to see. In fact, what we really desire to see with our eyes, according to Lacan, is not to see and, therefore, to remain within the passion for ignorance, a passion suspended by desire. In Seminar X *Anxiety*, Lacan connects this desire not to see with an anxiety that pertains to the role of the object a in fantasy, to which regarding the realm of the visible, the subject is always in a relationship of misrecognition:

> It is through zero of *a* that visual desire masks the anxiety of what desire essentially lacks. It is what condemns you never to be able to grasp any

living being in the pure field of the visual signal except as what ethology calls a *dummy,* a puppet, an appearance.
(Lacan, 2014/1962–1963, p. 254)

And here, with the presence of anxiety bearing a fundamental relationship to what is hidden within the visual field, we have a crucial link in considering the compulsion at the level of the imaginary pertaining to the symptomatology of the pandemic. In its complicated relationship to passivity, the screen has both masked and induced anxiety, an anxiety that is "not without an object" (ibid, p. 131).

## Anxiety and the Screen

The object of anxiety, as Lacan is referring to here, is that of the object a – in the field of the visible, this object a constitutes the gaze: "The object a is what lacks, it is non-specular, it cannot be grasped in the image" (ibid, p. 254).

The fact that the gaze is largely located in the field of the Real for Lacan, renders a difficulty for theorisation in moving from the realm of the arts to that of the subjective symptom, notwithstanding the view of art *as* a symptom. The difficulty, as Shepherdson (1997) points out, is that the gaze, as it functions in some film theory, is not the same as that which functions at the level of the drive. In other words, there is a disparity between how we can conceive of the gaze on screen and that which corresponds to the subject's symptomatology on the ground. The gaze does not correspond to the subject's look, but is a hidden object in the field of the visible. This is what Todd McGowan has addressed in his book *The Real Gaze* (2007), although I think imagining a certain emancipation through the "trauma of the gaze" remains problematic. Certainly, there appear to be slippages in Lacan's account of the gaze as that which cannot be grasped in the visual field and that which can be seen in anamorphic form in the Holbein painting. The point here with these elaborations is how to account for the lack of an embodied gaze throughout the pandemic, given the slippery localisation of this enigma of the visual field. The key is to think of this embodied gaze not simply as something material/physical, as we might imagine a person's look might be, but more in the field of lack and the object a. The gaze is that hole in the Real, stimulated by the visual field, through which we relate in fantasy to the cause of our desire. Paradoxically, the presence of the physical body, provides us with a certain lack of satisfaction that is important to the regulation of the drives. So, in this sense, the lack of the embodied gaze refers to the lack of lack within the virtual visual field – a lack substituted by technology as a seductive excessive presence that seduces by its very apparent absence of the material body. In other words, we know that there is something lacking in the screen, and yet this knowledge masks the excessive presence of virtuality where anxiety marks the fallout of this magnified techno presence. In other words, through the screen, the mask of desire is revealed as mask and with that, the chasm beneath the fantasy beckons.

In this regard, we can take a small example from the setup of the visual apparatus on Zoom. Although we may see our own video reflected back at us on the screen, we are still – from the point of view of the gaze – not actually seeing ourselves, seeing ourselves. In Seminar XI, Lacan explicitly differentiates the function of the gaze for psychoanalysis from that of philosophy and phenomenological enquiry through an analysis/critique of Merleau-Ponty's posthumous work *The Visible and the Invisible* (1964). The gaze is not related to a subject who can see itself seeing itself, not part of a reflexive egocentric consciousness, but derives from the split/the lack of castration inherent to the divided subject: "The eye and the gaze –this is for us the split in which the drive is manifested at the level of the scopic field" (Lacan, 1964, p. 73). Ironically, it is when the split in the scopic field is seemingly and possibly momentarily overcome that we encounter anxiety and the uncanny dimension of the visible field.

As Lacan says: "The Unheimliche is what appears at the place where the minus-phi should be. Indeed, everything starts with imaginary castration, because there is no image of lack, and with good reason" (Lacan, 2014/1962–1963, p. 42). That is, when what we don't expect to see, that which is hidden within the field of the visible, becomes seen or specularised in some way, we encounter a lack of lack where desire loses a foothold in the suspension of the fundamental fantasy. We encounter the anxiety of a presence usually masked or misrecognised, cloaked by the mirage or the screen that renders the gaze opaque. The screen, as Lacan states in Seminar XI, is that which distinguishes the human subject from the animal kingdom. The screen referred to in this seminar consists of the duality of both the material world and the inner world of fantasy; it is that upon which the painter paints and that through which technology is transmitted. Critically, the screen of fantasy interior to the subject functions as a mediation point of desire and the gaze. As Lacan says: "Man, in effect, knows how to play with the mask as that beyond which there is the gaze. The screen is here the locus of mediation" (Lacan, 1964, p. 107).

Could we deduce then that there is no gaze for the human subject that is not mediated by a screen? Whether it be the medium utilised by the artist, canvas, film or even writing, the very page upon which words are inscribed. From the above quote, the screen effectively is the mask, although we should be alert, as Maria Scott (2008) points out, to the equivocations of Lacan's style here and the difficulty of defining the subject of the written statement.

In Seminar XI, Lacan places great emphasis on the scopic field as the domain of the desire of the Other. As he says:

> At the scopic level, we are no longer at the level of demand, but of desire, of the desire of the Other. It is the same at the level of the invocatory drive, which is the closest to the experience of the unconscious.
>
> (ibid, p. 104)

As we have already seen, the scopic field is characterised by a split at the level of the eye and the gaze, this is a split which generates a lure, a hole or distortion in the visible toward which we are seduced:

> Generally speaking, the relation between the gaze and what one wishes to see involves a lure. The subject is presented as other than he is, and what one shows him is not what he wishes to see. It is in this way that the eye may function as *objet a*, that is to say, at the level of the lack.
>
> (ibid, p. 104)

If we take Lacan's definition of the screen as mediation and consider its application to the technological screen, we can imagine that the small screen is that which mediates the split between the eye and the look, and the gaze as the point of absence in the technological screen. The seduction of the visual field as it is represented by the materiality of the technological screen, both induces the fantasy of a scopic satisfaction where our needs and desires appear to be fulfilled by the all seeing appearance or "fullness" of the images presented to us. While Lacan states that man knows how to play with the mask, this presumably is not a conscious knowledge in the phenomenological sense of the word. Although we may know that we are "playing", we also want to remain ignorant of the lack at the heart of the visible while attempting to unmask it at the same time.

The complexity of the relation between knowing and seeing as filtered through the screen is certainly a moot point, and I am making an assumption here that embodiment is experienced differently in the space of the flesh as distinct from the space of virtuality. As Frankel and Krebs (2022) argue, "The virtual world provides a screen where we are tricked into believing that all our wishes and desires, our passions and aspirations can be fulfilled and hence made 'real' without the work and labor as they are required by actual life" (p.2). Indeed, the seductive fullness of the screen lures the subject into an encounter with the gaze (object a) as imaginary rather than Real,[6] where the work and labour required by actual life sustains desire at the level of lack, rather than the uncanny too-muchness of the image. In other words, we imagine that we are held by the gaze and place too much hope in this image, only to be disappointed at the aloneness that is encountered when the video is switched off. The anxiety that is both pacified and generated by the screen is fuel for paranoia, a paranoia that refuses a renunciation of enjoyment where the mis-recognitions of the imaginary are substituted for the Real loss of habitual jouissance. This paranoia has echoes of narcissism, a refusal to acknowledge the lack in the Other, and our inherent traumatic passivity as subjects of the drive.

## Paranoia and its Discontents

The pandemic has required us to make certain sacrifices as filtered through a demand of the Other and broadcast through the small screens of our domestic space. While for some subjects, the big Other is making unreasonable demands, warranting an obvious desire to resist and counteract these injunctions and restrictions, for others a more subtle and heightened sense of passivity is experienced – resulting in vague feelings of guilt and anxiety regarding transmitting the virus to others. The prevailing narratives of taking responsibility and protecting each other have had resonances of the biblical command to love thy neighbour as thyself, a command that Freud completely turns on its head in *Civilisation and Its Discontents*. Freud's account of neighbourly love incorporates the aggressive drives and hatred the human subject does not like to acknowledge. We are specifically commanded to love thy neighbour so that we can sublimate our aggressive tendencies toward this neighbour. As he says of the stranger:

> Not merely is this stranger in general unworthy of my love; I must honestly confess that he has more claim to my hostility and even my hatred. He seems not to have the least trace of love for me and shows me not the slightest consideration. If it will do him any good he has no hesitation in injuring me, nor does he ask himself whether the amount of advantage he gains bears any proportion to the extent of the harm he does to me
> (Freud, 1929, p. 57).

According to Freud's argument, humans do not take kindly to renunciations made in favour of their fellow humans, and even if they conform, there is always a question of love at stake, a fear of the loss of love or being outside of the herd, abandoned to one's fate. The superego lurks within many acts of renunciation and sacrifice, functioning as the arbiter of conscience, the judge of the distribution of jouissance. Either we make seeming acts of altruism or we are commanded to do so; either way the superego will have its say. Within the context of the pandemic, these demands concerning acts of renunciation have led to protests and wild conspiracy theories concerning the origin of the virus and the motives of the big Other behind the transmission of official information.

The present times have challenged the subject at the level of responsibility (what we could loosely call ethics) and at the level of the isolated body, what I have been referring to as a jouissance of the drive impulses. The more widespread uncertainty and confrontation with the lack in the Other has been a source of anxiety, paranoia and even violence for many. As Todd McGowan (2021) argues, paranoia involves a refusal to believe in the lack of the Other or the lack of knowledge inherent to the symbolic. Or, in other words: "that there is a hidden authority pulling the strings in the social order, a figure or figures that do not suffer from the limitations of everyone else" (p. 168).

In the recent anti lockdown protests RTE, the Irish national broadcasting network, has been the target of the protesters' grievances, including gatherings outside the RTE studios. Furthermore, RTE has been one of the means by which many of the signifiers used by the public health narratives have been conveyed to citizens. A little logo on the corner of the screen that tells us we should stay home has been persistently present during our viewing time. The protesters' accusations concern the view that RTE has been misrepresenting the facts of the pandemic and is in cahoots with the government narrative of the necessity of lockdown. While it is true that mainstream media often upholds the master discourses, such as science, some of the accusations are obviously bizarre conspiratorial constructions fuelled by a paranoia of a hidden other. This paranoia defends against the anxiety of a certain passivity in the face of the crisis; the impotence of the Other and the consequent existential responsibility left in its wake. In these paranoid protests, a question of meaning has been brought centre stage, either consciously or unconsciously. Through the pandemic, fate has proved itself to be a harsh taskmaster, and theories of causation and conspiracy abound to fill the gap wrought by the anxiety and increased awareness of mortality, uncertainty and need. In essence, we have experienced our passivity in the face of certain acts of contingent and outrageous fortune. According to Freud, the vicissitudes and misfortunes of fate, and the experience of being somewhat forsaken, fuels the superego with remonstrances which bolster narcissistic interpretations of events. General misfortunes are rarely perceived to be neutral by the human subject and can fuel the superego's admonitions and punitive tendencies. In Freud's words:

> Fate is regarded as a substitute for the parental agency. If a man is unfortunate it means that he is no longer loved by this highest power; and, threatened by such a loss of love, he once more bows to the parental representative in his super-ego – a representative whom, in his days of good fortune, he was ready to neglect.
>
> (Freud, 1929, 73)

In a sense, we could say that through the threat of our extinction as subjects, we take up an active position in fantasy regarding these contingent and unfortunate scenarios; often we bow down to the internalised gaze of the superego, a gaze that is never forgiving.

The demand for the average citizen to sacrifice certain satisfactions for the greater good, while possibly a source of enjoyment for some, is the cause of anger for others. The underlying narrative of some conspiratorial discourses amounts to a tacit narrative of dispossession, "we have lost our enjoyment, jouissance has been displaced, or stolen and somebody must pay". The imagined castrating Other is not lacking, helpless or passive but apparently actively and knowingly curtailing freedoms for its own ends. While for some, the small screen mediated a paranoid relation to the Other, where passivity is overcome through an outward projection, for others, the screen may have enabled the unfolding events of the current times – a "show" to be viewed passively at a distance. For others still, the small screen has rendered the symbolic present within the domestic space and has been used as a means to extend the more passively orientated body into virtual/domestic space.

Despite the many ambiguities of passivity as a signifier, it is true that fantasies of action thrive within scenarios where the body is in somewhat of a passive position, isolated and/or restricted. Given that fantasy is the screen which mediates the unconscious and the external world, could we say that the subject always takes up a position within the dialectic of fantasy and the object a, a position that could be deemed active? This might be why the film *Contagion* is one of the most downloaded films throughout the pandemic. If we cannot take heroic action in real life and are condemned to staying safe within a context that heightens feelings of vulnerability, then at least we can imagine heroic deeds by living precariously through the screen, a feeble defence as it may be against the anxiety of passivity, nonetheless. Ultimately, the subject of the unconscious as subject to the drive will always take up a position in fantasy when confronted with an experience of passivity, inactivity and frustration. Even if this position involves an imagined submission to the cause of the passivity, a cause interpreted as a paranoid gaze. The drive, including that bound up with the look, and the desire to see and be seen, will always seek satisfaction. Therefore, against the injunction to stay home and stay safe during the pandemic lockdowns, we can conclude that there is no safe place when it comes to the drive and the labyrinthine pathways of jouissance, no "staying home, staying safe".

## Notes

1 In a previous article entitled *Contagion and its objects: the body as an object in the world and its relation to the unconscious* published in *Lacunae* (2021), I argued that psychoanalysis could benefit from the insights of phenomenology as regards considering the impact of the external environment, (contingencies in the world) on the unconscious constellations of the subject. I will not go into the same detail here, suffice it to recognise that the domestic space is by its very facticity implicated within the "object" relations inherent to the dialectic of the human and the screen at this time of crisis.
2 In *The Project for a Scientific Discovery*, Freud says, "the original helplessness of human beings is thus the primal source of all moral motives" (Freud, 1895, p. 379).
3 In the category of television, I am including what is called linear TV, (in its function as a traditional broadcasting medium tied to national and international networks) and in its capacity as non linear or advanced, or as smart TVs, through which we can stream on demand services, such as Netflix, YouTube etc.
4 "Sex During Pandemic: Panic Buying of Sex Toys During COVID-19 Lockdown" Arafat & Kar, (2021); "TV streaming habits in lockdown" Oliver & Ohlbaum Associates (2020).
5 In Freud's 1915 paper, *Instincts and their Vicissitudes*, scoptophilia (the pleasure in looking) is categorised by Freud as one of the key sexual instincts, along with the pair of opposites sadism/masochism. Exhibitionism is the passive form of scoptophilia, where the subject's body becomes an object of the others look. There is a key

distinction, however, between these binary drives in that the scopophilic instinct/drive has a preliminary autoerotic stage, unlike that of sadism/masochism (see Freud 1915, p. 130).

6 It is important not to reduce the effects of technology to a negative/binary conception of good versus bad. Frankel and Krebs (2022) argue that Derrida's notion of the pharmakon, as both poison and solution, illustrates the complicated implications of its impact, both expansive and destructive.

## References

Arafat, SMY., and Kar, SK. (2021). Sex during pandemic: Panic buying of sex toys during COVID-19 lockdown. *Journal of Psychosexual Health*, 3(2), pp. 175–177.

Soderbergh, S. (2011). *Contagion*. Film. Los Angeles: Warner Bros.

Campbell, A. & Mathias, A. (2020). *Death to 2020*. Written by C. Brooker, A. Jones and T. Baker. Los Angeles: Netflix.

Frankel, R. and Krebs, J.V., eds. (2022). *Human virtuality and digital life: Psychoanalytic and philosophical reflections*. New York and London: Routledge.

Freud, S. (1895/1950). Project for a scientific discovery. *S.E.*, I, pp. 283–397.

Freud, S. (1915/1925). Instincts and their vicissitudes. *S.E.*, XIV, pp. 117–140.

Freud, S. (1920). Beyond the pleasure principle. *S.E.*, XVIII, pp. 7–64.

Freud, S. (1929). Civilisation and its discontents. *S.E.*, XXI, pp. 64–145.

Friedberg, A.L. (2021). *Through a screen darkly: Psychoanalytic reflections during the pandemic*. New York and London: Routledge.

Kourti, A., Stavridou, A., Panagouli, E., Psaltopoulou, T., Spiliopoulou, C., Sergentanis, T.N, Tsolia, M. and Tsitsika, A. (2021). Domestic violence during the COVID-19 pandemic: A systematic review. *Trauma, Violence & Abuse*, 24 (2), pp. 719–745.

Lacan, J. (1958–1959). *The seminar of Jacques Lacan: Book VI, Desire and its interpretation: trans C. Gallagher*. Unpublished.

Lacan, J. (2014/1962–1963). *The seminar of Jacques Lacan: Book X, Anxiety* (Ed. J.-A. Miller; Trans. A. Price). Cambridge: Polity Press.

Lacan, J. (1964/1978). *The seminar of Jacques Lacan: Book XI, The four fundamental concepts of psychoanalysis* (Ed. J.A. Miller; Trans. A. Sheridan). London: W.W. Norton.

Leader, D. (2022). *The drive*. Public Lecture at CFAR, 26 March. Available at: https://vimeo.com/ondemand/26032022leader/693063648.

Liu, W. (2021). Pandemic paranoia: Toward a reparative practice of the global psyche. *Psychoanalysis, Culture & Society*, 26(4), pp. 608–622.

McGowan, T. (2007). *The real gaze: Film theory after Lacan*. Albany, NY: State University of New York Press.

McGowan, T. (2021). Cinema's paranoid tendencies. *Psychoanalytische Perspectieven*, 39 (2), pp. 165–186.

Meehan O'Callaghan, S. (2021). Contagion and its objects: The body as an object in the world and its relation to the unconscious. *Lacunae*, 21, pp. 122–148.

Merleau-Ponty, M. (1945). *Phenomenology of perception*. London: Routledge.

Merleau-Ponty, M. (1964). *The Visible and the Invisible* (Ed. C. Lefort; Trans. A. Lingis). Evanston, Il: Northwestern University Press (1968)

Office for National Statistics, UK (2020) Coronavirus and how people spent their time under lockdown: 28 March to 26 April. Available at: https://www.ons.gov.uk/

economy/nationalaccounts/satelliteaccounts/bulletins/coronavirusandhowpeoplespen ttheirtimeunderrestrictions/28marchto26april2020.
Oliver & Ohlbaum Associates (2020). TV streaming habits in lockdown. Available at: https://www.oando.co.uk/insight/tv-streaming-habits-in-lockdown.
Scott, M. (2008). Lacan's "Of the Gaze as Objet Petit a" as anamorphic discourse. *Paragraph*, 31(3), pp. 327–343.
Shepherdson, C. (1997). A pound of flesh: Lacan's reading of "the visible and the invisible". *Diacritics*, 27(4), pp. 70–86.
Voruz, V. (2013). Disorder in the real and inexistence of the other: What subjective effects? The Irish Circle of the Lacanian Orientation, October. Published online. Available at: https://www.iclo-nls.org/_files/ugd/add8ea_8b8cff268592498a81a50b7c64a89472.pdf.
Zipfel, S., Schmidt, U. and Giel, K. (2022). The hidden burden of eating disorders during the COVID-19 pandemic. *The Lancet*, 9(1), pp. 9–11.
Žižek, S. (2020). *Pandemic! COVID-19 shakes the world*. New York: OR Books.

# Chapter 4

## *Undine:* Siren Screens

*Jessica Datema and Manya Steinkoler*

Christian Petzold's film *Undine* shows the dangers of small screen engagement without limits or empathy, a condition already in place with the globalization of social media and technology that multiplied during the pandemic. By small screens we mean the move from shared collective experiences of cinema to isolated screens. Our solitary endemic "society" where users log on in the privacy of their home to a small screen connects them to an ocean of people all the while separating them from a larger contextual engagement. This shift promotes invulnerability, the antithesis of the lack necessary for a social link, rendering our society more automated and robotic than ever.

*Undine* premiered at the 60th Berlin International Film Festival in February 2020 just prior to the start of the pandemic and was released via Curzon Home Cinema streaming in 2021. The film is the first in Petzhold's trilogy that transposes myth to show how it echoes and reflects contemporary life. The main character, Undine, is a water spirit, mermaid, siren, and muse, first dreamed up by the sixteenth-century alchemist Paracelsus, later developed by Friedrich de la Motte Fouqué, Hans Christian Andersen and more recently rewritten by Toni Morrison and Ingeborg Bachmann (Bachmann, 1987; Morrison, 2004).

As a water spirit, *Undine* marks the amniotic unity that must be sacrificed for symbolic life. The film analyzes fluidity and literal streaming in both form and content. A scene at the film's outset when the aquarium breaks, indicates the explosion of limits and the shattering of the mirror. Undine comes from nowhere (the sea) and leaves to nowhere, problematizing the distinction between life and death. Ultimately, the film underlines that life requires a loss and that loss is mythic, cf. Lacan's *Lamella*.

Set in Berlin, Undine is a city tour guide, robotically lecturing on German history. As her lectures explain, post-1989 Berlin is plural and diverse, demographically, and politically. The modern city after *Die Wende* is no longer part of the Eastern Bloc where citizens were deeply rooted in a collective "big screen". The lectures' dive into German history parallels *Undine's* amorous relationships. The first lover, Johannes, is a government worker with a big house and swimming pool, the site of his eventual demise. His character is

DOI: 10.4324/9781003272069-5

perhaps a nod to Berlin German Democratic Republic (GDR) rhetoric and the relation with Undine shows the dangers of forgetting or denying history. At the same time the film reveals the dangerous allure of small screens, it also shows how a recovery of lack and vulnerability in relation to the mirror, water, and technology might facilitate more humane encounters.

*Undine* (Petzold et al., 2021) opens with the two lovers staring at screens in a café on a Berlin cobblestone street while bickering about the phone message that prompted their meeting. She claims that Johannes said, "I must see you", while he insists that she said they must stop seeing each other. "Seeing" sets the stage for the watery mirror stage. They sit amongst stones and roses, a fitting memorial to their past affair. During their meeting, Undine tells Johannes, "You cannot go", adding "if you leave, I'll have to kill you; if you leave, you'll have to die". While sounding hysterical and surreal, we will discover that Undine's words are in fact a real threat. She will make good on this threat later in the film when she murders Johannes in his own swimming pool. What seems to be the language of a jilted and anxious woman turns out to be the very real voice of a modern mythic siren. Don't mess with a siren: welcome to the oceanic screen of the real.

Surfing the small screen involves an engagement with the siren who tempts the other with the promise of wholeness without separation. Undine is the siren's voice that calls out from screens where online users endlessly browse. She is emblematic of an oceanic feeling without separation or limit that is like what Freud describes as "a sensation of 'eternity', a feeling as of something limitless, unbounded—as it were, 'oceanic'" (Freud, 1962, p. 11). In Orwell's *1984*, we see the oceanic as dependency upon a super-state that is the vehicle for "an unending series of victories over your own memory. 'Reality control,' they called it, in Newspeak 'doublethink'" (Orwell, 2017, p. 34). What we are calling the "oceanic" refers to our small screen world of control through rhetoric, surveillance, and social media apps that incite addiction to the virtual.

In showing the relation between the oceanic and extremist politics, *Undine* is not new. Orwell named his state, Oceania, the super-state that controls the western world through newspeak, surveillance, and oppression. Correlatively, virtual reality provides oceanic screens that promise imaginary unity but are used for marketing, the gentler sway of surveillance and control. Big and small screen corporate ideologies both share the view that technology should unite and connect eschewing difference and lack. A small screen allows us the illusion that the personal is not political, denying its own partisanship. In small screen culture, the other exists even less than with big screens where we sit side by side watching; citizens exist in their own technological and social media bubble. Small screens give the illusion of intimacy yet there is no dialogue, negotiation of the other, or lack. Even before they were invented, tech devices were part of Oceania.

In *1984*, a narcissistic body politic exerts limitless control over its subjects and traps them in the imaginary; or as Lacan explains, it puts citizens in a state of being in "captivation by images" (Lacan, 2013, p. 35). Our world is becoming more like Oceania, a virtual reality world of imaginary tribes and projected states. Technological control through "narcissism" is seen in the very names of our everyday mobile devices: iPhone, iPad, or iMac. Every device contains the word "I" as a trick so that: "Narcissism can be indulged without the terror of being out of touch or out of control. This formula is a magnet for human longing. It's all about me, iThis and iThat" (Lanier, 2013, p. 205). The "i" is simultaneously a lure for the subject and the mechanism that controls them via the oceanic. Undine, like limitless technology, hooks users with the fluidity of mobile devices that appeal to their narcissism and promise to fulfil their every desire.

The oceanic small screen is now an inevitable part of our everyday relation to technology. The film shows surfing with sirens is far from an ancient myth, but rather alive and well at the bottom of our small screen seas. *Undine* uses water and glass to show how a lack of separation and a desire for imaginary wholeness is the dream of technology today. Virtual reality controls much of our everyday narrative. Jacques Lacan presciently claimed the signifier has become the apparatus of *jouissance* through Capitalist discourse "that consumes itself, that consumes itself so that [it] is consumed" (Lacan, 1978, p. 11). Little could he imagine how true that is today. The wish for narrative wholeness has shifted from face-to-face encounters in community, to the "safe space" of small screens. As the call of the small screen, Undine is a figuration of what eludes the user's sight. She embodies the mythic promise of complete unity as a projection of what refuses mirror alienation.

Today, with your Apple Watch, FitBit, and iPhone, the siren call is always present. If, as Slavoj Žižek has put it, "Cinema teaches us how to desire" (Fiennes & Žižek, 2009), the small screen presents new challenges to such a teaching. By small screens, we mean the move away from shared collective cinematic experiences to the isolation of personalized data-rich and data-gathering activities. Instead of being autonomous navigators, online users are targets tricked by oceania, e.g., the parasitic corporate and social networks. Small screens incite narcissistic *jouissance* and an unbound perusing that makes the internet an ocean all too real. Undine emerges from the water, e.g., the screen, as the partner, as *jouissance*. She deepens a condition already in place by way of modern technology that became viral during the pandemic.

Undine personifies the element of water as infinite that precedes and surrounds the less stable city, or *polis*. Her striking hair laden with blood overtones is a florid mermaid red. She tells visiting tourists that the city was founded by traders in the 13th century and the word "Berlin" means "marsh" or "dry place in the marsh". Layers of the past resurface in her speeches in the same way that Undine resurfaces as a mythic creature in modern day Berlin. Her narrated history suggests that the cultural-symbolic city is less stable than the more permanent surrounding waters.

The traditional hierarchy between culture and nature is reversed in *Undine*. Small screen culture, like Undine's lectures for tourists, hide the underwater real ruins in an imaginary unity. Her lectures attempt to create a fluid and unified narrative of Berlin's political history that obfuscates its fragmentation and separation. This view of history avoids dredging up shameful events that weigh on contemporary society. It glosses over the burdens of history and inheritance that Larkin famously wrote of in "This Be The Verse". If it's not worked through, intergenerational trauma is handed down as his poem states, "Man hands on misery to man. It deepens like a coastal shelf" (Larkin, 2004, p. 142). The war-torn past of Berlin and the monstrosities of previous generations resurface and deepen as the film and Undine's relationships escalate. While Undine the character avoids dredging up a difficult complex history, the film *Undine* dives further down into political amnesia.

As the embodiment of a material real, Undine's amours exemplify the relation of users to small screens, water to the city, and by proxy, the oceanic to the siren herself. The film highlights the perils of oceanic unity and shows that separation is necessary for understanding modernity, history, and subjectivity. The film figures the power of the oceanic as the power of modern technological engagements with overwhelming *jouissance* that threaten otherness and civic ties. It portrays this through its depiction of the love affair between Christoph, a city employee who is a diver/engineer working on the city's underwater power supply and Undine, a mythic marine siren.

At their meeting, soon after the scene with Johannes, an aquarium that is present inside the café, shatters, indicating an explosion of limits and the fragmentation of the imaginary dimension. The exploding aquarium reveals the oceanic of the drive that the ego tries to keep at bay. The shattered aquarium is the real reason for their romance. Initially bereft with Johannes gone, Undine stands up to stare at a large aquarium in the café which mythically calls out her name, underlining the other world from which we come, the maternal womb, and its relation to the lost home. A man approaches, invites her to coffee, and tells her that he's "usually underwater". Christoph is an underwater engineer. He spends most of his time sub-surface fixing bridges; it is no accident he is immediately drawn to Undine and she to him. As a figure between the oceanic and the symbolic, between desire and *jouissance*, an engineer and a deep-water diver, Christoph is trained to shepherd and cross the Lacanian registers of symbolic, imaginary, and real. Unlike Johannes, he will be able to survive Undine.

Undine stands with Christoph, who, overwhelmed, backs up and knocks into the wall as the aquarium shatters and they fall on the floor covered and pierced by broken glass and cascading water. The underwater engineer picks the shards out of Undine while dying fish flip about on the floor. Angered by the expensive accident, the bar owner bans Undine from returning to the café. Christoph and Undine's first drenched encounter illustrates the way love can be an immersion that shatters the mirrors of the ego. The film shows that such an encounter concerns the real from which subjectivity is appended. It is the real that grounds the whole chain of symbolic narrative, the sea from which the city of Berlin emerges.

The aquarium scene foreshadows the end of the film when Undine will save Christoph from drowning in the ocean. *Undine* reminds us that the oceanic dimension, while necessary, is at the same time, potentially lethal for humans. While the internet promises users a pre-symbolic maternal connection without subjugation to the elements, the film underlines the dangers of non-separation in the oceanic. Today, streaming services are the new umbilical cord promising a subjectivity beyond breath and death. People die, but their Facebook profile lives on. This is exactly the kind of watery simulacra that requires separation to engage reality. The internet, like the ocean, is a stream that can be a resource depending on how it is used. It is, like oxygen or the other elements (water, fire, air, earth) a resource that tends toward excess, deluge and saturation or dearth, scarcity, and emptiness. It reminds us of the real as a force of *jouissance* manifest in the material world that is not good or bad but depends upon how it is siphoned.

The casting of Christoph (Franz Rogowski) in the film is particularly interesting. The actor's speaking voice sounds as though he's holding his nose, and his face seems as though he may have been born with a cleft palate. This handicap is at the same time a power that signals his access and ability to negotiate the ocean and the city, the real and the symbolic, the "split" emblematic of the power he has in both worlds. Christoph repairs subaquatic bridges that allow people to cross over water. He visits Undine's apartment, (whose walls are green like the ocean) not long after their aquarium encounter. Undine's apartment, like the many train scenes that contain a lot of glass, looks as if she lives and moves underwater. In all these interactions, Christoph demonstrates the ability to live both above water as well as in the deep.

The film cuts to several days later when Undine leaves the city to meet Christoph, who gives her a diver toy that has fallen out of the aquarium for her return trip. This toy diver fell from the broken aquarium, which he retrieved from the bar floor after the aquarium shattered. A kind of Winnicottian blanket, the diver is both a transitional object and a double of Christoph himself as the aquanaut who can live on land and in the sea. The diver has a *savoir faire* with the drive and the elements. Prefiguring what happens to Christoph, the diver-figurine's legs are severed when it falls off the table after a colleague wakes Undine and orders her to give an extra lecture, as though waking her were disturbing the proximity to the watery depths. This destruction foreshadows the coma that Christoph will fall into which Undine will have to undo by exiting the symbolic realm and sacrificing her "human" life.

In *Undine*, Christoph's relation to the infinite oceanic element of nature is his work, not a sport or hobby. As such, we might point out that his know-how (*savoir-faire*) is not reducible to unbound *jouissance*. Christoph's facility diving underwater contrasts with the now popular sport of freediving. Free diving involves plunging underwater and descending as deep as possible without scuba gear for as long as athletes can hold their breath. The lure of surpassing bodily limits of breathing submerged farther and farther below makes the sport competitive, with winners often blacking out, draining oxygen reserves, taunting death, and even dying. The fact that doctors must be present in these competitions only points to the limitless *jouissance* and death-driven lure of this sport (Alfonsi, 2021). The sport parallels our small screen world where people take deep dives into the metaverse, gaming, tweeting, and Instagram to drown in virtual reality without taking a breath. Subsequently, in popular culture, everyone feels that they are drowning, stressed, and "need to exhale". We see this frequently nowadays in faddish coveted breathing apps like Headspace, Breathing, Wim Hof, Yoga, or any other new practice that perpetuates programmed servitude of the neoliberal body in late capital. These apps illustrate how the film relates to our time by revealing the inundation of the oceanic drives in our everyday lives. Unlike enthusiasts of these apps or sport divers, Christoph does not free dive and brings supplemental equipment, including a snorkel, to breathe underwater.

We could ask: If breath cuts water, and water cuts breath, what cuts internet streaming? Drowning, or having the air cut off is analogous to losing oneself while submerged in virtual reality without limits. The word or breath, as separation, is a bodily limit cutting oceanic *jouissance*. Breath cuts the maternal primordial waters out of which we are born. In one scene when Christoph and Undine dive together, she disappears until he finds her body floating on the surface and fishes her out of the water. Since she is unable to breathe, Christoph performs CPR on Undine while singing "Staying Alive". Once revived, she laughs and exclaims "revive me again!" Undine is not afraid of death; insofar as she is part of elemental nature, she is already dead.

Undine's rebirth also shows the power of love via the instrument of the voice that crosses realms of oceanic pre-symbolic and the symbolic. Her laugh upon reviving is a pre-symbolic expression of life in death. It not only indicates she is not human but that she does not inhabit the world of lack, separation, or otherness. Similarly, the small screen obsessed lack separation and the symbolic constraints required for shepherding streams of the oceanic internet. For Christoph, a human with a job to go to and a girlfriend he's not too fond of, the oceanic is what threatens to overwhelm and submerge both him and the city. It is his job to maintain breathe and voice even while sub-aquatic, fixing generators that ensure the survival and safe passage of Berliners.

As shepherd and custodian of deep currents, the name Christoph is a nod to Christ, and his character is literally born again. At the end of the film when Christoph emerges from his coma, he sucks in oxygen as if taking a first breath and cries out like a newborn. This shout, and his emergence from the dead, depends upon Undine's sacrifice, i.e., her killing of Johannes and return to the water. Unlike Christoph, Johannes underestimates Undine's power as a death driven force of the oceanic. His denial of the power of the oceanic elements returns Undine from the real as repressed. This contrasts with Christoph whose revived respiration literally depends upon Undine's withdrawal to the water. Her departure creates a separation that allows Christoph to breathe, become a father, and continue fixing underwater bridges that preserve culture.

Initial alienation in mirroring reflection is what allows one to "not drown" in the virtual ocean. The film shifts perspective between scenes of limitless and moving windows, water, and broken aquarium glass, which all foreground the lamella-like bottomless fluidity of Undine as a mythic figure of the oceanic. This *lamella* is the

> hitherto unheard-of that bathes speech. Freud gives it a mythical name, *libido*, and Lacan one that is also mythical: *lamella (lamelle)*. *Libido* is a word to be thought in the language where love is called *Liebe*, it is the Freudian myth.
>
> (Braunstein, 2020, p. 146)

The reason we don't have to breathe in the womb is because we have the umbilical cord, a link which Undine embodies. While the filmic screen and mirror provide a frame for subjectivity and history, Undine offers invisibility and infinite fluidity. Ingeborg Bachmann writes of her own character, Undine; she is an "indifferent mirror that forbids me to see you differently" (Bachmann, 1987, p. 172). Undine, as the embodiment of the aquatic element, is the denial of difference.

Modern users of technology, like Homer's sailors, risk succumbing to imaginary capture whilst surfing the Internet. An example of parsing the oceanic occurs in *The Odyssey*; Odysseus warns his sailors not to succumb to the siren call. *The Odyssey* features myriad siren figures, including Circe, Calypso, and the sirens themselves (Homer). After Odysseus escapes the island of Circe, he must then overcome the sirens, a double departure from imaginary capture. Forewarned this time, he has his shipmates plug his ears with wax and bound him to the mast, making them promise not to untie him. What is the equivalent of Odysseus' restraints via the wax and fettering to the mast today?

Technological devices and platforms including iPhones, Facebook and social media all host the siren call that makes unfettered users feel immortal, powerful, and connected. Ancient mythic sirens tempted the sailors much like modern siren servers, the machines that vacuum up personal data to harvest information. Jaron Lanier explains how companies like Amazon, Facebook, Twitter, and Google began using siren servers to capture and hold data in "gigantic facilities, located in obscure places where they have their own power plants and some special hookup to nature, like a remote river that allows them to cool a fantastic amount of waste heat" (Lanier, 2013, p. xv). These siren servers make users feel in control even while being tracked. Perhaps more powerful than Homer's siren song, the siren servers' call is silent, so we often do not even hear a voice or know how to circumvent being seduced. In the "Silence of the Sirens", Franz Kafka wrote that "from the sirens' silence, there was no resistance" (Kafka, 1988, p. 431).

Tech company's siren servers work like the sirens in Homer's *Odyssey* through a stealth blackmail where you can't really see or hear clearly what's in front of you on the Internet. They work outside what's visible, e.g., in Virtual Reality (VR), a phrase created by the computer scientist Jaron Lanier. When someone signs up for a social network service like Facebook or Twitter, all their data, and user information is captured in company siren servers. All of this is done with the illusion that everything is free for the user, so "the deal looks sweet, but you don't see everything that should be [seeing]in front of you" (Lanier, 2013, p. 55). When putting information into one of these servers, one becomes captured data, as one encryption expert in *Cypherpunks* explains:

> Most of the time we are not even aware of how close to the violence we are, because we all grant concessions to avoid it. Like sailors smelling the breeze, we rarely contemplate how our surface world is propped up from below by darkness.
>
> (Assange et al., 2012, p. 3)

These servers that prop up virtual reality steer through an invisible gaze that conceals who is at the helm.

The film *Undine* is about shepherding the oceanic, not via rationality or predictability, but by preserving otherness and separation despite the allure of complete connectivity. Christoph, Undine's lover, like Odysseus, goes into the eye of the siren storm, hears the singing "chatter" only to live, become a father and pass on his name at the end of the film. Like the bound Odysseus who lets his crew know when the ship has passed the realm of the sirens, Christoph intentionally and sacrificially, as a Christ figure, goes underwater to fall in love with the beautiful, jilted siren. When they quarrel, Christoph has a diving accident and blacks out after being deprived of oxygen for twelve minutes. He becomes a follower of Undine, making a *symbolic* sacrifice true to his name, Christoph. In response to his devotion, Undine engages in her own *real* sacrifice for Christoph. It is real precisely because as a mythic creature, Undine does not exist in the symbolic realm and is unable to lack, but out of love, dies a human death. The reference to Christian monotheism both embracing and trumping the pagan gods couldn't be more evident.

Frantic that he misunderstood her, Undine leaves a message on his voicemail saying that she wasn't waiting for Johannes, she was waiting for him. We discover that Christoph phoned Undine when he was already in a coma. As if by magic, he was able to speak to her from this border state between life and death. Later, she is informed by his diver ex-girlfriend that he was brain dead at the time of the call. This underscores how Christoph and Undine are engaged in relationships beyond speech. Not wanting him to really die, Undine sacrifices herself to reconfigure and recast their relationship. She returns to the water to save Christoph. Her act releases him from his powerless position to show the power of the oceanic stream. Their relation is a bond, like Odysseus' binding, of chosen restriction – analogous to a modern-day tech user who offset their time online to be with others. What is needed today is an ascesis, or ritual practice of taking breaks and separation from small screens. This type of praxis is the equivalent of binding the siren call like Odysseus to curb internet usage and mitigate virtual saturation.

Undine shows how the ocean, like the internet, is a stream whose value as a resource depends upon the way it is handled. Our use of technology, like oxygen or the other elements (water, fire, air, earth), determines its value. Today's practices of technology tend toward the excessive – being online all the time – or scarcity, being on the wrong side of the digital divide where online access is difficult. The oceanic controls through deprivation or deluge, not transparent political and cultural apportioning. Users spending a lot of time online contract a limitless feeling of connection without community, which leads them to cancel culture. After all, a. negativity must be created somewhere.

For example, the author Toni Morrison has been banned in some parts of America for writing about how people prefer fabricating myths of the noble past to the realities of present-day racism. Morrison modernizes and rewrites the Undine myth in her novel *Tar Baby*. The novel portrays the love affair of Jadine and Son, two Black Americans abandoned by their mothers who grow up in very different class structures. Jadine is adopted by a wealthy family who owns a home in the Caribbean, where the story is set. Son is from the impoverished South yet uses his trickster cleverness and good looks to travel all over the world, including to the Caribbean Island where Undine resides. The struggles of Jadine and Son exemplify the illusions or self-deceptions regarding race, class and gender that support their worlds until they do not.

Going further than Christoph who shepherds the lure of Undine, Morrison's *Tar Baby* narrative exposes the hypocrisy of those powers that claim to offer imaginary freedom while entrapping in the oceanic. Jadine's adopted father, Valerian Street, is like the mythic fox and owner of the field uses tar baby to entrap the rabbit. This happens when Valerian hosts an interloper, devoid of a name excepting "Son," as a guest in their home after he breaks in and watches the women for several days from a closet. After becoming an invited guest Son and Undine swap roles as figures of the classic Tar Baby myth, both playing the lure who entraps or the rabbit who sticks. They recognize the decoy of the fox's trap – Valerian's invite sets up their meeting – but pretend not to know after falling in love and getting caught up in the seduction. The owner's "generosity" effects a lack of boundaries that ultimately disenfranchises everyone in his orbit and upends the whole island manor.

Morrison's novel reworks the Undine and Tar Baby myths to show how fluidity in identification and stereotyping is part of the self-deception and stickiness of symbolic authenticity. It shows how Valerian's generosity is a product of his egoism, vanity and attempts to satisfy his own curiosity about the uninvited guest. Separately, the maid named Ondine becomes the hero who avoids the stickiness of illusory conceits to reveal the rotten truth about the patron Street family. Ondine discloses how Valerian's wife cuts their biological son from birth with a razor that draws blood from his legs until he was old enough to resist. She exposes the bizarre torture at a Thanksgiving meal where – since the Streets actual son didn't attend – their adopted child Jadine, the interloper "Son", and servants like Ondine and her husband were invited. In a double exposure of the plantation proprietor as a good father, patron and plantation owner, Ondine serves up a candid reality that cuts through the Streets illusory, elevated, and unchallenged rhetoric.

Ondine, unlike the mythic rabbit who gets caught up in the deception of the Tar Baby decoy, deposes the planter/fox and uncovers the whole myth. Morrison's brilliant novel portrays Ondine, the servant cook as the wise and capable woman who cuts through all deceptions. Valerian Street, the plantation owner and fox, made his money from a sugar store in Philadelphia, catching customers with the ultimate culinary lure. Ironically, it is his cook who remains unsusceptible to Valerian's snares. In the preface to Morrison's novel, Ondine is described as one of those "African-American women [who] are not side-tracked by seduction and cynical about 'authenticity'" ... They are the ones able to "witness, as challenge, as judges intent on the uses to which stories are put and the manner of their telling" (Morrison, 2004, p. xiv). *Tar Baby* complicates the Undine myth with Ondine, who knows not only how to parse the elemental for all its layers and resources but how to witness the hidden stories that surface out of the glistening and smothering waters.

Correlatively, both *Undine* and Morrison's *Tar Baby* show how negotiating elemental *jouissance* is less a rational activity than a bodily practice of cultivating and allocating creation as a resource. Habits of separation and limitation are necessary to parse out and share the elemental streams of the earth's economy and technology, e.g., the oceanic. The unfair allocation of resources and ongoing historic racial inequity that finally surfaced in the pandemic with cultural disasters like the death of George Floyd incited protests. "I can't breathe" still resounds. Voices witnessed and finally called the one-sided chokehold of law enforcement upon Floyd, which was a visual reminder of drowning without limits in both an inequitable justice system and divided community. It is no wonder people took to the streets during the pandemic. Crowds of protestors are the flip side of small screen usage, e.g., quarantine isolation and mass protest mobilise as a group, drowning individuals in a crowd. *Undine* and *Tar Baby* are a reminder to remember the dangers of forgetting a shameful history. They challenge us to recover vulnerability through lack, to breathe and step away from the decoys until we can see society, others, and ourselves clearly.

*Tar Baby,* like *Undine* exposes the siren call that hides a more lethal fox and planter, i.e., Valerian Street, and military tech companies that use siren servers to control users. Oceanic culture thrives where there is no lack of lack or subjective restraints that would create technological limits. "Liking" content is the way we assent to the new cultural misappropriation. Moreover, following Freud's observation, we can consider technology as a set of artificial organs or an extension of our natural body. He noted early on that "the relationship between us and our tools is often blurred and frequently intimate" (Rybczynski, 1985, p. 4). Mobile devices like cell phones, tablets, and smart watches are what Jacques Lacan calls *lathouses* in that they disconnect us from symbolic reality while making us feel as though we are connected. Undine and Tar baby are a lure akin to *lathouse,* a lethal object that makes us forget the structure of power to which we are subjected. As a small part of a terrible whole, "one mustn't tease *lathouse* too much" (Lacan, 2007, p. 187). Technology like iPhones and other iThings tap into anxieties about the self as a post-modern construction. In modern day society the benefit of technological usage accrues to the owner of the server and not to the creation or the improvement of society. Governmental and corporate proprietors prey upon the desire for wholeness that is offered through a spiritual and totalizing vision, as for example created by tech company founders like Apple's Steve Jobs.

After spending time after dropping out of college in India, Steve Jobs saw gurus as the focal point of love and respect. He then modelled himself as Apple CEO upon the guru model, a narcissistic structure where followers are often treated harshly or badly to make them more devoted. Undine, like the guru, is a prophetess and enticer of desire, the ultimate seducer whose allure and trap is death. Simulating a watery realm with no borders, Job's Apple Store interior was originally designed to look like an ashram. The idea was it would be all white to model transcendence and take humans to a place beyond boundaries. Jaron Lanier explains the Apple architecture, "At the same time, the white space must be highly structured and formal. There must be a tangible aura of discipline and adherence to the master plan" (Lanier, 2013, p. 204). Tech stores as temples are new in terms of the form but not in terms of the social and political power structure that drowns users in addiction is as ancient as Homer. The twist is that in Homer's time, memory and narrative keep Odysseus from drowning, but today memory and narrative are being erased and drowned by the undoing of civilization.

As navigators of the oceanic, programmers have an adage for overthinking a solution, "Don't boil the ocean". That's because they know the ocean cannot be contained for boiling. Now it is not just programmers but everyday online users whose health depends upon bodily separation or self-imposed restraints to steer through the swelling promises of connectivity that appeal to our narcissism. Small screen devices are sold as decoys, tar babies, and limitless joy devices that social media companies use for entrapment purposes of marketing, tracking, and listening. Solitary small screen culture depends upon people surfing to feel connected to an ocean of people. Yet, modern machine culture makes people more isolated, without the other even while being submerged online in an imaginary world with millions of virtual users on their smart devices. This shift promotes the illusion of invulnerability, the antithesis of the castration necessary for the social link, risking a society more automated and robotic than ever. Technology creates users not agents or subjects.

Like other mythic permutations of the *lamella*, Undine is a water spirit that marks the amniotic unity that must be sacrificed for symbolic life. Water is symbolic of screens without limits where people imagine unity and complete connection is possible. The duped online subject prefers to be in a relation to Undine, via their oceanic phone or computer screen, swimming in an imaginary puddle of narcissism rather than with real others. The film demystifies and critiques the seductive dream of pure oceanic connectivity of streaming in form and content. Undine like the internet comes from nowhere and goes nowhere, undoing distinctions of otherness, subjectivity, and community. Ultimately, Undine exemplifies the undone. The film underlines that life requires a loss (castration) and that loss is mythic, as Lacan posited with the *lamella*. In the end no one, not even Christoph, knows what happened to Undine. *Undine* is about the entropy of the death drive as the oceanic and the constant undoing, e.g., Undine-ing, of culture, subjectivity, and history.

Petzold's *Undine* revivifies the siren from her German Romantic roots into a primary mythic figure of modern life. In the classic tradition, Undine is the water spirit, or mermaid, siren, muse, first dreamed up by the sixteenth-century alchemist and medical doctor, Paracelsus. The physician and alchemist imagined that the elements were personified in beings. Paracelsus' idea would flower in German Romanticism and 19th century versions of the Undine myth, including the Little Mermaid. For Paracelsus, the earth was represented by gnomes, the air by Sylphs, fire by salamanders and water by Undines. An alchemist, prior to the scientific revolution, believed the spiritual element inhabited the material and concerned the soul, and believed elemental beings had no soul. For the Romantics, this "element" is the object, like Novalis' *blaue Blume*. Paracelsus' tale was developed by Friedrich de la Motte Fouqué and is a prime example of the uncanny genre with doubles, *deja vu*, repetition and the presence of what should be repressed.

In the post-modern tradition, writer Ingeborg Bachmann breaks from the German tradition of letters and philosophy. "Undine Goes" is a short story monologue entirely from the perspective of Undine. It begins with her repudiation of Hans and humans in general as monsters. She is a siren, or real inhuman voice, highlighting her distance from Hans. German tradition treats encounters with Undine as a striving for unification of the spiritual and corporeal, living and the dead. Contrarily, Bachmann's in "Undine Goes" Undine declares to Hans – "You monsters named Hans" – but in an address that emphasizes their distance and separation (Bachmann, 1987, p. 171). Bachmann's text speaks from the water to reject symbolic womanhood and oceanic femininity. Her Undine eschews reproductive womanhood as the continuance of a phallic name and legacy, e.g, phallic femininity.

As a mythic figure in opposition to the distinctions of symbolic maternal life, Undine's spirit harbours no phallic desire. Bachmann's text shows how for "Undine, this whole notion of personal ego-identity becomes irrelevant. Her lack of demands, caution, and intention or future attest to a non-lack: her rejection of the Law of the Father" indicate her desirelessness (Scrol, 1994, p. 241). "Undine Goes" exposes the whole myth of Oedipal security and stability in maternal phallic femininity. Like Morrison's Ondine, Bachman's Undine inverts the whole Oedipal triangle in a three-way undoing of Undine, Hans and Woman to expose the real that pokes a hole in the symbolic. Like Undine, Ingeborg Bachman herself eschewed traditional female roles, died suddenly, and wrote "Undine Goes" after the death of her lover, the poet Paul Celan. Given Bachman's Austrian father was a fervent Nazi, the writer's frustration with history and the work of *Gruppe 47* – an informal association of German speaking writers founded in 1947, hence its name – the writing was also personal, perhaps aimed at atoning or undoing her own bad history.

What is important in all these mythic retellings for us, is that *Undine* represents the real voice of death that is sacrificed in symbolic representation. In traditional accounts of the mythic story, the man is caught up, killed, or consumed by Undine. Petzold's film shows something different; Christoph lives and is saved by Undine. Even though he turns away from Undine (like Orpheus), in the end, he remains in a relation of loss to Undine and the death drive she embodies. To hear the siren's voice, is to realize death is the unacknowledged and unsung partner of our desire. Despite that reckoning, Christoph embraces fatherhood, his partner who is carrying their child, and his profession. He separates finally from Undine who exists for eternity by having worked through a relation to death.

*Undine* is a cautionary tale about diving into the totalizing oceanic virtuality of the real. On the one hand, the film shows how contemporary subjectivity and history are being submerged by the Oceanic infinite jouissance of streaming as exemplified in Christoph's relation to Undine as a real relation to death. On the other hand, *Undine* shows how civilization depends upon separation and an awareness that screens do not unify or provide the imagined hoped-for invulnerability. A recovery of lack and restraints is fundamental for human connection, culture and avoiding the repetition of disaster in history. Like air, water is an uncontained element, that involves a *jouissance* which must be shepherded as an excessive part of being. Christoph dives into the oceanic past and becomes brain dead in the present. He displays the danger of diving too deeply into the oceanic of virtual and historic screens, a signal of our need to surface for air. *Undine* reveals how if we do not shepherd the elements and face the oceanic real (of self, other, history) at intervals we cannot reckon or see ourselves clearly in the mirror. *Undine* is a warning to be attentive to repetition and avoid drowning in the oceanic to forget history, which repeats itself. We have to stop saying "water under the bridge" and viewing the other as superfluous to remain submerged in oceanic small screen culture. This means heeding the real (other/history) that keeps calling us back, again and again, as Undining/Undoing.

## References

Alfonsi, S. (2021). Alexey Molchanov on diving more than 39 stories deep while holding his breath for four and a half minutes. *CBS News*, 26 September 2021. Available at: https://www.cbsnews.com/news/free-diving-alexey-molchanov-60-minutes-2021-09-26/.
Assange, J., Applebaum, J., Müller-Maguhn, A., and Zimmermann, J. (2012). *Cypherpunks: Freedom and the future of the internet*. New York: OR Books.
Bachmann, I. (1987). Undine Goes. In M. Bullock (Trans.), *The thirtieth year: Stories by Ingeborg Bachmann* (pp. 171–181). New York: Holmes & Meier.
Braunstein, N. A. (2020). *Jouissance: A Lacanian concept* (Trans. S. Rosman). New York: State University of New York Press.
Fiennes, S., and Žižek, S. (2009). *The Pervert's Guide to Cinema*. Documentary. Amoeba Film, Kasander Film Company, Lone Star Productions.
Freud, S. (1962. *Civilization and its discontents* (Trans. J. Strachey). New York: W.W. Norton.
Kafka, F. (1988). *The complete stories* (Trans. N. N. Glatzer). New York: Schocken Books.
Lacan, J. (1978). On psychoanalytic discourse. In *Lacan in Italia, 1953–1978* (Trans. J. Stone) (pp. 32–55). Milan: La Salmandra. Available at: https://web.archive.org/web/20140729192754/http://web.missouri.edu/~stonej/t67894312xxxv.html.
Lacan, J. (2007). *Book XVII: The other side of psychoanalysis*. New York and London: W.W. Norton.
Lacan, J. (2013). *On the names-of-the-Father* (Trans. B. Fink). Cambridge: Polity Press.
Lanier, J. (2013). *Who owns the future?* New York: Simon & Schuster.
Larkin, P. (2004). *Collected poems* (Ed. A. Thwaite). New York: Farrar, Straus and Giroux.
Morrison, T. (2004). *Tar baby*. London: Vintage International.
Orwell, G. (2017). *1984*. London: Signet Classics.
Petzold, C., Beer, P., Rogowski, F., and Zaree, M. (2021). *Undine*. Drama, Fantasy, Mystery. Schramm Film, Les Films du Losange, Zweites Deutsches Fernsehen (ZDF).
Rybczynski, W. (1985). *Taming the tiger: The struggle to control technology*. New York: Viking Penguin.
Scrol, V. (1994). Return to "0": A Lacanian Reading of Ingeborg Bachmann's "Undine Goes". *Studies in 20th & 21st Century Literature*, 18(2). Available at: https://doi.org/10.4148/2334-4415.1352.

Chapter 5

# Prohibition and Power

## *Normal People* as Pandemic Pornography

## Erica D. Galioto

"It's not like this with other people" serves as an apt tagline for the powerful relationship featured in the TV adaptation of the groundbreaking novel *Normal People* (2018) by Irish author Sally Rooney. The novel's bingeworthy small screen adaptation directed by Oscar-nominated Irish director Lenny Abrahamson and Hettie McDonald riveted viewers who hungrily consumed Marianne and Connell's millennial relationship and its intermittent intensity during the spring 2020 uncertainty of the global COVID-19 pandemic. *Normal People*, as a novel and as a televisual representation, removes sex from the pastoral idealisation of total union and places it in a more complicated and shifting nexus of desire, power, pleasure, and pain. This chapter argues that Marianne and Connell construct a shared fantasy of prohibition and power and thus experience the epitome of psychoanalytic desire, a mutual desire at risk due to the ubiquity of internet pornography, the endless swiping of dating apps, and the superegoic command to gorge on the physical act of sex while simultaneously guarding against "catching feelings". "It's not like this with other people" because with each other, Marianne and Connell exist within the fantasy of the impossible sexual relation, a unique constellation of unconscious drives only accessible in/with/through each other. Their nuanced psychic interplay installs a mutually-agreed upon fantasy that is created from within their internal relational dynamic and not imposed by the external Other, and it is electric whether viewed on the screen or read on the page.

*Normal People*, I argue, is synonymous with pandemic pornography, a much-needed psychoanalytic retroversion to the preservation of impossible, yet necessary, relationality at a time when interpersonal intimacy is often viewed as superfluous or even detrimental to a sexual encounter. As pandemic pornography, *Normal People* represents desire and stimulates our own because it enacts an authentic desire predicated on prohibition and power. This intense authenticity stands in sharp contrast to the 21st-century imperative to enjoy technologically-driven and relatively anonymous sex. Marianne and Connell, at the height of our modern-day quarantine, urge us to reject this pervasive imperative to eliminate desire, and instead prioritise interpersonal and interpsychic desire in our post-pandemic world. Drawing support from Lacan's

DOI: 10.4324/9781003272069-6

*Seminars XX* and *XVII* as well as other psychoanalytic thinkers, this chapter illustrates how within their impossible relation – not despite it – Marianne and Connell construct a fantasy where boundaries, shared power, and awareness of lack eroticise them and arouse us to consider the ways in which we might engage, rather than avoid, psychoanalytic desire in our new reality.

## I

Following her highly-acclaimed debut novel, *Conversations with Friends* (2017), Sally Rooney's *Normal People* (2018) broke barriers between the general reading public and the literary intelligentsia with its appealing and heady modern love story. Winning Rooney a host of literary praise, such as the 2018 Costa Novel Award, as well as the unofficial "first great millennial novelist" label, *Normal People* was already contributing to the ever-evolving landscape of popular culture two years before its small screen launch (Barry, 2018). *Normal People* spans four years in the lives of the central characters, Marianne Sheridan and Connell Waldron, as they negotiate their interdependent relationship first at a Catholic high school in Carricklea, County Mayo and then at Trinity College Dublin. Despite its ostensible classification as a campus novel, *Normal People* rejects the adolescent disillusionment that typically attends the genre and instead focuses on the central relationship and how it transforms Marianne and Connell as individuals from within their shared intimacy. As millennials on the cusp of adulthood, Marianne and Connell communicate through spoken conversations, of course, but also through emails and text messages that reveal the depth of their discourse, a discourse illustrating a relationship existing within a network of ideological decisions and through rising awareness of class consciousness. Their small typecast lives continually engage in casual self-revelation, and virtual communication is central to their examinations of one another and their relationship.

They also have sex, and a lot of it. First in secondary school when their relationship is kept secret at Connell's request so he doesn't lose his social status by a too-close affiliation with Marianne's pariah-like alienation. And later in college when their roles have reversed and Marianne's upper-class family background allows her to easily slide into the privileged undergraduate social scene Connell feels barred from due to his working-class roots and his single mother, Lorraine, who works part-time cleaning Marianne's family home. In neither high school nor college is each other's social capital quite coincident, yet their magnetic intimacy persists and embeds in mutual constructions that endlessly punctuate through time, despite their lack of official relationship title. Marianne and Connell are always working on who they are together and in this shared space of investigation and negotiation, they are figuring out who they are as individuals. Rooney explores their interdependency through language and sex, and of course how language and sex interpenetrate each other. Sex, then, is not the product or proof of their love, but rather the terrain that allows them to discover their relationship and their individual transformations. Sex as discovery, not as endpoint, manifests potently on the small screen in the BBC/Hulu limited series that pushed *Normal People* from a book in our hands to the show before our eyes and became pandemic pornography for the world in spring 2020.

The twelve episode small screen rendition of *Normal People* gave the existent novel readers a satisfyingly faithful adaptation, due largely to Rooney's contributions to the writing and production of the series, as well as Abrahamson and McDonald's precise and realistic directing. For those viewers who were unfamiliar with the novel, Rooney scored legions of new fans who instantly found themselves transfixed by the steamy sex shared by the beautiful and smart Marianne, played by Daisy Edgar Jones, and the equally beautiful and smart Connell, played by Paul Mescal. It is the manifestation of these two human bodies engaged in shared and mutual sexual awakening onscreen that catapulted *Normal People* from its status as a smart book to a blockbuster small screen series. While spoken dialogue was often culled directly from the pages of the novel, the bold and explicit naturalistic sex featured in the series exceeds far beyond the novel's often unadorned sexual depictions, such as "they have sex again, not speaking very much", to the bodies and sounds and glances – the language of spoken and unspoken intimacies – comprising Marianne and Connell's emotional and physical intimacy on the small screen (Rooney, 2018, p. 93). What Rooney does with language in the novel to highlight the interdependent psychic space of Marianne and Connell, Edgar-Jones and Mescal do with their sexual expressions following the direction of Abrahamson and McDonald and the collaborations from Rooney herself and Ita O'Brien, the show's intimacy coordinator now known as "a guru of screen sex" (Kinchen, 2020). Simply put, the onscreen meticulously-scripted sex between Marianne and Connell resonated as "normal" sex between "normal" people.

The combination of quarantine-inflicted isolation and *Normal People*'s normal sex turned the show itself into a global turn-on: the much-needed pandemic pornography for those who craved new pathways to old arousals. Slavoj Žižek's foundational article "Pornography, Nostalgia, Montage: A Triad of the Gaze" (1991) offers an early critique of the "show everything" methodology of filmic pornography, even before its internet ubiquity, and provides rationale for the vast appeal of *Normal People*'s "normal" sex. His well-known argument establishes the central distinction between show all pornography and cinematic nonpornographic sex. On the one side, pornographic sex shows everything, conceals nothing, and turns the spectator into an object; whereas on the other side, nonpornographic normal sex hits up against a limit of visibility where not all is shown because not all can be shown when it comes to sex, and this gap inaugurates not only the desire of the featured couple but also that of the spectators. "In contrast to this limit of representability defining the 'normal' love story or melodrama", Žižek emphasises, "pornography goes beyond, it 'shows everything'" (1991, p. 110). Yet, he continues, "The paradox is however, that by trespassing the limit, it always *goes too far*, i.e., it *misses* what remains concealed in a 'normal,' non-pornographic love scene" (1991, p. 110). It is significant that in Žižek's discourse "normal" is antithetical to pornography; "normal" sex contains a necessary barrier to full representation that actually engages and arouses desire, while show all pornography effectively extinguishes desire by exceeding beyond the boundaries that constitute desire in the first place.

By showing everything, pornography plugs up the gap on which the libidinal economy initiates and perpetuates. Bringing Žižek's argument into the present-day makes his dichotomy between normal and pornographic sex only more poignant. 24/7 on-demand accessibility to internet pornography that is ever-increasing in specificity continues to obliterate the self-same limit Žižek urged us to reinstall in the nineties. By quickly and effortlessly and repetitively showing penetrative sexual acts often through close-ups of organs and orifices, otherwise known as "the thing itself", in Žižek's parlance, show all pornography effectively eliminates the desire it supposedly intends to induce and prolong (1991, p. 110). Pornography's constitutive failure to engage and maintain desire is proven by how viewers continue to seek more various and explicit content. Each escalating attempt ultimately fails because this brand of pornography explodes the barrier of representation and turns the viewer into the gazed-upon object, whose arousal is manufactured through scripted illusion. For Žižek, there is another way for pornography to function. He explains,

> The fantasy ideal of a perfect work of pornography would be precisely to preserve this impossible harmony, the balance between narration and explicit depiction of the sexual act, i.e, to avoid the necessary *vel* that condemns us to lose one of the two poles.
>
> (1991, p. 111)

As Žižek explains here, when it comes to sex onscreen, viewers are presented with either explicit sex acts very loosely tied to flimsy storylines or tepid sex scenes overshadowed by detailed plotlines.

*Normal People* exists as close to Žižek's ideal as possible, and in so doing, became pandemic pornography for millions of viewers who found themselves alone and aroused watching Marianne and Connell on the small screen. This exquisite balance between story and sex, or shall we say language and sex, manifests onscreen before our eyes of course, but the same coincidence also pertains to the epitome of psychoanalytic desire, the shared space of a mutually-agreed upon fantasy, whereby each individual accepts the Other's fantasy as their own. To emphasise this dual point further: *Normal People* achieves an ideal equilibrium for viewers because its power is reached through mutually-reinforcing plot points and sex scenes, and the featured couple,

Marianne and Connell, also highlight the value of interdependent desire and its necessity for climactic arousal. *Normal People* is a pornographic ideal, then, precisely because it maintains the harmony between language and sex by preserving the delicate balance between self and other on which it rests.

Take Marianne and Connell's first time in Episode 2 as the foundation for the series' achievement as pandemic pornography. This representative early scene takes place in Connell's bedroom; Marianne sits on his bed, and Connell on his desk chair. They face each other awkwardly with some nervous energy and establish their signature flirtatious banter based on Connell's posters before discussing how they are viewed by others at school, and then easily slide into their own judgments of each other. "You always know what you think, and I like that," Connell states explicitly as a firm contrast to his own inability to deliberately structure his own shapeless thoughts, despite the present moment's exception (Episode 2). In response, Marianne innocently offers, "You must know what you feel though," seemingly unaware of the moment's charge (Episode 2). When he replies, "Most of the time I don't have a clue," and she quickly follows with "What about now?," viewers see and feel the effects of spontaneous naturalistic dialogue that operates on more than one level at once (Episode 2). When Connell stands and moves toward Marianne, we know that the sexual level of knowing how each feels and what each desires has overtaken the level of their discourse that refers to school-based classroom discussions. The kiss he initiates follows an intense stare into each other's eyes and is accompanied by the sounds of breathing and smacking resonant with a passionate French kiss.

As viewers, we are keenly aware that this exchange is not explicitly constructed for the benefit of our arousal as in show all pornography. This effect is also achieved due to the cinematic usage of montage as a filming decision. As Žižek writes, "Montage is usually conceived as a way of producing from fragments of the real – pieces of film, discontinuous individual shots – an effect of 'cinematic space,' i.e., a specific cinematic reality" (1991, p. 116). The montage emerges due to the inability to show everything; it's the leftover pieces that remain around the void that cannot be shown. This cinematic decision is exemplified most obviously in *Normal People* through the various vantage points from which the viewers see the scenes, particularly the sexual ones. In the present example, sometimes viewers are aligned with Connell's perspective, and at others Marianne's. We sometimes see both bodies in a long shot, while at other moments, we experience extreme close-ups of individual limbs and touches and adjacencies.

The overarching effect of this montage is that viewers are prevented from a stable point of identification; these discontinuous and shifting shots permit viewers to remain in their positions as subjects, not objects, of desire. The combination of our blocked identification with one of the two central characters, along with their unbroken focus on each other, piques our arousal without granting it either an immediate outlet or extinguishing it by rendering us objects. The viewer's desire also rests upon the failure to show all – as in explicit sexual images of organs, orifices, and fluids – and this delicate balance keeps viewers and their desires pleasurably poised. It is important to note that Connell's famous chain is prominent in this early scene as a focal point contrasting against the pair's naked skin and silently gesturing to that inexpressible void that they can't quite access and we can't quite see. For Žižek the identification of Connell's chain as a symbolic object for viewers emerges as a byproduct of the montage shooting strategy that originates with Hitchcock and "elevates an everyday, trivial object into a sublime Thing" (1991, p. 117). Connell's chain certainly did this for viewers who tracked its appearance in photos and videos throughout the series and even devoted an Instagram account to its whereabouts. "By purely formal manipulation, [montage] succeeds in bestowing on an ordinary object the aura of anxiety and uneasiness", Žižek writes (1991, p. 117). Present in the space, yet not attached to a position of stable identification, Connell's chain became an ordinary object that for viewers, occasioned not so much anxiety and unease, as desire's arousal. The fetish object necessary for desire to emerge, Connell's chain, both sturdy and delicate, stands for the ideal intimate attunement between partners in exquisite balance.

The scene's continuation supports the foregoing explanation, and Connell's chain is present through it all. Marianne and Connell whisper and laugh about taking each other's clothes off, and Marianne even gets sort of tangled in her bra as Connell attempts to raise it over her head. Amidst their kissing, their talking continues. Mere inches apart and topless, Marianne questions whether Connell "do[es] this a lot" with other girls, and Connell jokes back that it was really she who "seduced [him]" (Episode 2). "I just like talking to you," he says with a smile (Episode 2). That he says this exact statement at the moment of their first sex is extremely significant because it is through their entwined discourse and sex that their relationship approaches the epitome of psychoanalytic desire, as this article will continue to reveal. Their talking leads to sex, of course, but their sex also is their talking; likewise, their talking is also sex. Quieting their spoken discourse with more kissing and more undressing, Connell and Marianne look in each other's eyes and at each other's bodies. Viewers observe through the discontinuous montage shots that prevent absolute identification with either character, but also privilege Connell's chain as synecdoche. Marianne and Connell don't care about us; they are constructing a world with their bodies and minds: a mutual space that is not for us and can't be seen by us.

Part of this mutuality, of course, is their shared enthusiastic consent, an explicit affirmation that is certainly noteworthy in its depiction onscreen. Not only does Marianne ask for Connell to use a condom, but Connell also verifies with "Is that what you want?" (Episode 2). And continues to tell Marianne that the first time often hurts and if it does and she wants to stop, that they will. "It won't be awkward," he assures her as evidence of his care for her (Episode 2). They continue to talk and laugh quietly during penetration about whether it hurts ("It's nice," she says), and at the moment their sexual noises turn to moans of pleasure, the scene cuts to the next school day and their deliberate and absolute avoidance of one another (Episode 2). Next, there's another quick splice to Marianne being on top and riding Connell, sweaty and enjoying herself. They seem connected physically and emotionally, deep kissing and talking. When Marianne says that she wants to watch him have sex and questions if she's weird, Connell replies, "Yeah. Yeah, that's really weird, Marianne. But I think I understand it" (Episode 2). The juxtaposition between their school-based refusal to acknowledge each other and the intimate tenderness and care in private moments of shared sexual pleasure and honest talking is glaringly obvious, yet its cinematography serves to highlight that the school agreement, based on Connell's request, is integral to their expressed sexual fantasy. Psychoanalysis maintains that one's desire comes from the desire of the Other, as Lacan asserts in *Seminar XI*, so it might be argued that Marianne and Connell's avoidance of each other at school strengthens their shared intimacy because it highlights their recognition and acceptance of the Other's desire. Marianne agrees to take on this aspect of Connell's desire as her own by willingly giving her power to him, and Connell agrees to take Marianne's desire for submission by putting himself in the position to hold her power. Though this notion of shared power gets complicated through the series, as we will see, it is their joint negotiation of power and mutual willingness to take each other's desire as their own that allows *Normal People* to both arouse viewers as pandemic pornography and also role model the value of desire at a time where its necessity seems to be downplayed.

## 2

Undoubtedly, Marianne and Connell's pandemic pornography also appeals to viewers because their entwined physical and psychic intimacy is so contrary to the supposed goals of modern romance which advocate the avoidance of emotional closeness above all else. The foundational article "Tinder and the Dawn of the 'Dating Apocalypse'" (2015) by Nancy Jo Sales was an early exposé of the dating apps that are now central to most sexual lives. As her cheeky title borrowed from one of her twenty-nine-year-old female interview subjects indicates, Sales' well-researched journalism illustrates how dating apps like Tinder, Grindr, Hinge, and Bumble have eradicated dating as it was once known and have replaced those rites of passage from the previous century with hookup sex with strangers. Central features of this new reality, of course, are the ability to swipe hundreds of people a day, the access to 24/7 sexual contact, and the consumer mindset creating endless competition and instantaneous replacement. In contrast to the sex as discovery model that I'm suggesting exists between Marianne and Connell, the sex as product model advocated through these apps exists when users exclude feelings from their sexual encounters. The sex had in these moments of contact with strangers, then, is characterised as purely physical, not emotional. There is no expectation for a relationship; there is not even the former expectation of dinner and a movie before the event. Put simply, dating apps turn sex into mutual acquisition and exchange. "Dating apps are the free market come to sex", Sales concludes; "the art of choosing consumer brands and sex partners has become interchangeable" (2015, p. 4).

The shopping metaphor Sales develops here is a powerful one despite its simplicity. Like so many products in our 21st-century-high-capitalist economy, the market for sexual partners has become flooded. There are endless options to choose from, and few are actively pursuing the ideal conditions often required for a mutually-meaningful and pleasurable sexual experience. "It's straight efficiency," states one of Sales' interviewees bluntly (2015, p. 6). In addition to eliminating feelings and challenge and effort, these dating apps and their model of sexual efficiency also eliminate desire. Not only does this absence of desire have real physical consequences like men losing erections and women not experiencing orgasms, but there is also a pronounced "lack of intimacy in hookup sex" (2015, p. 13). Most profound, of course, from the vantage point of psychoanalysis, is how the removal of desire from a sexual encounter renders the whole experience negligible. Like the tagline I've proposed for *Normal People* states, feeling like "it's not like this with other people" is exactly the type of sexual encounter we should be courting (Rooney, 2018, p. 93). Marianne and Connell incarnate their intimate singularity for and with one another at the height of their mutual desire. The dating apps, of course, advocate the polar opposite in their insistence that there is nothing unique to be pursued; there is nothing special to desire; there is no deeper connection to be shared. Like the all-access show all porn already elaborated here, the endless swiping of dating apps effectively neuters desire. The combination of new technology and easy accessibility is the same in the realm of pornography and dating apps. In the words of one of Sales' subjects, "People are gorging. That's why it's not intimate. You could call it a kind of psychosexual obesity" (2015, p. 15).

In both cases, the explosion beyond the limit of representability and accessibility has removed the necessary impossibility on which desire rests. Marianne and Connell are firmly imbricated in their network of limits and prohibitions, and it's this network that causes and strengthens desire for them, as it enacts an economy of exchange that is distinct from the one dominating the current landscape of modern romance. Therefore, their pleasurable representation of the impossible limit of psychoanalytic desire also arouses viewers who have likely found themselves unsatisfied by the expectations, if not actuality, of sex with strangers, as well as trapped in pandemic lockdowns and separated from human touch. Physical touch, whether the inability to have it in lockdown or the removal of its intimate communication in hookup sex, emerged during the pandemic as a rekindled desire for meaningful human contact felt acutely when lost and features prominently in the shared fantasy of Marianne and Connell.

In a timely update to his earlier treatise on pornography, Žižek's recent article "Sex in the Age of Social Distancing" (2020) maintains that the pandemic's demand for social distancing has only highlighted our reliance on real human bodies and their necessity for our pleasure. As in the previously explicated article that divided pornography from normal sex, this article separates virtual sex in all its forms from real sex shared by human bodies. Like the dating app business model explained above, virtually-mediated sexual experiences whether via a screen or a sex doll, for instance, are typically thought to prioritise the physical body engaged in the carnal acts of sex. In the well-worn theorisations of the mind/body duality, these acts of physicality are thought to exist as natural biological urges apart from the thinking mind. For Žižek, however, he actually reverses the foregoing assumptions about the physical body in sex. In his psychoanalytic framework, "sexual love is more bodily than sex without love" (Žižek, 2020, 53). Instead of demoting the physical body in sex to the level of animalistic mating, Žižek argues that the physical body oriented in sexual love is evidence of the ultimate harmony between mind and body, and not proof of the body's ability to detach from the mind. Though, it should be noted, the material body need not be present for the experience of shared desire, both Žižek's recent article and *Normal People* prioritise the body of substance, as I will here.

The body of the Other contains the fantasmic support necessary to access one's pleasure. As pathway to one's own *jouissance*, the Other's body is where "I use the flesh and body of my partner as a prop to realise and enact my fantasies" (Žižek, 2020, p. 53). The Other's body, then, for Žižek is worthy of respect, admiration, and tender care. "When one makes love with someone they truly love", he says, "touching their partner's body is crucial" (2020, p. 53). The touch referred to here is not the variety of dating app sex with strangers, but rather is touch predicated on shared mutual fantasy found in and through the body of the Other. This mutual touch, as shown by Marianne and Connell in *Normal People*, highlights the body as a place of reverence and surely contributes to the appeal of an idealised pandemic pornography that shows how bodies are shared and worshipped and simply loved. "If sex is always, up to a point, masturbation with a real partner", then bodily touch in sexual love makes intersubjective what might otherwise be viewed as solipsistic (2020, p. 52). The body of the Other is absolutely central to one's experience of the self. While the ubiquity of dating apps and their supposedly safe anonymity proposes that sex with strangers provides easy access to ultimate pleasure, it is actually, according to psychoanalysis, dependence on the multiple signifiers of the Other that permits access to the highest pleasure: a pleasure that is only available due to shared and negotiated relationality.

Take *Normal People*'s Episode 5. In this episode, Marianne and Connell are at Trinity College and have recently reconnected. Marianne is now in the socially superior position, and Connell is struggling to adjust. "I think about home, school, and I just, I can't connect this life and that life. It just doesn't fit," he reveals as he opens up to Marianne about his insecurities (Episode 5). It is during this conversation that a mutual reckoning of their secondary school falling out transpires. Each puts to language what has never been spoken before, and ultimately this linguistic signification leads to the sexual expression of their bodies at the end of the episode. Their secondary school rupture occurred when Connell, intent on keeping his relationship with Marianne hidden, asked another girl to the Irish high school graduation dance, *Debs*, despite the ongoing sexual and emotional relationship he and Marianne shared. Now at college, Connell questions whether Marianne would be embarrassed if her new friends found out about their previous relationship. Though she says she would be embarrassed, it's not because of Connell or who he is, it's because of how she views herself in the past iteration of their relationship. "Because it was humiliating," she states, and then continues with "And ... Just the fact that I put up with it" (Episode 5). After revealing that he had not even thought of inviting Marianne to the Debs, Connell obliviously continues with "Would you have said yes?" (Episode 5). Overcome with tears, Marianne seems flabbergasted that he would even ask such an inane question, while Connell rambles about how their classmates apparently knew about their secret relationship anyway. Bumbling forward in starts and stops, he attempts to explain with "I still think about it all the time. I still ... think about why I acted in such a fucked-up way and I'm really sorry. Marianne, I ... I really am sorry" (Episode 5). After Marianne whispers, "I forgive you," the scene cuts to a prompt break-up scene between Marianne and Gareth, her then-boyfriend, and then on to a house party (Episode 5). At the party, Marianne drinks too much and Connell rejects her blunt sexual entreaties but remains until the next morning.

Back at her flat, Marianne takes a shower and returns to her kitchen where Connell waits. Sober and damp from her recent shower, Marianne stands before Connell who undoes her robe and kisses her belly worshipfully. When she directs, "Come to bed then," it seems as though his touch occasions the type of meaningful communication Žižek attributes to the care provided to the Other's body in physical contact (Episode 5). The scene shifts to Marianne on her bed looking attentively at Connell who goes directly toward her in a kiss that looks like a conversation, back and forth, given and taken. Connell's body is also revered with kisses and touches; his chain on full display as a talisman to their ongoing discourse. Though this scene proceeds without speech, their gazes at one another, along with their rapt attention to various parts of each other's bodies through fingertips, tongues, breasts, and simply flesh, continues to express the conversation first begun with their kiss on the bed, hearkening back even further to their truth telling conversation the day before, and projecting even deeper backward to their earlier conversations in Carricklea. As evidence of Žižek's ballad to the body in sexual love, Connell exemplifies the theorist's conditional statement, "If he were passionately in love with his sexual partner, her body would have mattered to him since every gesture of touching her would disturb the core of her subjectivity" (2020, p. 53). From start to finish of this scene dominated by tender touch, Connell and Marianne prove this conditional statement as possibility, if not fact. For each, the body of the Other matters because it is the encasement of the subjectivity on which the access to pleasure for each resides. It is not separate from that place; it is the place; "a path to the spirit," even (2020, p. 55).

After their sex, in a beautiful repose of pale bodies overlapping as one contiguous shape, not two, and with Mescal's revealed penis balanced with Edgar-Jones' exposed breasts, my oft-repeated tagline is spoken by Marianne in the small screen rendition of the novel's dialogue. "It's not like this with other people," she says, eyes closed and absentmindedly playing with Connell's hair. Also eyes closed, he replies, "I know. I think we'll be fine," and then the episode fades to black (Episode 5). The ultimate singularity of the Other and the prominence of the Other's body and physical touch manifest equivocally in Marianne and Connell with and for the Other. That their spoken discourse and their sexual discourse entwine emphasises the primacy of their mutual fantasy as an ongoing evolving language spoken only by them. Their intimate body contact in the age of social distancing reminds viewers that touch is integral to mutually-agreed upon shared fantasy and urges us all to really feel the Other in our new reality. In sharp contrast to the pre-pandemic insistence on the instantaneous access to sex without feelings, Marianne and Connell remind viewers that the greatest access to pleasure actually comes through the negotiated shared discourse of prohibition and power advocated by psychoanalysis.

## 3

*Normal People*, I have argued, exists as potent pandemic pornography due to its arousing portrayal of the balanced harmony between story and sex and between self and Other. The discourse and touch captured onscreen between Marianne and Connell resonate as interrelated practices suturing intersubjectivity amidst the presence of persistent miscommunications and lacks and failures. Their relationship is not, it should be emphasised, ecstatic unity, but rather is more akin to Lacan's notion of love in *Seminar XX* which famously attributes the inevitable conclusion of failure, impossibility, and disappointment for two to ever become one. From the perspective of psychoanalysis, however, and as evidenced by *Normal People*, this disjunction is a place of immense potentiality because mutual desire is a space of coincident movement where pleasurable relationality exists, though the merging of two into one never will. Put simply, Lacan's famous theorisation that "There is no such thing, that it is impossible to found a sexual relationship" stands as an anchor of psychoanalysis because it points to the absolute incommensurability of any amorous encounter (1998, p. 9). There is no penultimate annihilation of lack or obliteration of castration in human subjectivity; instead there are two sexuated positions that never relate in synchronicity, regardless of the gender or sexuality of each individual subject.

Satisfaction is attainable nonetheless, for "What makes up for the sexual relationship is, quite precisely, love" (Lacan, 1998, p. 45). Instead of the merging of two soulmates into one, we have fantasy: fantasy to both give and receive what is never properly had. In place of the sexual relationship, love exists as a negotiated discourse launched through desire, testifying that "this sexual relationship, insofar as it's not working out, works out anyway" (1998, pp. 32–3). In other words, the failure of absolute coincidence is the prerequisite for ultimate success. Alenka Zupančič's *What Is Sex?* (2017) offers a fully elaborated explication of Lacan's theories on the sexual and their ontological importance. In cogent prose, she maintains, and Marianne and Connell prove true, "It is only the inexistence of the relation that opens up the space for relationships and ties as we know them" (2017, p. 24). Impossibility, she emphasises echoing Lacan, founds relationality and opens the potential for intersubjective pleasure. These are not substitutive or partial pleasures reliant on impossible fantasies unable to be located in reality, but rather real-world fantasies of *jouissance* that exist in reality due to their *reliance* on the structure of the impossible sexual relation. To put it in yet another way, the non-relation provides the necessary condition for the fantasy that does exist in reality. Zupančič eloquently explicates, "non-relation is not simply an absence of relation, but is itself a real, even the Real" to emphasise the structuring negative potentiality of the incommensurability of the sexual relation (2017, p. 18). For sex to reach the dimension of the Real, impossibility must remain integral to the fantasy structure. At this juncture, my goal is to articulate how Marianne and Connell exist in their own fantasy of the impossible sexual relation.

The achievement of their shared fantasy is perhaps most obvious when reflected in contrast to other sexual relationships explored in *Normal People*. Marianne's unfulfilling forays into BDSM with Jamie and Lukas strikingly contrast her pleasurable cycle of power exchange with Connell. Despite their high level of satisfaction with one another, Marianne and Connell continue to experience external obstacles that interrupt the flow of their relationship, such as geographical separations, unspoken insecurities, health struggles, and even other partners. These tangible manifestations of their psychic impossibility prevent ongoing monogamy, yet Marianne and Connell still exist to each other. Their linguistic and sexual discourse is never completely severed, just paused perhaps, as Rooney highlights in the novel with chapter titles such as "Six Months Later" or "Three Months Later" to indicate the time spans of absence. During some of these gaps, Marianne explores her sexuality: first with Jamie, a fellow student at Trinity, and then with Lukas, a photographer in Sweden. With both men, she engages in BDSM and then attempts to relate those physical experiences to the kinds of power dynamics she and Connell share on a psychical level.

In Episode 7 at a café in Dublin, an edgy Marianne dressed all in black and smoking sits at a small outdoor table with Connell. They have recently agreed to be friends during this stretch of disengagement and briefly discuss the upcoming Scholars' exams before turning their attention to Marianne and her relationship with Jamie, whom Connell also knows. She asks Connell whether he wants the details and after he nods, Marianne opens with, "He's into pain. Like, inflicting it. Turns out he's a bit of a sadist." Connell seems surprised that she likes this type of sex and asks what Jamie does specifically, so Marianne continues with "[He] slaps me. Uses a belt. Things like that" (Episode 7). A noticeably agitated Connell admits, "It sounds fuckin' horrible" and mentions that Marianne never indicated these desires when they were having sex, but she explains how "Things were different" with Connell (Episode 7). And continues:

> I didn't have to play any games with you. It was just real. With Jamie, I don't know ... It's a bit like I'm acting a part. I just pretend to feel a certain way. Like I'm in his power. But with you I actually had those feelings. I'd have done anything you wanted me to.
>
> (Episode 7)

With these powerful words lingering in the air, the scene pivots to rough sex between Jamie and Marianne. He's pulling her hair strongly from behind, and she's gasping audibly, still mostly clothed and looking at the ceiling. Interspersed with these rough sex scenes, we first see Connell walking the streets of Dublin alone and then we observe both Marianne and Connell sitting for their exams as they exchange a quick smile. Marianne's words from earlier in the café conversation resonate as viewers contemplate the divergent sex scenes superimposed on the backdrop of the academic environment: "We had mutual, equally involved kind of sex. It's different with Jamie" (Episode 7). With Jamie, Marianne *acts* as if she has given him her power and he *acts* as if he has taken it, which is arousing to him and not her, as indicated by her pleasureless affect during their sex; yet with Connell, Marianne consciously offers her power and he holds it cautiously which is arousing to them both. Connell and Marianne have an authentic negotiation, while Jamie and Marianne merely a façade.

Marianne repeats this type of relationship in a slightly different way the following year while studying in Sweden. Episode 9 details her experiences with a photographer named Lukas, who begins mistreating her sexually after Marianne tries to break up with him. In an attempt to change the course of the formulaic break-up conversation, Lukas directly states, "I really like you," and seems genuinely confused when Marianne replies, "That. I don't, I don't want that. I don't want you to say that ... I want, if anything, the opposite of that" (Episode 9). Rather than concluding the relationship as Marianne had intended, this unusual conversation permits the entanglement with Lukas to carry on under different circumstances. From Lukas' perspective, the opposite of a relationship is his absolute power over Marianne through domination and bondage.

Like the sex with Jamie, this sex is also rough, but now Marianne is often shown restrained with her hands tied together and then clamped by Lukas, and she is also subjected to verbal assaults by him, such as "Don't ask me for stuff" and "I'll tell you when it's over and you can have a shower" and even "You're worthless. You're nothing" (Episode 9). With Jamie, Marianne felt as though she were acting during their sex, while with Lukas, she now feels dissociated from herself, a hollow vacancy that erodes her sense of stable existence. In a voice-over reading of an email to Connell, she says,

> I feel so not myself at the moment ... Not in a bad way, I just feel outside of my own life somehow ... Sometimes someone will make eye contact with me, like a bus conductor or a person looking for change, and I'll feel shocked that anyone can actually see me, and there's something comforting about it. Something good about feeling sort of numb. Detached from it all.
>
> (Episode 9)

Physical bruises attest to Marianne's corporeality, though her mutual participation in these activities is questionable.

During a staged photoshoot on Christmas, Lukas exploits Marianne and her shrunken power further by posing her topless body immobilised with bondage ties. All the while viewers are confronted with Marianne's flat facial expressions and closed eyes; then we hear Connell's voice-over of emails attesting to her value with "You are a good person and I say that as someone who really knows you" (Episode 9). It is with Connell's words in her head that Marianne's small resistances accumulate to one final "I don't want to do this" and "No," as she leaves the shoot (Episode 9). In this instant, Marianne marshals her power, wields it in the way she desires, and refuses to be reduced to the pornographic abused subject of Lukas' art. Both Jamie and Lukas exert explicit power over Marianne by engaging physical violence, verbal abuse, and deliberate humiliation, but these forms of domination do not work for Marianne or her desire because they cause the same pain her father and brother cause(d) her and her mother. Rather than working through trauma, these similar patterns merely repeat it. For Marianne, her fantasy is not one where her power is wilfully taken over by someone else, as we see with Jamie and Lukas, but rather one where she has power that she elects to give up to someone else, as she does pleasurably with Connell.

Marianne knows that she and Connell can have the kind of intersubjective transference that is at the pinnacle of psychic functioning, and she knows that it can come through the surrender of her body to him. Her often repeated, "You can do whatever you want with me", attests to this understanding, yet she initially struggles to find a form of dominance pleasurable to them both that is different from the unpleasurable physicality enacted by Jamie and Lukas (Episode 11). When Marianne asks Connell to hit her during Episode 11's powerful resurgences of linguistic and sexual intimacy, he declines, so both are left alone to reconsider the absolute impenetrability of the Other and each's failure to fully satisfy their impossible lacks. As Lacan theorises and Zupančič extends, this complete and utter incommensurability is the prerequisite for the negotiated real-world fantasy that Marianne and Connell may choose to launch as their shared discourse. Marianne's consciously given power becomes the master signifier on which their intersubjective transference depends, a theorisation that Lacan elaborates in *Seminar XVII*. In correlation with Lacan's theory, when Marianne gives her power to Connell, she engages in a signifying act that provides access to shared *jouissance* that is only made possible due to self-imposed boundaries, limits, and conditions. As we learn in *Seminar XVII*, the master signifier is a prerequisite for desire's movement; without this master signifier – in this case, Marianne's power transfer to Connell – the fantasy does not initiate, as with Jamie and Lukas, and neither does the desire predicated upon it. As Lacan states, "The signifier becomes articulated, therefore, by representing a subject to another signifier. This is our starting point for giving meaning to this inaugural repetition that is repetition directed at *jouissance*" (2007, p. 48). Thus, the relationship between *jouissance* and the signifier is constitutional and as such, the signifier opens the path to *jouissance* at the same time as it marks that attainment as impossible.

As has already been explicated, Marianne and Connell both mark their impossibility and negotiate a joint fantasy that permits access to shared *jouissance*. Marianne's transferal of power and Connell's tender acceptance of it is the signifying act necessary for their fantasy. Lacan would say that Marianne and Connell have become subjects of *jouissance* because they have installed the parameters of their fantasy together and jointly uphold the illusion of their own limits and transgressions. Their impositions of prohibitions and wilful power shifts permit them to experience *jouissance* within the contours they have determined. This, indeed, "creates a discourse", a language spoken on multiple levels of bodies, psyches, and words (Lacan, 2007, p. 189). In the BBC/Hulu limited series' final episode of *Normal People*, viewers see Marianne and Connell come to the psychoanalytic conclusion that their shared fantasy is a choice: they may continue their pleasurable shared fantasy as long as Marianne consciously transfers her power to Connell, and he consciously accepts it without abusing it. This shared negotiation is the mutual acceptance of the Other's desire as one's own. Connell chooses to let

Marianne submit her power to him, and Marianne chooses to do so with the understanding that it is not necessary for him to physically hurt her.

When Connell finally kisses her at the New Year's Eve party back at home in front of the Sligo public he once concealed their relationship from, Marianne acknowledges that their fantasy is, in fact, mutual. He wants to please her through this safe psychic form of domination as much as she wants to please him through submission. Therefore, they both accept their shared fantasy and its existence in reality, yet also realise the constitutive impossibility at the centre of their discourse. Marianne's repetitious signifying act occurs when she gives her power to Connell, and their fantasy persists when Connell receives the power as it is given without abusing it.

This is why, in the final scene, Connell gives Marianne the opportunity to deny him the decision to move to New York City. Marianne knows that he gives her this option to please her, but she also knows that their continued fantasy depends on returning this power to him. If she were to tell him to stay in Dublin, it would ultimately undermine their shared negotiation of power to the point where it would be unlikely for them to maintain their delicately cultivated discourse. Marianne's carefully spoken "I want to stay here. I want to live the life I'm living" marks not the destruction of their fantasy, as many viewers lamented in spring 2020, but rather its enduring continuation in a phase of prohibition (Episode 12). Connell's "I go," quickly followed by Marianne's "and I'll stay and we'll be okay" testifies to their blended discourse and their shared commitment to remain in their essential, mutually-agreed upon power dynamic (Episode 12). As epitomised in this powerful and emotional conclusion, *Normal People*, as pandemic pornography on the small screen, portrays what is possible when we engage, rather than negate, impossibility, and offers us a "new normal" where we might become people who eroticise reality through jointly constructed fantasy.

## References

Abrahamson, L. (2020–2020). *Normal People*. TV mini-series. Dublin: Element Pictures and Screen Ireland.

Barry, E. (2018, August 31). "Greeted as the first great millennial author and wary of attention". *The New York Times*, August 31. Available at: https://www.nytimes.com/2018/08/31/world/europe/sally-rooney-ireland.html.

Kinchen, R. (2020). "The fairy godmother who showed her normal people the joy of sex scenes". *The Sunday Times*, April 26. Available at: https://www.thetimes.co.uk/article/normal-peoples-intimacy-co-ordinator-made-sex-on-set-a-joy-w3qhl7qtd.

Lacan, J. (1998). *Book XI: The Four Fundamental Concepts of Psychoanalysis*. Ed. Jacques-Alain Miller. Trans. Alan Sheridan. London: W.W. Norton.

Lacan, J. (1998). *Book XX: On Feminine Sexuality, The Limits of Love and Knowledge (1972–1973)*. Ed. Jacques-Alain Miller. Trans. Bruce Fink. London: W.W. Norton.

Lacan, J. (2007). *Book XVII: The Other Side of Psychoanalysis (1969–1970)*. Ed. Jacques-Alain Miller. Trans. Russell Grigg. London: W.W. Norton.

Rooney, S. (2018). *Normal people*. London: Faber & Faber.
Sales, N. (2015). "Tinder and the dawn of the 'dating apocalypse'." *Vanity Fair*, August 6. Available at: https://www.vanityfair.com/culture/2015/08/tinder-hook-up-culture-end-of-dating.
Žižek, S. (1991). "Pornography, nostalgia, montage: A triad of the gaze". In *Looking awry: An introduction to Jacques Lacan through popular culture* (pp. 107–122). Cambridge, MA: MIT Press
Žižek, S. (2020). "Sex in the age of social distancing". In *Pandemic! 2: Chronicles of a time lost* (pp. 51–55). New York: Polity Press.
Zupančič, A. (2017). *What IS sex?* Cambridge, MA: MIT Press.

Chapter 6

# Weeping On and Off Screen
## Truth, Falsity, and Art

*Miles Link*

There is something strangely revealing when we weep at an artwork that has moved us – revealing, in the sense that it has the flavour of truth, but strange, because it is hard to locate where that truth actually lies. What we might take as an artful enchantment that leads us to tears may not apportion truth and falsehood in the way we think it does. Against an understanding of the artwork as an affirmation of all that is true in ourselves by means of presenting us with a beautiful lie, instead we could posit the artwork as a fatal encounter with what we are not, one that upends everything we thought we were.

This chapter explores these two different understandings of the aesthetic encounter, using Jacques Lacan's psychoanalytic concept of the gaze and Theodor Adorno's aesthetic theory as a guide. I argue that Lacan and Adorno share the view that our encounter with artworks does not affirm any inner truth about its audience, but actually confronts us with the falsity of our sense of self. When an artwork moves us to tears, there has been (in Lacan's terms) a collision with the real, or a passage from truth into falsehood (in Adorno's). Crucially, in both thinkers' views, a screen stands between artwork and audience, both as a point of inversion and doubling. Rather than assigning truth or falsity absolutely to one side of the screen or the other, what matters for both thinkers is the very encounter between artwork and audience, an encounter in which the self is negated, only to be reconstituted.

However, this is not the notion of the aesthetic encounter that we most commonly see today. In the discourse surrounding art, media, and our virtual lives, there is no reconstituting of the subject in the encounter with the artwork. In this opposing notion of the experience of art, the screen stands as a solid barrier between the real world and the world of the artwork, a stark separation between the true and the false that must be maintained. This rather rigid notion of the aesthetic encounter lies at the bottom of both the fear of the virtual world's corrupting influence, and the orgy of entertainment into which it seems to invite us. But how might we otherwise conceive of our experience of art?

The chapter begins with a detailed examination of an episode from Book VIII of Homer's *Odyssey*. Through Odysseus's repeated encounters with a

DOI: 10.4324/9781003272069-7

work of art, and his repeated reaction in a remarkable gesture of grief, this episode demonstrates first a notion of art that affirms the truth of self, and then the unravelling of this notion. On his long journey home, Odysseus hears a bard sing of Odysseus's own exploits in the Trojan War. The first song spurs him to try and recapture something of his heroic stature as depicted in the song. However, in an eerie repetition, Odysseus then listens to a second song from the bard, and his sense of self is shattered, forcing him to re-narrate his history and identity. Both times, Odysseus is moved to tears by the bard's songs, screening his weeping face with his cloak. At first, Odysseus's gesture appears to be a way for him to preserve his true self against the artifices of the bard's music. In its repetition, however, this self is revealed as always falling short of the ideal presented in these songs, always lacking, never quite itself – and so his tears take on an entirely new meaning. These scenes raise crucial questions about how we are to understand the aesthetic encounter, and how to grasp the motion of true and false across the screen of Odysseus's cloak.

Turning from the expansive world of myth to the present day, a world vastly reduced by the coronavirus pandemic to the 'small screens' of our virtual lives, we might ask if our understanding of the aesthetic encounter has also shrunken. That is, just like the critics of the television medium in a previous era, we seem committed to an idea of the encounter with art in which the viewer always occupies the side of the true, constantly on the defence against the corrupting influence of fantasy. But is the problem of the aesthetic encounter a problem of the screen medium alone?

Finally, in another strange aesthetic encounter that echoes Odysseus's, a discussion of the 1945 film *Scarlet Street* returns us to Lacan and Adorno's conception of the aesthetic encounter. Fritz Lang's film demonstrates that the screen that separates art and audience is more properly seen as the point where the latter is doubled and inverted, in a *camera obscura*. That is, perhaps what awaits us within the artwork is precisely an image of what the world is not, but could have been or is not yet.

In this exploration of Lacan and Adorno's theory of the aesthetic encounter, I hope to show how the encounter with art allows new understandings of the self to emerge – all the more salient at a cultural moment when, worldwide, the screen has become not just ubiquitous but necessary for art, entertainment, and social discourse.

## Odysseus weeps

Homer's *Odyssey* contains many encounters with art (particularly song), but one episode in Book VIII is particularly interesting when considering the nature of the aesthetic encounter. Odysseus, shipwrecked after his departure from Calypso, washes up on the island of Phaeacia. There he is discovered, naked and bereft, by Nausicaa, the daughter of Alcinous, king of the Phaeacians. Nausicaa feeds and dresses Odysseus, then brings him to Alcinous, where a banquet is held for him in a grand gesture of hospitality. Importantly, when his hosts ask who he is, Odysseus tells of how he had been shipwrecked alone and held on Calypso's island for seven years, but reveals neither his name nor anything of his background. At the banquet, the blind bard Demodocus is led in front of the company and sings a song about the Trojan War – in fact, about Odysseus himself. Upon hearing the song, Odysseus is overwhelmed, and covers his face with his cloak to weep:

> Odysseus drew his purple mantle over his head and covered his face, for he was ashamed to let the Phaeacians see that he was weeping. When the bard left off singing he wiped the tears from his eyes, uncovered his face, and, taking his cup, made a drink-offering to the gods; but when the Phaeacians pressed Demodocus to sing further, for they delighted in his songs, then Odysseus again drew his mantle over his head and wept bitterly. No one noticed his distress except Alcinous, who was sitting near him, and heard the heavy sighs that he was heaving.
> (Butler, 2022, modified)

The scene is equally poignant and the strange. Here is a man, reduced to nothing and travelling incognito, who hears a song about himself at the height of his fame, a time that has already receded a good distance into the past. It is not so difficult to understand why this juxtaposition would leave Odysseus overcome – at the same time, however, it is not immediately clear what it is about the song that moves Odysseus to tears.

So, what can we learn from the song itself? Demodocus sings about 'the feats of heroes' (Butler, 2022), specifically about 'the quarrel between Odysseus and Achilles, and the fierce words that they heaped on one another as they sat together at a banquet' (Butler, 2022, modified). So, does Odysseus weep because the song is *truthful*? That is to say, is this song so painfully close to his own memories and experience that the tale affects him as if he were reliving the same events? Or, maybe it is not so much the song's content as it is the way in which it is performed that moves the hero. The bard's music is repeatedly described as well-sung: Demodocus is 'the famous bard Demodocus, whom the muse had dearly loved', she having 'endowed him with a divine gift of song' (Butler, 2022). Perhaps, then, it is not the song's proximity to truth that touches Odysseus but the very gap between the past as it was truly lived and how that past is rendered, a fissure that runs deeper the better the artwork is crafted. That is, does Odysseus actually weep because the song is a beautiful rendition of the truth – not, in other words, because it contains falsities, but because it *falsifies*?

A relationship between the song, its audience, and the truth is beginning to emerge, prompting us to reframe the initial question: does Odysseus weep because the song is *true* or because the song is *false*? We know, for example, that accounts of warriors' 'glorious deeds' often play fast and loose with the truth. On the other hand, we could equally argue that any artistic treatment seeks in its rendition the truthful essence of its subject, and so an artwork's truth is not to be judged by the fidelity of its appearance. However, the greatest surprise in this scene does not come from the manner of the bard's song but from the circumstances of its telling: Demodocus relates an event from years past, in another land, among men who have since died or disappeared. Perhaps Odysseus's tears simply carry a sense of outrage that even after all his trappings of glory have been stripped from him, and he has washed up naked and nameless on a foreign shore, a song could still turn his private memory into a public performance, and speak him into a discourse.

But if the question of truth still hangs in the air here, we can at least make a distinction between Odysseus's two reactions, his weeping and his screening of himself. The former is in response to the song, the latter is in response to his sense of shame: 'he was ashamed to let the Phaeacians see that he was weeping' (Butler, 2022). When Odysseus is noted for his cunning, this is the same as noting his inwardness and interiority, and here in Book VIII even the poet is not privy to what about the song has so affected Odysseus. It seems something meaningful has been hidden behind the hero's cloak, something that he further covers through a social gesture, pouring out a libation each time Demodocus pauses in his song.

The inwardness of Odysseus and the ignorance of the rest of the song's audience might push us to place truth on the hero's side. We might conclude that the bard's song is an artful fiction – the song is false, and Odysseus's tears are true, the emanations of a private knowledge of a public untruth, even a double untruth: the war wasn't really like that, and the song's artifice does violence to any truth it may nonetheless contain. Perhaps Odysseus weeps because of some deep inward self-regard, as his 'consciousness' 'turn[s] back upon itself', like '*seeing oneself seeing oneself*' (Lacan, 1964/1986, p. 74, italics in original): faced with an image of himself in his glory days, Odysseus is lost in a narcissistic self-regard.

This way of framing the scene – an independent observer receives the artwork and inwardly works their judgment upon it – is, however, exactly what Lacan wishes to overturn in his discussion of the gaze in his Seminar XI. If we accept the reading of Odysseus as an independent observer, we pass over not only the function of the gaze, but also the very issue that leads Lacan to the discussion of the gaze: that is, this weeping scene *repeats*. Alcinous the king notices Odysseus's tears and politely cuts the song short, in another gesture of hospitality. He invites the company to a series of public contests, in which Odysseus demonstrates his strength and skill, surpassing the abilities of his Phaeacian hosts. Odysseus is then bathed, clothed, presented with copious gifts, and finally wined and dined again, proving himself an excellent guest. He thanks Alcinous's daughter Nausicaa for her care towards him, accepts the apology of the young nobleman Euryalus, who insulted him, and, in high spirits, asks Demodocus to sing again, this time about the famous Trojan Horse:

> Now, however, change your song and tell us of the wooden horse which Epeius made with the assistance of Athena, and which Odysseus got by stratagem into the fort of Troy after freighting it with the men who afterwards sacked the city. If you will sing this tale aright I will tell all the world how magnificently heaven has endowed you.
> (Butler, 2022, modified)

Demodocus duly tells the tale, singing of how Odysseus battled heroically in the fighting that followed the subterfuge, and the sack of the city. Once again, Odysseus covers his head with his cloak and weeps at the song, but more violently this time:

> Odysseus was overcome as he heard the bard, and his cheeks were wet with tears. He wept as a woman weeps when she throws herself on the body of her husband who has fallen before his own city and people, fighting bravely in defence of his home and children.
> (Butler, 2022, modified)

Again Alcinous is the only one to notice his guest's tears and asks for the music to cease. 'From the moment that we had done supper and Demodocus began to sing, our guest has been all the time groaning and lamenting' (Butler, 2022). This business with the stranger's grief can no longer be taken as his own personal matter, but is now a state affair – that is, it risks the Phaeacians' reputation as good hosts. For his own part, Alcinous has tolerated this stranger's anonymity until now, but he is driven by this man's strange behaviour to ask for his identity: 'do you on your part affect no more concealment nor reserve in the matter about which I shall ask you' (Butler, 2022). Odysseus reveals his identity, and tells the story of his journeys from Troy.

With this second scene we once again find ourselves in the dark about what exactly moves Odysseus to tears. However, in addition to this question, and the question of what truth or falsity the bard's songs contain, now we must also ask: why does the scene with the bard repeat? The accident of Odysseus hearing a song about himself was remarkable enough, but Odysseus even invites the same encounter again, subjecting himself a second time to the unaccountable effect of the bard's song. Odysseus's repetition possesses an 'element of poignancy', an eerie quality of destiny, that constitutes what Lacan calls '*tuché*, the encounter' (1964/1986, p. 69). This *tuché* indicates a 'veiled meaning' lurking disguised within a seemingly accidental repetition; *tuché* names an encounter with the real that is always a 'missed encounter', due to the real's unrepresentable nature (Lacan, 1964/1986, p. 69; Foster,

1996, p. 132). Odysseus has *missed something* in this glancing blow with the real, something that is located neither in the song nor in Odysseus but in their very meeting. This something is 'ordered in the figures of representation' and 'slips, passes, is transmitted, from stage to stage, and is always to some degree eluded' in this relation between artwork and audience (Lacan, 1964/1986, p. 73). Altogether, the style, content, and circumstances of the bard's songs suggest something of the nature of this encounter: the tychic encounter with the bard's songs reveals what Odysseus is not – it draws into sharp relief the distance between the glorious hero of the tale and the divided subject who listens to it.

When Odysseus hears the bard's first song, then, he is still in a position to receive it as a kind of reassurance. The song seems to offer an encouraging artifice: Odysseus is presented in the song not as he is but as he was and could be again. Though he has suffered some wear and tear through externally-imposed hardships, it appears to say, his true self is nonetheless whole and secure. Even if the reminder is a painful one, Odysseus receives the song as something assistive, salutary, uplifting, instructive. The gaze looks back at Odysseus and catches him up in what he supposes he is meant to be, since, as Lacan says, 'the gaze operates in a certain descent, a descent of desire [...] a sort of desire *on the part of* the Other' (1964/1986, p. 115). Reacting to the first song, Odysseus hides his weeping from a wish not to have seen by others the distance between what he was and what he is now. He pulls his cloak over his head in an attempt to preserve what in himself is true, and he ratifies the social dimension of this attempt – to be what the Other wants him to be – with libations poured out to the gods. Odysseus then tries to embody the hero that the song has depicted, and his attempt even works for a time, earning him the praise and the gifts of the Phaeacians.

The bard's second song, however, melts this conceit away. In hearing this second song, Odysseus again feels the separation between what he is and what he was. However, though his reaction to the second song appears identical to the first (except in its intensity), Odysseus's position relative to the song has shifted. This time, his shame comes from a recognition that he *cannot help but* fall short of the song's heroic image. When he again hides his face to weep, this time the screen of his cloak covers the *false*, rather than preserving the *true*. Alcinous detects this falsity and now recognises its disruptive potential. His demand for Odysseus to disclose his identity is, from the king's side, a demand to re-stabilise the relationship of hospitality between guest and host; from Odysseus's side, the king's demand for the stranger to identify himself is a prompt to re-symbolise what for Odysseus has erupted from the real – to explain again who he is.

What this repetition shows is that Odysseus cannot adequately answer the strangeness of this encounter that feels all at once like accident and destiny, the hero hearing his own song. As Lacan says, 'That is why it is necessary to ground this repetition first of all in the very split that occurs in the subject in relation to the encounter', the split between this *tuché* and the 'factitious fact' that is erected in reply to it (1964/1986, pp. 69–70). Really, the tychic encounter undermines not only this facticity but also any notion of the artwork as a salutary and uplifting experience for the self, which remains secure in its wholeness. This notion of the aesthetic experience becomes a kind of lure, the 'pacifying, Apollonian effect' behind which lurks the shattering encounter with the gaze (1964/1986, p. 101). The bard's songs cannot inflict the fullness of this encounter while Odysseus occupies a position of the universal 'stranger' – only when he has misread the bard's first song as a bolster to his inner spirit can the second song pierce this factitious fact he has raised up and enacted for a day.

Importantly, the bard's two songs about Odysseus even contain warnings against self-serving misreadings. In the first song, Agamemnon, leader of the Greek forces, looks on pleased at a quarrel between Achilles and Odysseus, believing that the argument fulfils the oracle he heard at Delphi. 'Here was the beginning of the evil that by the will of Jove fell both upon Danaans and Trojans' (Butler, 2022). The quarrel suggests to Agamemnon that his great exploit is going to plan, a judgment that ages rather badly. The second song's warning is even more blatant, taking as its subject the most famous deception in history, the Trojan Horse: within the song, presented in the guise of yet another gift to the Phaeacians' surpassing guest, Odysseus's grief is smuggled back in, too.

These repeated scenes of weeping thus establish three important points. We see how Odysseus's weeping shifts from a mark of authenticity to one of an internal lack, we see how the bard's songs show Odysseus what he is not, and we see how the cloak stands between these artworks and their audience as a divider or filter – as a screen. When Odysseus twice covers his weeping face, he moves from, firstly, asserting the falsity of an artistic lie to, secondly, avowing himself as false. His encounter reveals him as a divided subject, unreconciled to the image in the bard's songs, which are held out to him first as an exhortation and then as a rebuke. In the last instance, however, Odysseus's tychic encounter with the bard's music prompts him to tell his own tale, a task which demands that he not only recognise what in him is false, but also that he rediscover some promise of reconciliation with the true.

## Real world, screen world

False and true: these are not Lacan's terms, of course, but Adorno's. It is useful to bring together the two thinkers' concepts here. If the bard's songs reveal something in Odysseus that lies on the side of the false, or 'that which is not itself in the first instance', as Adorno defines it (2008, p. 28), this is the same as saying that Odysseus's brush with the real demonstrates that a perfect reconciliation of the self is impossible – that is, the divided subject can never resolve their lack. Odysseus's encounter is not only an illustration of Lacan's notions of *tuché* and the gaze, then, but also an illustration of Adorno's notion of the aesthetic encounter, of which he says: 'Although artworks offer themselves to observation, they at the same time disorient the observer who is held at the distance of a mere spectator; to him is revealed the truth of the work as if it must also be his own' (2002, p. 269). Artworks, says Adorno, reveal to us a version of ourselves that exceeds what we merely are, and in that sense, the cloak pulled over Odysseus's weeping face ultimately signifies a subject who is false, i.e. who is not himself.

So what about the artwork, then? As a mere representation, says Adorno, the artwork, too, is false. But, in so much as it shows how the real world falls short of the promise that the artwork represents, the artwork is also true. Both artwork and audience, in Adorno's terms, occupy a position of false and true in different ways.

Adorno emphasises the back-and-forth passage of truth and falsity across the screen erected between art and audience, rather than apportioning truth and falsity to one side or the other, because, as Lacan points out, what matters is the encounter of the one with the other.

These notions of the aesthetic encounter, however, are not the prevailing ones of today. Lacan and Adorno's focus on the meeting of art and audience, on the shifting distribution of false and true, rather than their locations on one side of the screen or the other, can be difficult to sustain. Shifting our attention to our pandemicised present, we are perhaps more willing these days to a see a hard truth in mere reality; we perhaps more easily believe that the artwork, the world beyond the (increasingly digital) screen, is sublimated fantasy. From this perspective, real life must be the criterion by which we judge digital life. Digital life itself even appears to concede its own falsity in the automatic notices above social media comments sections, as with this forlorn plea, recently seen on Twitter: 'Conversations like this can be intense. Don't forget the human behind the screen'. Just as in Odysseus's encounter with the bard's first song, we can detect the presence of some element of falsity in this encounter between real life and digital life, but we are unwilling to locate it in ourselves, and we surmise that the false world beyond the screen must be parasitising our inner truth.

The screen that stands between real life and digital life thus has this power of inversion. Considering several high-profile cases of bad behaviour on Zoom just in the first year of the pandemic – two Irish lecturers badmouthing their students, a masturbating *New Yorker* journalist, an Argentine lawmaker sucking his partner's breast – shouldn't we say that the screen is able not only to cover the false, but also to *reveal what is true* (Carroll, 2020; Goñi, 2020; Diaz and Paybarah, 2020)? Doesn't the screen lure us into disclosing more of our hidden selves, safe as we feel with a medium between us, seduced into dropping our guard? Doesn't the screen expose the repressed wishes that our public presentation would otherwise carefully efface?

But with thoughts like these again we are mapping a spuriously neat distribution of truth and falsehood onto real life and digital life, as divided by the screen. Even as we assert that the screen can draw out embarrassing truths about ourselves – things that, like Odysseus, we thought would remain within the silent recesses of our interior lives – we insist on the unreality of that screen world. However, here we are stuck in Odysseus's repetition. In Adorno and Lacan's terms, the point is not to locate truth or falsity on one side of the screen or the other, but to see what the encounter elicits when truth and falsity pass across the division of the screen. What, then, would today constitute a tychic encounter that would undermine our conviction in such a static distribution of the truth, and tip that falsity back onto our own heads?

Where does this insistence on dividing false and true along the screen come from? A parallel example from the past might help clarify. Our collective re-reckoning of online life during the coronavirus pandemic, in which, we aver, we are confronted from outside by the false, is often reminiscent of talk from the not-too-distant past about another screen medium, the 'small screen' of television, and especially the discourse in the 1980s around television's social power. Then, writers like Neil Postman and Jerry Mander aimed their critiques not at any particular television content, but instead located the source of its dubious influence in the nature of the medium itself (Postman, 1985/2006; Mander, 1978). That is, these writers did not aim their criticisms at the quality of television's entertainment – the danger, they said, was precisely that nothing on television could rise above the level of entertainment. In so doing, they framed television's aesthetic encounter as one in which the rational, independent, democratic subject, properly on the side of the true, met a false fantasy in the entertaining world of television, an encounter in which the subject was inevitably diminished. Again, this was a question of medium, not content: speaking in 1980 of the media landscape in which television was firmly embedded as a 'howling blizzard of signals', the art critic Robert Hughes noted that '[w]hole societies have learned to experience the world vicariously, in terms of swift montage and juxtaposition' (1981/1991, pp. 344–345). Television's quintessential mode of presentation, montage, was thus constitutionally false, not itself.

George W.S. Trow, a journalist for *The Atlantic* magazine, was even more declarative in his 1981 book *Within the Context of No Context*. 'Art requires a context', he pleaded, defining this context as 'the power of this moment, the moment of the events in the foreground, seen against the accumulation of other moments. The moment in the foreground adheres to the accumulation or rejects it briefly before joining it' (1981, p. 63). Here is a fairly durable definition of the artistic tradition: an expansive universal that sooner or later embraces all particularities. The trouble with television, says Trow, is that it works to destroy this universal: 'The work of television is to establish false contexts and to chronicle the unravelling of existing contexts; finally, to establish the context of no-context and to chronicle it' (1981, p. 82). Trow's book even demonstratively re-stages this unravelling in its written form. Rather than presenting his argument in a coherent text, Trow breaks up his observations on television, celebrity, and pop culture into discrete lines and paragraphs, in no particular order and seemingly unconnected, with headings like 'The Decline of Adulthood' and 'World's Fair' that bear only a tangential relation to the words they introduce. In other words, *Within the Context of No Context* reproduces in print the experience of channel surfing, in which one non-context follows another.

Trow's book works as a rejoinder to the reading of Odysseus's weeping as the product of a tychic encounter. Trow instead attempts to orient us back towards a preservation of the autonomy of the self against a blizzard of accidental events. Rather than the screen used to cover Odysseus as the divided subject, the television screen, says Trow, locates that lack outside the subject, in their social, historical, and cultural context. Television then proceeds to 'unravel' this context, in the service of 'establishing false contexts'. Television, he argues, circumvents the aesthetic necessity for a universalising context '[b]y the use of ad hoc contexts', introduced with the jarring phrase of so-called continuity announcers, 'And now, this':

> Just for the moment. We're here together, in a little house. It makes such good sense. But just for a moment. We're playing Password! Do you remember when we played Password? Do you remember Johnny? Yes, you do. When he squirted whipped cream on Burt Reynolds, into his trousers? Remember that? Now This.
>
> (Trow, 1981, p. 63)

Specifically, says Trow, television establishes 'false contexts' by providing an illusion of access: 'The lie of television has been that there are contexts to which television will grant an access'. Eventually, Trow says, television will even drop the pretence that truth abides just offstage, and 're-form around the idea that television itself is a context to which television will grant an access' (1981, pp. 82–83). In practice, television's illusion of access signalled things like backstage broadcasts at awards ceremonies, living room interviews with prominent politicians, and so on: you appear to be admitted into a space reserved for the select, but this admission is a mere conceit. It is 'champagne wishes and caviar dreams'.

So, what is this false context – that is to say, what is a television programme?

> It's a little span of time made friendly by repetition. In a way, it doesn't exist at all. Just what does, then? A certain ability to transmit and receive and then to apply layers of affection and longing and doubt.
>
> (Trow, 1981, p. 63)

Repetition here has nothing to do with a surprise and a reformulation of the subject's desire, but with the establishment of a pseudo-totality that can only be sustained through 'a very complex kind of work, involving electrons', a 'coldness' that television must cover over 'with a hateful familiarity'. 'Why hateful?', asks Trow. 'Because it hasn't anything to do with a human being as a human being is strong. It has to do with a human being as a human being is weak and willing to be fooled' (1981, p. 63). Trow and the critics of the television medium tend to speak of television audiences in this way, as the hapless victims of a medium of universal negativity. The television for them possesses a sort of gaze, but it is the equal and opposite to what Lacan calls the 'annihilating subject, correlative of the world of objectivity' (1964/1986, p. 85): the television medium, in this view, de-formulates and nullifies what the self has constructed and raised up.

Trow and the critics of the television medium thus present the screen, standing between us and virtuality, as the boundary line between true and false. That is why the moments on the screen in which truth seems to break through the falsity are so significant for us. Today we share videos of newscasters in intensive care units breaking off to weep, and nurses, doctors, and medical officials affirming the truth of the pandemic. Perhaps it seems right to us, in a macabre way, when COVID patients must say goodbye to their families on video conference screens – right, because this is the screen world reined back in to a properly subservient position to the truth. Life on screen, apparently, has not changed from its television days: today, unlike the voices of the television critics who cried out in the wilderness, the lurking danger of a virtual life untethered to reality is proclaimed everywhere. For example, Patricia Lockwood writes in the *London Review of Books* of her experiences in the 'snowy white disintegration' of the internet, 'which felt also like the disintegration of my own mind'. She speaks of her sense of the screen world as broken and breaking our minds as it draws us further into the 'the blazing endpoint of a civilisation', a morass of memes, clickbait, posts, comments, and all the detritus of an extremely online life. She asks, 'What, in place of' this morass, 'marched in the brains of previous generations?' (2019).

There is, then, a ring of familiarity between the critics of yesteryear's indictments of the television medium and our contemporary anxiety about what the internet is doing to our brains. If that is so, then the internet loses its status as an unprecedented epistemological whirlwind. For television and the internet, the division is apparently the same: the screen world, on the side of the false, can only negatively influence the real world, on the side of the true. Truth is therefore expressed in the failure of this conversion. The newscaster who breaks down in tears offers us, we suppose, the truest moment of all: something from the universal 'accumulation of moments' has escaped into visibility by its failed conversion into the false, the false context of nothing but particularities. What animates this notion of Trow's universal accumulation, and the general notion of the screen world as false, is the belief in totality as a sort of centripetal force that draws everything in, against the centrifugal force of scattering particularities.

Following this notion, does this mean that Odysseus, in hiding his weeping face, is really hiding his particularity? As a nameless foreigner, is he adopting a universalised persona, the guest who must be met with hospitality, in order to fix the identity of his hosts in place, and to raise the possibility that anyone could be subject to the same fate as Odysseus? If, in his vulnerability as he weeps under his cloak, Odysseus is attesting to the universal vulnerability of all human beings, then this suggests that artworks with a healthy respect for Trow's 'accumulation of moments' generally work in this fashion – cutting across and overturning particularities, and drawing out the universal from them. Surely Odysseus's reaction needn't only be read as a socially inconvenient moment that the conventions of hospitality must contain: instead, everyone can sympathise with the desolated Odysseus, because everyone is susceptible to the same desolation.

But, once again, can that notion of art account for what Odysseus finds so affecting in these two songs performed by the blind bard? It emerged from our exploration above that neither the content nor the form of the bard's songs had in themselves moved Odysseus to tears. As Lacan says, 'it is not a question in painting of a realistic reproduction of the things of space' (1964/1986, p. 92). The power of an artwork is not a matter of the artwork's fidelity to reality. Quite the opposite, in fact: the songs Odysseus hears are all the more affecting to him because they call up so strongly what is not so (or, in his case, what is no longer so), and why they both allude to misreading and deception – Agamemnon and the oracle, Odysseus and the Trojan Horse.

However, if we stopped at the notion that art calls up what is not so, we would arrive at the idea that art (or virtual reality, or fantasy) is just a photo negative of the world, and all we must do is invert its colours to get the real thing. (Similarly, of the passage from the unconscious to the conscious, Freud reminds us that 'not every negative necessarily becomes a positive, nor is it necessary that every unconscious mental process should turn into a conscious one' [1916/1981, p. 295]). Insisting that the difference between subject and artwork – or between real life and screen life – is the difference between truth and falsehood leads us to a rigid, value-laden distribution of truth and falsehood that can say little concerning Lacan's tychic encounter. Something else has to be involved in what art presents to the subject, and this something else has an overpowering effect on the subject that is unaccountable in terms of the pure autonomy of the self. As Lacan says, 'we are beings who are looked at, in the spectacle of the world [...]. The subject does not see where it is leading, he follows' (1964/1986, p. 75).

So, how is this process effected by the encounter with the artwork? That is to say, how does art catch us up and represent us as subjects? For, as Lacan describes it, 'the subject who concerns us is caught, manipulated, captured, in the field of vision. [...] as subjects, we are literally called into the picture, and represented here as caught' (1964/1986, p. 92). Here is why the example from the *Odyssey* is so revealing. When we say that art shows us what the world is not, this 'is not' includes what the world might have been, could be, and has not become yet. In this way, the artwork does not just show the subject what is not so but implicates them in that unreality. Especially in the case of Odysseus, the artwork implicates the subject by pointing to what the subject has lost. In psychoanalytic parlance, we can trace the identity of this object that has been lost to the primal object, reformulated by Lacan as the *objet a*. It is this object cause of desire that gazes back at Odysseus and places him unawares in relation to these two songs that, explicitly and implicitly, represent for him who he is; Odysseus is 'determined by the very separation that determines the break of the *a*, that is to say, the fascinatory element introduced by the gaze' (1964/1986, p. 118). When Odysseus then attempts to live up to this image of the hero, he is attempting to fulfil the promise that art holds out, to reconcile its audience with what they have lost. We find here an echo of Adorno's claim that 'All art aims to end art' (2005b, p. 75). By this statement Adorno means that art intends to realise the potential it embodies and to make itself superfluous, even if this a task that art can never itself carry out:

> [I]f the Idea of Beauty appears only in dispersed form among many works, each one nevertheless aims uncompromisingly to express the whole of beauty [...]. Beauty, as single, true and liberated from appearance and individuation, manifests itself not in the synthesis of all works, [...] but [...] in the downfall of art itself.
>
> (2005b, p. 75)

## Camera obscura

In conceiving of the encounter with artwork as the subject's encounter with what they are not (but had been or could be), we arrive at the not-unfamiliar metaphor of the *camera obscura*. That is, the screen between artwork and audience does indeed establish an inversion – not simply to divide the false from the true, as the television critics and our contemporary anxieties about the internet suppose, but to set up for the subject a double of themselves, passed through a focal point and reconstituted upside-down. As the French philosopher Sarah Kofman observes in her short work on the *camera obscura*, 'to see is always to obtain a double' (1998, p. 21). Kofman observes that in Freud's use of the *camera obscura* metaphor, the passage from unconscious to conscious always 'entails an ordeal, a test, and this is always a showdown of sorts' (1998, p. 22). In very similar terms, Lacan describes the way in which the gaze catches up the subject:

> That which is light looks at me, and by means of that light in the depths of my eye, something is painted [...] something that is an impression, the shimmering of a surface that is not, in advance, situated for me in its distance.
>
> (1964/1986, p. 96)

Something in this process upends the idea we have of ourselves.

Adorno's characterisation of art similarly involves not only an opposition but an essential conflict. Artworks are not just in conflict with each other over the true expression of beauty, but are also in conflict with their audience, artworks being so many undeveloped negatives awaiting their photo-chemical reaction with what the subject supposes they themselves are. Adorno calls this inversion in the aesthetic encounter – this encounter with art that overturns everything we thought we knew about ourselves – the 'aesthetic shudder', and argues that this encounter is precisely what preserves the possibility of a symbolic re-reckoning of whatever is met in the real:

> The aesthetic shudder [...] rescues subjectivity, even subjective aesthetics, by the negation of subjectivity. [...] If in artworks the subject finds his true happiness in the moment of being convulsed, this is a happiness that is counterposed to the subject and thus its instrument is tears [...].
> (2002, p. 269)

This is, finally, why we cannot divide the relationship of the subject and the artwork into true and false: it is in this *tuché* that the artwork stages that subjectivity is rescued by the negation of subjectivity. We pass through the *camera obscura* of this encounter and emerge upside-down, not ourselves, but with an ever-disappointed promise of reconciliation with an inverted double.

Let us turn to a final example to illustrate this process of inversion in a different context. In Fritz Lang's 1945 film *Scarlet Street*, Edward G. Robinson plays Chris Cross (an 'inverted' name if there ever was one), a sweet-hearted but naïve department store cashier and hobbyist painter whom Katherine 'Kitty' March (Joan Bennett) mistakes for a rich artist. At the prompting of her shiftless boyfriend Johnny Prince (Dan Duryea), Kitty wheedles money and then an apartment from Chris, who is forced to steal first from his wife and then from his employer to bankroll his paramour. When Johnny tries to sell some of Chris's 'outsider art' paintings, they are discovered by a famous art critic by chance. Johnny passes the works off as Kitty's, launching her to fame. Chris, however, is delighted, and agrees to paint works for Kitty to sign, including a large, bewitching 'self-portrait'. While professing her deep love for Johnny, Kitty continues stringing Chris along. However, after Chris walks in on Kitty with Johnny, who promptly departs, she finally rejects Chris, who then murders her in a fit of pique. Chris pins the crime on Johnny, who is tried and executed. Chris, now jobless and alone, is tortured by the mocking voices of Kitty and Johnny in his head. The guilt for his deed drives Chris to a life on the streets, where, in the final scene, he witnesses his 'self-portrait' of Kitty, sold for ten thousand dollars and being carried off from a high-end art gallery, as he hears Kitty's whispered cry: 'Jeepers, I love you, Johnny' (Lang, 1945).

*Scarlet Street* (an adaptation of Jean Renoir's 1931 film *La Chienne*) is a weird second take on *The Woman in the Window* from the year before, another Fritz Lang film featuring Robinson staring longingly at a portrait in a gallery window. As in *Scarlet Street*, Robinson in *The Woman in the Window* meets, seduces, and kills the woman in the portrait (played again by Joan Bennett) – only, here, to awaken and discover that the entire affair was a dream. Drawing upon Lacan's discussions of Zhuangzi's dream of being a butterfly and the dream of the burning child from Freud's *Interpretation of Dreams*, Slavoj Žižek characterises *The Woman in the Window* as a film in which a dreamer 'awakes *in order to continue his dream* (about being a normal person like his fellow men), that is, to escape the real (the "psychic reality") of his desire' (1991, p. 16, italics in original).

In *Scarlet Street*, we also see overlapping fantasies that skirt the real of their subjects' desire. Deeply engrained in Chris's feeling of guilt is his belief that Kitty and Johnny really did love each other, and that he has destroyed a genuine love for the sake of his fantasy. 'He brought us together, Johnny, forever', Kitty whispers in his penitential thoughts; 'See Chris, she loves me,' returns Johnny. Chris's overweening interest in fantasy is signalled throughout the film. He sheepishly admits to Kitty that he believes 'feeling' is the most important thing about an artwork: 'I just put a line around what I feel when I look at things. [...] Every painting, if it's any good, is a love affair'. Johnny, aping an art appraiser's technical judgment, throws Chris's fantasising back in his face: 'You have a little trouble with perspective, don't you?'. When Chris discovers the two lovers together, he attempts to convince himself that Johnny had forced himself on her, which finally spurs Kitty's scornful derision: 'I've wanted to laugh in your face since I first met you. You're old and ugly, and I'm sick of you – sick, sick, sick! [...] You kill Johnny? Why, I'd like to see you try. He'd break every bone in your body! He's a man!'. Here, Kitty presents – to herself, as much to Chris – Johnny as her ideal love, despite her boyfriend's openly declared intention to sponge off her success. Chris, then, is far from the only fantasist in *Scarlet Street*. Only Johnny tries to save himself by abandoning the fantasy: during his trial, he exposes the whole fraud, but no one believes him, partly due to the testimony of Chris, who 'admits' he had only ever copied Kitty's paintings.

But *Scarlet Street* is not just a film *about* art; it is a film that stages the *encounter* with art, especially in its final scene, one that is remarkably like the scenes of Odysseus weeping from the *Odyssey*. As the portrait of Kitty is carried out in front of Chris, the painting's subject, this artist who never existed, is born in truth, as the synthesis of his painting and her persona. The art that Chris has created, and which has been sold under Kitty's name, is not 'false'; in fact it is the only truthful thing that their relation has produced. Neither the shabby con artist couple nor the hobbyist painter could have created the work alone, and it stands for an existence – a reconciliation – that neither could attain separately. As it is carried out of the gallery, the portrait is literally a screen between Chris and the empty street, where ahead of him lie only obscurity and death.

Consider the parallels between this final scene of *Scarlet Street* and the image of Odysseus weeping: a broken and desolate man, faced with an uncertain prospect, is confronted by an artwork that calls up his past. This work of art is all the more strange because its exact provenance is obscure, and its effect is unaccountable. As if by inverting his whole life in a *camera obscura*, this artwork, and the gaze that stares back at the subject from within it, reveals all the things he could have been but was not, all the things he could be but is not yet.

Here, then, is the power of Lacan and Adorno's notion of the aesthetic encounter: the subject is shifted onto the side of the false, and while the nameless potential that this art represents remains unrealised, its appearance forces the subject into the pursuit of a new truth for themselves. With this shared notion, Lacan and Adorno both recognised, each in their own way, the peculiar alchemy that the artwork performs on us. Lacan, with his concepts of *tuché* and the gaze, names the poignant sense of destiny that the encounter with artwork can raise in us, while Adorno argues that the mark of this poignancy, with its power to negate subjectivity only in order to rescue it, is the tears that the artwork evokes in us (as here, in his discussion of Franz Schubert's *Winterreise*):

> We cry without knowing why, because we are not yet what this music promises for us. We cry, knowing in untold happiness, that this music is as it is in the promise of what one day we ourselves will be. This is music we cannot decipher, but it holds up to our blurred, over-brimming eyes the secret of reconciliation at long last.
>
> (Adorno, 2005a, p. 14)

If this reconciliation – with the real beyond representation, with the truth that art represents – is for the subject impossible, then the aesthetic encounter, at least, remains possible, and with it the continually open chance that art gives us to reconsider who we are.

## References

Adorno, T. W. (2002). *Aesthetic Theory*. Eds. G. Adorno and R. Tiedemann. Trans. R. Hullot-Kentor. London: Continuum.

Adorno, T.W. (2005a). Schubert. Trans. J. Dunsby and B. Perrey. *19th-Century Music*, 29 (1), pp. 3–14.

Adorno, T.W. (2005b). *Minima Moralia: Reflections from Damaged Life*. Trans. E. F. N. Jephcott. London: Verso.

Adorno, T.W. (2008). *Lectures on Negative Dialectics: Fragments of a Lecture Course 1965/1966*. Ed. R. Tiedemann. Trans. R. Livingstone. Cambridge: Polity Press.

Carroll, R. (2020). Irish lecturers overheard insulting students on video call. *The Guardian*, 15 December 2020. Available at: https://www.theguardian.com/world/2020/dec/15/irish-lecturers-apologise-for-offensive-remarks-about-students-on-video-call.

Diaz, J. and Paybarah, A. (2020). New Yorker suspends Jeffrey Toobin after Zoom incident. *New York Times*, 19 October 2020. Available at: https://www.nytimes.com/2020/10/19/business/media/jeffrey-toobin-new-yorker-suspended.html.

Foster, H. (1996). *The Return of the Real: The Avant-Garde at the End of the Century.* Cambridge: MIT Press.

Freud, S. (1916). Introductory Lectures on Psycho-Analysis (Part III). *S.E.* XVI.

Goñi, U. (2020). Argentinian politician quits after kissing partner's breasts in online legislative session. *The Guardian*, 25 September 2020. Available at: https://www.theguardian.com/world/2020/sep/25/argentina-politician-breasts-online-debate.

Homer, *The Odyssey*. Trans. S. Butler. Available at: https://www.gutenberg.org/files/1727/1727-h/1727-h.htm (Accessed 2 August 2022).

Hughes, R. (1981/1991). *The Shock of the New.* New York: Alfred A. Knopf.

Kofman, S. (1998). *Camera Obscura: Of Ideology.* Trans. W. Straw. Ithaca, NY: Cornell UP.

Lacan, J. (1964/1986). *The Four Fundamental Concepts of Psycho-Analysis.* Trans. A. Sheridan. Harmondsworth: Penguin.

Lockwood, P. (2019). The communal mind: Patricia Lockwood travels through the internet. *London Review of Books*, 41 (4) (February 2019). Available at: https://www.lrb.co.uk/the-paper/v41/n04/patricia-lockwood/the-communal-mind.

Mander, J. (1978). *Four Arguments for the Elimination of Television.* New York: Quill.

Postman, N. (1985/2006). *Amusing Ourselves to Death: Public Discourse in the Age of Show Business.* New York: Penguin.

Lang, F. (1945). *Scarlet Street.* Los Angeles: Universal Pictures.

Trow, G. W. S. (1981). *Within the Context of No Context.* New York: Atlantic Monthly Press.

Žižek, S. (1991). *Looking Awry: An Introduction to Jacques Lacan through Popular Culture.* Cambridge, MA: MIT Press.

Chapter 7

# "The thing did not dissatisfy me"?
## Lacanian perspectives on transference and AI-driven psychotherapeutic chatbots

*Michael Holohan*

There can be so many barriers to getting help with your mental health. It can be expensive – whether you're an individual looking for a private therapist or a health service administrator looking for a cost-effective way to provide mental health services. There can be a stigma to getting help, which makes it even harder to reach out when you need it. And even if you can manage to cover the cost and overcome the stigma, you're more than likely going to have to wait – sometimes many months – before you can get an appointment. But what if you didn't have to? – Cue some upbeat advertising music – What if there were a simple solution to the problems of cost, stigma, and scarcity, that was cheap, easy to access, and abundant? And what if you could have it in the palm of your hand, right now?

This is the promise offered by the most recent crop of AI-driven psychotherapeutic chatbots. With names like Woebot, Wysa, or Tess, these virtual psychotherapy technologies aim to provide their user-patients with easy access to inexpensive (or free) chat-based platforms, accessible via mobile phone apps, where they can talk about their problems and receive responses designed to mimic those of a psychotherapist. This kind of promise – of technological solutions to intractable individual and/or social problems – is not unique to the field of psychotherapy, and both mental health professionals and the public might be surprised to learn that it is not exactly new to their field, either. But two significant sociotechnical changes have led to a relatively recent acceleration and proliferation of technologies such as AI-driven psychotherapeutic chatbots. On the one hand, this has to do with recent developments in the field of artificial intelligence (AI). On the other hand, there is the giant social experience/experiment of widespread lockdowns and remote living in response to the COVID-19 pandemic that shifted so much of our social life onto the small screens of our laptops and mobile phones. The two together represent a specific moment of increased availability and acceptance of these specific technologies and openness to new paradigms.

While the moment appears to be ripe for a growing acceptance and expansion of this new technology, there has so far been little in the way of careful reflection about what this new technology is, what it means for the

DOI: 10.4324/9781003272069-8

field of psychotherapy, or how to think about it from the perspective of psychotherapy – or rather from the many different perspectives that make up the psy professions, including psychoanalysis. And while it is unlikely that AI-driven chatbots will ever be able to conduct a psychoanalysis or replace psychoanalysts any time soon, there is much that psychoanalysis can contribute to the consideration of this new technology and new clinical modality. In particular, psychoanalysis is ideally positioned to provide reflections on the theme of transference in its vast variety and clinical specificity.

The question of transference in relation to AI-driven chatbots has been raised before, but only briefly or without reference to the specific term (Bickmore T., Puskar K., Schlenk E., et al., 2010; Bickmore T., Mitchell S., Jack B., et al., 2010; Fiske, Henningsen and Buyx, 2019; Scholten, Kelders and Gemert-Pijnen, 2017). Elsewhere (Holohan and Fiske, 2021), I have provided a general overview of this theme from the point of view of Science and Technology Studies (STS) and feminist epistemology. In this chapter, I want to build on my earlier effort and provide a further consideration of AI-driven psychotherapeutic chatbots and transference from a Lacanian psychoanalytic perspective. In doing so, I also hope to contribute to this volume's focus on the recent shift of so much of our lives and experiences (spurred on by the pandemic) to the small screen. The increased prevalence of remote therapy (via the phone, Zoom, text messages, etc.) is part of this shift, and AI-driven psychotherapy chatbots represent a unique and curious form of remote therapy. In what follows, I will first provide a brief discussion of the origins of the technology in the 1960s to show that the question of transference was there at the beginning but was later neglected. Then I will consider the different aspects of transference that may occur between a person and a chatbot from the point of view of the three Lacanian registers of the Imaginary, Symbolic, and Real. Finally, I will close with some reflections on and further considerations of the small screen as a specific sociotechnical assemblage and how this influences transferential relations with AI-driven chatbots.

## ELIZA – The first chatbot

We can define a chatbot as a software application used to facilitate a text-based interaction between a user (usually human) and a computer. Admittedly, this definition might sound a little clunky. I could have said "conversation" instead of "interaction" or simply "a human" instead of "a user (usually human)." But it's important not to assume too much at the outset, since "In their output, machines capable of communication give the appearance of machine-level cognitive ability. At present, chatbots do not literally think, but rather give the illusion of intelligent conversation by imitating it" (Fulmer, 2019, p.4). The interaction between the user and the computer produces something that may look or feel like a conversation, and thus it is better not to say that it is a conversation, but that the impression of a conversation is an effect of the interaction. As I have discussed elsewhere from an STS perspective, the presence of a certain technology has specific effects on the interaction, which allows us to consider, among other things, the agency of non-human actors in this context (Holohan and Fiske, 2021). And the user who interacts with the chatbot is usually human, but need not always be so.[1]

Although the term chatbot[2] is generally understood to date back only to 1994 (Mauldin, 1994), the first computer program designed to mimic a natural language conversation between a human user and a machine was ELIZA, developed by Joseph Weizenbaum at MIT in 1964 (Weizenbaum, 1966). It worked as follows: A user sat in front of a typewriter which was remotely connected to a mainframe computer. A sort of conversation would take place, with the user typing in a statement and then receiving a typed reply "from" ELIZA. Using an early form of Natural Language Processing (NLP), the program was able to analyse the content of the user's statement by identifying certain keywords and, based on those keywords, the program generated a new sentence that had the appearance of a reply (Weizenbaum, 1966). The replies generally were questions based on an identified keyword or, if not, they were generic responses. The actual process was in fact very basic, especially in comparison to today's examples, but was nonetheless able to produce a passable impression of a conversation (see Weizenbaum, 1976, especially pp. 6–7).

Here is a sample conversation, as provided in Weizenbaum's original paper. The user writes first. ELIZA's responses are in all caps:

> Men are all alike.
> IN WHAT WAY
> They're always bugging us about something or other.
> CAN YOU THINK OF A SPECIFIC EXAMPLE
> Well, my boyfriend made me come here.
> YOUR BOYFRIEND MADE YOU COME HERE
> He says I'm depressed much of the time.
> I AM SORRY TO HEAR YOU ARE DEPRESSED
> It's true. I am unhappy.
> DO YOU THINK COMING HERE WILL HELP YOU NOT TO BE UNHAPPY
> I need some help, that much seems certain.
> WHAT WOULD IT MEAN TO YOU IF YOU GOT SOME HELP
> Perhaps I could learn to get along with my mother.
> TELL ME MORE ABOUT YOUR FAMILY
> My mother takes care of me.
> WHO ELSE IN YOUR FAMILY TAKES CARE OF YOU
> My father.
> YOUR FATHER
> You are like my father in some ways.

WHAT RESEMBLANCE DO YOU SEE
You are not very aggressive but I think you don't want me to notice that.
WHAT MAKE YOU THINK I AM NOT VERY AGGRESSIVE
You don't argue with me.
WHY DO YOU THINK I DON'T ARGUE WITH YOU
You are afraid of me.
DOES IT PLEASE YOU TO BELIEVE I AM AFRAID OF YOU
My father is afraid of everybody.
WHAT ELSE COMES TO MIND WHEN YOU THINK OF YOUR FATHER
Bullies.
DOES THAT HAVE ANYTHING TO DO WITH THE FACT THAT YOUR BOYFRIEND MADE YOU COME HERE

(Weizenbaum, 1966, pp. 36–7)

ELIZA was designed to approximate a conversation with a Rogerian psychotherapist (I will return to why this was a bit later), but it was not intended to act as an actual psychotherapeutic technology (Weizenbaum, 1966, p. 42). Rather it was simply designed as an early demonstration of the ability of a computer to mimic a conversation (Weizenbaum, 1976, p. 4). However, in the same year that Weizenbaum published his paper on ELIZA, Kenneth Mark Colby, a psychiatrist and disenchanted psychoanalyst turned computer scientist, published his description of a program named SHRINK which was, in fact, designed to "conduct a psychotherapeutic dialog" (Colby, Watt and Gilbert, 1966). Colby and his son Peter would later develop and market a dialog-based psychotherapeutic computer program named "Overcoming Depression" in the 1990s (Zeavin, 2021, p. 160). This program and ones like it were essentially similar in design to ELIZA, in that they utilised Natural Language Processing to produce script-based responses based on a particular database of vocabulary and response structures. This is more or less where the state of the art remained until very recently.

What has driven the development of the newest generation of AI-driven chatbots (including psychotherapeutically oriented chatbots) is a vast increase in the complexity of Natural Language Processing, which is able to produce a more effective simulation of (and responsiveness to) human language (Fulmer, 2019). In addition to improvements in NLP, there is the utilization of Machine Learning. A subfield of artificial intelligence, Machine Learning describes a machine that is able to improve on its tasks and predictions (or "learn") through its own practices and its interactions with its environment (e.g. with a user). Chatbots like ELIZA or Overcoming Depression were able to produce script-based responses based on what a user typed, but were not able to incorporate and learn from that user input. In other words, the chatbots' responses could not change over time based on their interactions with a specific user, or from previous interactions with past users.

Newer applications that employ Machine Learning represent a major shift in the technology, making them "paradigmatically dissimilar from their predecessors" because a machine that can learn and produce output based on that learning "may possess skills and abilities unknown to its human originators" (Fulmer, 2019, p. 3). In other words, a chatbot that employs Machine Learning would be capable of producing not only content that might be novel and surprising to the user who interacts with it, but to its designers as well. The introduction of Machine Learning into chatbot programs introduces a truly aleatory element into the interaction and represents the possibility of a chatbot producing something that could be considered properly singular, unexpected (and unexpectable), and unique to itself and its practices, as we will see with the Real of transference, later in this chapter. It must be said, however, that in some ways this currently remains a theoretical point about the possibilities of Machine Learning in the near future for two reasons. First, Machine Learning as a technology is still very much in its infancy (Fulmer, 2019, p. 3) and second, since many current AI-driven chatbots are proprietary, it is not often possible to determine the extent to which a given chatbot utilises Machine Learning, if at all.

## Chatbots and the transference

It is notable that the arrival of chatbot technology is nearly coeval with the attempts to utilise it as a psychotherapeutic tool. Even though Weizenbaum had no interest in making ELIZA function as an actual psychotherapist, and was ultimately quite scandalised that anyone would actually try to do so, his choice to employ the therapist persona is quite significant. He was very upfront about his reasoning: Because the ELIZA program was not very sophisticated in its ability to produce coherent responses, he intentionally chose the "psychiatric interview" as a mode of communication that did not necessarily ask or assume too much of one of its interlocutors (the therapist) and in which the other (the patient) would expect and tolerate a certain level of opacity from the outset.[3] It is worth quoting Weizenbaum in full here:

> This mode of conversation was chosen because the psychiatric interview is one of the few examples of [...] communication in which one of the participating pair is free to assume the pose of knowing almost nothing of the real world. If, for example, one were to tell a psychiatrist "I went for a long boat ride" and he responded, "Tell me about boats," one would not assume that he knew nothing about boats, but that he had some purpose in so directing the subsequent conversation.
>
> It is important to note that this assumption is one made by the speaker [i.e., the chatbot user]. Whether it is realistic or not is an altogether separate question. In any case, it has a crucial psychological utility in that it serves the speaker to maintain his sense of being heard and understood.

The speaker further defends his impression (which even in real life may be illusory) by attributing to his conversational partner all sorts of background knowledge, insights and reasoning ability. But again, these are the *speaker's* [the chatbot user's] contribution to the conversation. They manifest themselves inferentially in the *interpretations* he makes of the offered responses.

(Weizenbaum, 1966, p. 42)

ELIZA's designers relied on the human user to provide the bulk of the content and perform the significant interpretive work. In particular, they relied on the user to create an imaginary construct of their interlocutor. Users were informed that ELIZA was a machine and thus were not participating in a classic Turing test of artificial intelligence, which seeks to fool or convince users that their interlocutor is human. However, it is not entirely clear whether users were informed that ELIZA was going to talk like a Rogerian therapist in advance, in which case they would enter into the interaction with an expectation already, or whether they developed their imaginary construct as a result of the interaction itself. In either case, the success of the interaction explicitly depended on the human user's ability to produce a mental image of their interlocutor, including specific expectations about what that imaginary interlocutor might or might not say, the way in which they might speak, and the user's own expectations about how to interpret ELIZA's responses. In the example given regarding boats, "Tell me about boats" would likely be an odd or inappropriate response in most other kinds of conversations. But the user's expectations provide an interpretive framework that contextualises and makes sense of the otherwise strange remark.

Lacanian-oriented readers will also likely have heard an echo of Lacan's "subject supposed to know" (alternately translated as "supposed subject of knowing") in Weizenbaum's statement that a person would "assume" their interlocutor "had some purpose in so directing the conversation." In Lacan's work, the concept of the subject supposed to know represents "the constitutive element of the transference" starting in the 1960s and afterwards (Nobus, 2000, p. 125). In Weizenbaum's example, as a result of the patient's construction, the psychiatrist is permitted (by the patient) to pretend to know nothing about the world (ELIZA, of course, need not pretend) while at the same time, they are imbued (again, by the patient) with the power of knowledge about the patient and the proper direction of the treatment. In Lacanian theory, of course, the analysand's attribution of the subject supposed to know to the analyst is but one (early) moment in a complex dialectic of transference. Significant moments in this dialectic include the analyst's refusal of this attribution and the analysand's eventual realisation that such an attribution "was but an avatar of her own fantasmatic belief in the power of knowledge" (Nobus and Quinn, 2005, p. 4).[4] Even though Weizenbaum doesn't ever mention the word transference, and it is not certain that he was aware of it, it is clear that a form of transference is not only present in the human-chatbot interaction, but intentionally provoked.

It is a curious historical fact that this machine and its potential for transference did not, in fact, escape Lacan's attention. The same year that Weizenbaum's article was published, Lacan gave his fourteenth seminar, on *The Logic of Fantasy* (1966–67). In the third week of that seminar, Lacan makes a digression to say that he had read the article and goes on to provide a very brief but useful commentary:

> Elisa [sic] is, as you know, the person who in a well-known play – Pygmalion – the person who is taught to speak properly; she was a little flower seller on a busy London street and it is a matter of training her to be able to express herself in the best society, when it is noticed that she does not belong to it. It is something of this order which emerges with this little machine; in truth, what is involved is not, properly speaking, that a machine should be capable of giving articulated answers, simply when one speaks to it – I am not saying when one questions it – it is something which now proves to be a game and which puts in question what can happen in terms of obtaining responses from the one who is speaking to it. [...] [I]t is very interesting because, when all is said and done, there is something suggested which may be considered as a therapeutic function of the machine and in a word, it is nothing less than *the analogue of a sort of transference* which can be produced in this relationship, about which the question is raised. The thing did not dissatisfy me.
>
> (Lacan, Seminar XIV, Session of November 11, 1966, emphasis mine)

In this brief gloss, two related things become apparent. First, we can see that Lacan is more interested in the user side of the user-machine relationship. Rather than focusing on the novelty of a machine that might be "capable of giving articulated answers," he is more interested in the human user's interaction with the machine, which "puts in question what can happen in terms of obtaining responses from the one who is speaking to it." In other words, it is a question of how a subject's interaction with ELIZA puts the subject to work and obtains "responses" from that subject.

The second thing that becomes clear in this passage is that Lacan identifies the subject's responses as a kind of transference. Unfortunately, as far as I am aware, Lacan would not return to this theme again. And it seems that neither Weizenbaum's nor Lacan's forays into this topic were much taken up by later computer scientists or psychoanalysts, at least in terms of the question of transference. It seems safe to say this theme was largely forgotten. Or rather, it would be more accurate to say that it was misrecognised. This is evident in Weizenbaum's own later reflections on it, which show that he didn't quite recognise what he had stumbled upon:

I knew of course that people form all sorts of emotional bonds to machines, for example, to musical instruments, motorcycles, and cars. [...] What I had not realized is that extremely short exposures to a relatively simple computer program could induce powerful delusional thinking in quite normal people.

(Weizenbaum, 1976, p. 7)

The interpretation of the user-machine interaction as one of delusion, illusion, or distortion is at the heart of discussions about what became known as the "ELIZA effect," or the tendency of users to attribute human-like qualities of thinking and understanding to computers. This has generally been the predominant interpretive framework for understanding this topic in the field of Artificial Intelligence (see, e.g., Turkle, 1995 and Hofstadter and FARG, 1995).

## A Lacanian perspective on the Imaginary, Symbolic, and Real transferential possibilities of psychotherapeutic work involving AI-driven chatbots

All the more reason, then, to focus on the neglected question of transference as an alternate framework for understanding the interactions between human users and chatbots, in particular chatbots that aim to operate psychotherapeutically. We may therefore ask what kind of transference is at play in the relationships that develop between users and contemporary psychotherapeutically oriented AI-driven chatbots. In particular, the Lacanian framework of the Imaginary, Symbolic, and Real will allow for a certain level of granularity here. I will now briefly identify and analyse some transferential possibilities of psychotherapeutic work involving AI-driven chatbots, with reference to the three Lacanian registers. As Lacan himself put it, "I prefer to leave the notion of transference its empirical totality, while stressing that it is polyvalent and that it involves several registers: the symbolic, the imaginary, and the real" (1988, pp. 112–113). Cauwe, Vanheule and Desmet add that the polyvalence of the transference means that "it is related to the signifier, to images of other and self, to the body, and to what is beyond representation" (2017, p. 6). I want to be clear that my aim here is not to be prescriptive. I have no interest in enumerating what an AI-driven psychotherapeutic chatbot *should* do, and it would be foolhardy to criticise these chatbots for failing to follow Lacanian psychoanalytic practices. Rather, my aim is to utilise the explanatory potential of the Lacanian theory of the three registers to analyse and better understand the specific modes of transference that are, or at least might be, at play in users' interactions with AI-driven psychotherapeutic chatbots.

Beginning with the Imaginary, this describes the register built on "recognition supported by an image in the outside world," which involves a degree of both self-awareness and misrecognition, since one is the flipside of the other and "we wrongly assume that we 'are' the image" (Cauwe, Vanheule and Desmet, 2017, p. 3). Yet despite having misrecognition at its core, our perceptions and understanding of ourself is built out of these identifications, and we live our lives within the swirl of identifications that constitutes the Imaginary. It may come as no surprise that making interventions at the level of the Imaginary is often a major function of current AI-driven chatbots. Generally, such interventions take the form of encouraging and enumerating various user self-identifications. Identifying and naming specific aspects of oneself, including behavioural responses, are a central part of the current chatbot protocols, which are often based on the principles of cognitive behavioural therapy (CBT). For example, Woebot is designed to employ CBT-oriented responses based on the principles of empathic response, tailoring, goal setting, accountability, motivation and engagement, and reflection (Fitzpatrick et al., 2017, p. 3), and the Tess chatbot employs "interventions rooted in a variety of psychological modalities such as CBT, mindfulness-based therapy, emotionally focused therapy, acceptance and commitment therapy, motivational interviewing, self-compassion therapy, and interpersonal psychotherapy" (Fulmer et al., 2018, p. 4). In addition to supporting various self-identifications, the Imaginary aspect of transference is currently utilised to foster a therapeutic alliance. In the instances of Woebot and Tess, the focus here is on creating a bond between chatbot and user based, in particular, around the image of the bot becoming a friend and/or helper. For example, these two chatbots respond to users' declarations of loneliness with scripted responses such as "I'm so sorry you're feeling lonely. I guess we all feel a little lonely sometimes," or they show excitement by replying, "Yay, always good to hear that!" (Fitzpatrick et al., 2017, p. 3; Fulmer et al., 2018, p. 4). These kinds of imaginary relations are "characterized by mutuality, narcissistic love, and hate/rivalry" (Cauwe et al., 2017, p. 5). An example of this can be seen in statements from a participant in a recent clinical trial on the effectiveness of using Woebot to treat symptoms of depression and anxiety in young adults: "Woebot is a fun little dude" and "I love Woebot so much. I hope we can be friends forever. I actually feel super good and happy when I see that it 'remembered' to check in with me!" (Fitzpatrick et al., 2017, p. 8).

Of course, from a Lacanian point of view, the main aim of an analytic treatment at the level of the Imaginary lies not in establishing and fostering a patient's imaginary identifications (though there are instances in which such might be a short- or even medium-term intervention), but in challenging and countering them. In doing so, it is a matter of bringing to the fore the misrecognition that is at the heart of every recognition. Such imaginary identifications then become objects of analysis, not aims in themselves. It is through the analysis and working through of the analysand's identifications, including transferential identifications, that much of the psychoanalytic work is done, where a shift in the analysand's relationship(s) to themself and others becomes possible. From the psychoanalytic point of view, it is not sufficient to build up an analysand's identifications, and strengthening such identifications can even at times have a detrimental effect. Nevertheless, it is certainly possible to demonstrate that, with regards to AI-driven psychotherapeutic chatbots, transference can be established at the level of the Imaginary. In addition, such imaginary transferences are often intentionally provoked by the chatbots' designers, though it is not referred to by this term.

Interestingly enough, it has often been remarked that, with AI-driven chatbots, the "ELIZA effect" eventually breaks down, often due to the limitations of the technology (Fitzpatrick et al., 2017, p. 7; Fulmer et al., 2018, p. 9; Turkle, 1980, p. 19, Weizenbaum, 1966, p. 42). Perhaps we may see in this a technologically-specific form of the analyst's fall from knowledge, as was mentioned by Nobus and Quinn (2005 p. 4) above, where the analysand "comes to recognize that the attribution of the 'supposed subject of knowing' was but an avatar of her own fantasmatic belief in the power of knowledge." The question, then, would be: Is it possible to design a chatbot that would be capable of identifying this dialectical move and taking it into account, and what would be the clinical implications if it were? Just because the technology is not capable of such an operation now does not mean it won't be in the future. More importantly, just because something like this is not currently considered by today's chatbot developers doesn't mean it couldn't become an area of interest in the future.

In contrast to the register of the Imaginary, the Symbolic describes the aspect of subjectivity governed by language and the law, by social relations and "symbolic commitments" (Nobus, 2000, p. 66) with names like husband, mother, student, citizen, etc., where these titles signify symbolic positions which are only intelligible in the presence of an Other. In comparison to the Imaginary, in which relations are dyadic, the Symbolic register is triadic. Social relations between individuals, like marriage or kinship, are always mediated by the presence of a third (culture, law, family, state, professional societies, etc.). In Lacanian parlance, relations between others (with a small *o*) are mediated by the presence of the Other (with a big *O*). Such relations are deeply rooted in the unconscious. Descriptively, these are relations the meaning of which (or even sometimes the existence of which) we are not always aware of, and which we might even struggle to fully articulate, but which shape and direct our thought and actions. Structurally, the unconscious "core of subjectivity is constituted by otherness [...] the Symbolic is characterized by lack, the perpetual movement of the signifier, giving rise to a divided subject that can never coincide with itself" (Cauwe et al., 2017, pp. 4–5). This is perhaps best summarised in Lacan's statement that "the unconscious is the discourse of the Other" (Lacan, 1957/2006, p. 10).

Clinically, the register of the Symbolic operates through "the determining effects of language and [...] the repetition of signifiers. If we associate 'freely,' the same old stories, words, themes, and preoccupations return" (Cauwe et al., 2017, p. 11). In other words, the Symbolic is at play in the moments of repetition, when elements of old relationships to others (sometimes fragmentary, sometimes in their entirety) appear in the consulting room and are redirected onto the analyst. These Symbolic repetitions can manifest in the transference, for example, in a patient's speech, demeanour, attitude, or patterns of behaviour (Fink, 2007). This is a central element of the psychoanalytic understanding of transference and originates in Freud's earliest theorisations of the concept (Freud, 1912/2001). As I have written elsewhere, we can imagine

> a patient for whom the therapist's haircut or tone of voice resembles the hair or voice of her father, with whom she has a poor relationship. Based on this trivial similarity, the patient begins, sometimes without even meaning to, to act toward her therapist with the same kind of denial and protest that she did with her father. This transference of feeling from the father onto the therapist can lead the patient to complain about the therapist, find it hard to trust him, or even start to miss sessions.
> (Holohan and Fiske, 2021)

As a matter of working with the Symbolic aspects of transference, both the analyst and analysand are tasked with identifying and distinguishing these moments of repetition. The analytic process here consists, in large part, of tying what has arisen in the transference back (in)to the analysand's history.

At first glance, we might wonder what kinds of Symbolic transference could be possible with a chatbot. So much of the repetition in transference we are familiar with lies in a kind of mistaking the analyst (or the therapist more generally, since such is not the sole purview of psychoanalysis) for *someone* else. Yet a chatbot is quite literally *no one* else. It is not a person, and the user-patient knows this from the start. It is a built thing. But at the heart of Lacan's concept of the Symbolic register is the primacy of the form and not the content of the relation. It is therefore the chatbot's formal position, as addressee of the subject's speech, that matters here.[5] Certainly, there is no haircut or other personal characteristics that might act as a material kernel for the crystallisation of a transference, but even something like a tone of voice can be a characteristic of an AI-driven chatbot. In fact, we can imagine that even the patient's awareness that the chatbot is not human can be a cause of transference:

> [I]magine the following scenario: A patient using a psychotherapeutic chatbot feels relief in not being judged, since they know they are interacting with a robot. On the one hand, this makes them feel safe, making it easier to talk about difficult topics. On the other hand, the patient might at the same time contrast this absence of judgement with the overly judgmental attitude of their mother, to whom they still attribute a strong

degree of authority despite the fact that they suffer under her judgmental gaze. In this case, the patient might ultimately fail to take their chatbot therapist seriously, or even treat it with disdain because, through their transference, they ascribe a lack of authority to the chatbot, even though interacting with it makes them feel safe and cared for.

(Holohan and Fiske, 2021)

In this scenario, the transferential relationship between the user-patient and the chatbot therapist at the level of the Symbolic revitalises and brings into the therapeutic space an aspect of the patient's relationship with their mother, and this is due precisely to the non-human aspect of the patient's interlocutor.

Of course, in this example, the transference engages in what is often called a "negative therapeutic reaction" and would constitute a moment of trouble for the therapy and could even lead to its early termination. It is precisely at moments like this that the transference, once evoked, must be acknowledged, analysed and worked through if there is to be any hope of the therapy continuing. Such a moment, if handled carefully, might instead represent a significant moment of possibility and transformation in the course of the treatment. While different psychotherapeutic approaches might differ on what counts as careful handling of such a moment of Symbolic transference, it is nonetheless widely understood to be an important factor in psychotherapeutic treatment, including in approaches less commonly associated with the handling of the transference in general, such as CBT, which is currently the most common model for psychotherapeutic chatbot design (Prasko et al., 2010; Folk et al., 2016).

At the moment, it is both helpful and necessary to think through the question of Symbolic transference using speculative examples like the one above, since there are currently no empirical studies or case histories that have explored this phenomenon in situ. Such scholarship is greatly needed and would contribute to an advance in our understanding of the workings of this new technology and techno-human relationality, and would provide much-needed specificity about the actual experiences of actual user-patients. At the same time, it is striking that even one of the earliest conversations with ELIZA on record, in Weizenbaum's original paper, suggests anecdotally that Symbolic transference is at play with a machine that functions in the role of addressee and that seems to speak back. Recall the following part of the conversation quoted above (again, ELIZA's responses are in all caps):

WHO ELSE IN YOUR FAMILY TAKES CARE OF YOU
My father.
YOUR FATHER
You are like my father in some ways.
WHAT RESEMBLANCE DO YOU SEE
You are not very aggressive but I think you don't want me to notice that.

> WHAT MAKES YOU THINK I AM NOT VERY AGGRESSIVE
> You don't argue with me.
> WHY DO YOU THINK I DON'T ARGUE WITH YOU
> You are afraid of me.
> DOES IT PLEASE YOU TO BELIEVE I AM AFRAID OF YOU
> My father is afraid of everybody.
> WHAT ELSE COMES TO MIND WHEN YOU THINK OF YOUR FATHER
> Bullies.
>
> (Weizenbaum, 1966, p. 37)

It is not clear from the published information whether the person who participated in this exchange was in earnest or conducted it as a kind of demonstration model. All that is said of this person is that she is "a young lady," likely either a student or one of the administrative staff who were said to be keen on chatting with the program (Weizebnaum, 1976, p. 3 ff.). Regardless of the actual status of the conversation – since even if the user was not in earnest, it would be significant that she chose this theme as somehow appropriate or characteristic of a therapeutic conversation – we can see intimations of both Imaginary and Symbolic aspects of transference represented here.

The third and final Lacanian register to consider is that of the Real, which "refers to human experience to the extent that it cannot be articulated through language and discourse, nor turned into an image" (Cauwe et al., 2017, p. 5). For the subject, it can be used to describe experiences of the body, including the drives, that do not seem to have a place in discourse and yet insist as a kind of excess. Not the same as reality as such, the Real is a concept used to describe that part of human experience that does not or cannot have a place in the other two registers. Clinically, whereas the analyst in the transferential relation functions both "as effigy (Imaginary), then as a relation to absence (Symbolic)," as we have seen above, these do not represent the totality of the Lacanian understanding of transference in Lacanian psychoanalysis (Cauwe et al., 2017, p. 13). In addition to their Imaginary and Symbolic functions, the analyst "can become a real presence. It is a presence differing from the supposed subject of knowing (Symbolic) and the analyst as a person or a familiar mirror image (Imaginary)" (Cauwe et al., 2017, p. 15). I rely on the work of Cauwe et al. (2017) here, as I find their discussion of transference, in particular their articulation of the Real aspect of transference quite illuminating in general, and particularly apt for my consideration of the transferential possibilities of AI-driven psychotherapeutic chatbots. Central to their discussion of the Real aspect of transference is the importance of contingency, of chance and the unexpected or unexpectable in the treatment, and in particular in the analysand's relation(s) to the analyst. It is the element of contingency that allows for something new and even creative to emerge in the analysis. Without this element, they argue, the function of the transference in the treatment would amount to nothing more than a kind of mechanical repetition in which the presence of the analyst did not matter at all. It is the potential for the presence[6] of the analyst to appear enigmatic, as capable of surprise and thus to "introduce novelty" (Cauwe et al., 2017, p. 15).

For many readers, this may seem a step that a technology like an AI-driven chatbot would be incapable of taking. As a fellow psychoanalyst once remarked to me, there must be a limit here because, after all, the chatbot is a fully built thing, and the patient knows, at some level, that their artificial interlocutor was ultimately designed and programmed by a human being and is therefore fundamentally reducible to that design, and thus incapable of enigmatic surprise. At the current level of the technology, this may be more or less true. Though it must be said that even the question of what the humans who design AI machines know about them has become more complicated: Such projects and the specialised collaborative design process involved are often so complex that no single individual is familiar with or could even explain how aspects of the program that they were not directly involved with work. Moreover, as I mentioned above, the incorporation of Machine Learning into psychotherapeutic chatbot AI has already begun. Once it is more robustly established, the technology will be further capable of learning from its own practices, including its own interactions with specific individuals, as well as with all of the previous conversations it (or any other program or person included in its dataset) has ever had. In doing so, it would produce content that would be novel and surprising to the user who interacts with it, as well as being fundamentally not explainable by its designers. This truly aleatory element, singular, unexpected and unexpectable, would represent something unique to itself and its practices that may be comparable to a Real aspect of transference.

## Further considerations

Currently, there are no detailed studies of transference in real-world AI-enabled psychotherapeutic settings. However, as I have pointed out elsewhere (Holohan and Fiske, 2021) there have been anecdotal suggestions of this in some recent clinical studies of specific chatbots, where we can see that some users develop a human-like connection with the chatbot that can form the basis of a transference. In one study, a participant wrote, "Woebot felt like a real person that showed concern" (Fitzpatrick et al., 2017). In another study of the chatbot Tess, a participant wrote,

> Based on our interactions I do somewhat feel like I'm talking to a real person and I do enjoy the tips you've given. In that sense, you're better than my therapist in that she doesn't necessarily provide specific ways I can better myself and problems.
> 
> (Fulmer et al., 2018)

The latter statement is written in the second person singular because, at the end of the study, the Tess chatbot itself asked users for feedback on their experiences interacting with it.

In both studies, participants were clearly informed at the outset that they were interacting with a machine, not a human. In the case of Woebot, the program is so named in order to emphasise its non-human nature (Fitzpatrick et al., 2017, p. 9). The founder and president of Woebot Labs, Inc., Alison Darcy, frames the fact that the user knows they are speaking to a machine as both intentional and beneficial. As she describes it, it is not only a matter of ensuring that users are not deceived or confused, but that knowing they are talking to a robot can influence how they speak to it and what they feel allowed to say:

> It's just a chat bot [sic]. So it can see you on your worst day. You know, you can actually literally say anything to Woebot. And he very clearly does not understand or he's not going to be offended. There is no person there. There's no emotion there. And the experience is so much more mundane and friendly and warm and occasionally funny as well, because I do think humor is important.
>
> (Howard, 2020)

Here we can see, again, an understanding that what the user "knows" about their interlocutor strongly shapes their interaction with it/them. And again, it is apparent that the specificity of the medium of the interaction and the sociotechnical assemblage of an app accessible via the small screen of a user's mobile phone influences the specific modes and articulation of transferential relations to a chatbot. The implication in this example is that, as I discussed above, the question of being judged is obviated by the knowledge that Woebot is not a person and thus cannot pass judgement on the user's behaviour towards it.[7] Also seemingly removed from the equation is the possibility of the user's aggression having an effect on their interlocutor in terms of offending it/them.[8] This is only one example, but it may perhaps be indicative of how the designers imagine users will relate to their technology. While Woebot's designer presents this as a kind of fun feature, it is important to examine more carefully how these kinds of assumptions on the part of the user are fundamentally constitutive of while simultaneously being products of the material-discursive apparatus that the encounter between user and chatbot represents (Holohan and Fiske, 2021).

Additionally, how Woebot's creator talks about it points to a seeming disconnect in the way that AI-driven chatbot designers represent their technology in public. The passage cited above comes from a pop psychology podcast in an episode titled "Surviving Coronavirus Using a Free Mental Health App," which was recorded in the context of the early days of the COVID-19 pandemic, shortly after many countries first imposed lockdowns. In that podcast episode, discussion focused on the possibility for chatbots such as Woebot to play a role in the increased need for mental health services as a direct result of the pandemic, as well as the decrease in – or outright disappearance of – the availability of meeting with in-person mental health practitioners. While she touts the ability of Woebot to "help" people in mental distress, in the interview, Darcy often focuses on the offhand fun of Woebot and how it's not meant to do or "replace therapy" (Howard, 2020). This can be difficult to square with the fact that the Woebot company is actively researching the clinical effectiveness of the chatbot in delivering CBT to treat symptoms of depression and anxiety (Fitzpatrick et al., 2017). I have focused here on Woebot, but this is a common practice among chatbot development teams.

It may even be that this technology represents something genuinely new and will not ultimately fit into current paradigms, including that of psychotherapy. It may be that an admittedly ungainly term like "AI-driven psychotherapeutic chatbot" will someday come to seem as old-fashioned and future-blind as "horseless carriage." Even a gifted futurist like Carl Sagan was not immune from this kind of thinking when, in 1975, he envisioned "the development of a network of computer psychotherapeutic terminals, something like arrays of large telephone booths, in which, for a few dollars a session, we would be able to talk with an attentive, tested, and largely non-directive psychotherapist" (Sagan, 1975, as cited in Cristian, 2011). It was not possible for him to imagine at that time the rise of the personal computer, let alone our current world, in which so many of us have internet-connected computers in our pockets. Nor was he able to envision the contemporary tech industry profit model where users are able to access services for free because they themselves are the product, in the form of their data, which is collected and sold on to other entities or utilised for other purposes and projects within the company.[9] These sociotechnical details matter. As does the affective specificity that a techno-mediation like AI-driven chatbots foster. Hannah Zeavin (2021, p. 133) has recently proposed the concept of "auto-intimacy" as a way of thinking about automated therapies as "a closed circuit of self-communication, run through a relationship to a media object [...] a specifically therapeutic relationship to the self that is mediated by a program and its process." We will likely need to develop more concepts like this in order to better understand and analyse this technology and its potential forms of novelty from within.

It is important to note here that so much of the current discussion about how users think about, respond to, and act towards AI-driven psychotherapeutic chatbots is speculative. Chatbot designers often talk about how they expect or imagine users will or do interact with their creations. In this chapter, much of my discussion has also been hypothetical and speculative, based on clinical and theoretical principles. While this kind of speculative thinking is valuable and important, it must eventually be supplemented with empirical and clinical studies of the experiences of actual users. This will be necessary in order to pay attention to the radical specificity of individual user-patients and how they make use of and make sense of this new technology, likely in unique and unexpected ways.

To conclude, as we have seen, AI-driven psychotherapeutic chatbot technology promises a cheap, easy to access, and abundant means of providing mental health services. And perhaps there can and will be a place, or many differing places, for this technology in the broad and varied mental health landscape. But it is clear that many complex questions remain to be considered, not least among them the question of transference in all its variety. In this chapter, I have offered an initial intervention by considering how we can use the Lacanian theory of the three registers to better understand how transference is, or might be, at play in users' interactions with this unique technology. As I have shown, in some ways things appear to be quite the same; in other ways that remain to be fully explored, they are likely to be very different. Further inquiry into this question might even have the potential to reshape the psychoanalytic understanding of transference. The arguments and analysis presented in this chapter are intended to be exploratory, to help orient further inquiry into the psychotherapeutic potential and specificity of AI-driven psychotherapeutic chatbots. These chatbots may appear to be new, and in their current and near-future iterations they are undeniably head and shoulders (while possessing neither) above previous generations. However, as I have shown, the theme of transference was present at the birth of this technology almost 60 years ago yet just as soon fell into obscurity. As a result, it has remained under-researched and under-theorised. With the renewed interest in and proliferation of psychotherapeutic chatbot technologies that has coincided with our recent shift to the small screen, it is essential that more work be done to better understand the specificity and complexity of transference as it pertains to this sociotechnical asssemblage that is both old and new.

## Notes

1 In a surreal and curious moment in the early days of the technology, computer scientists engineered a "conversation" between a chatbot designed to mimic the speech of a paranoid schizophrenic (PARRY) and one designed to mimic that of a therapist (ELIZA) (Cerf, 1973).
2 Just as the common English word "chat" is a truncation of "chatter," "chatbot" is a shortening of the original form, "chatterbot."
3 It appears that Weizenbaum, as a computer scientist, selected the therapeutic conversation not because it represented a solution to a problem in the field of mental health, but to a problem in the field of chatbot technology. This can be understood as a technology-centred approach (see Breuer et al., 2022). In the case of ELIZA, the mental health context was important primarily because it encouraged the user to fill in the gaps created by the technological limitations of the chatbot and therefore demonstrate the capabilities of the system.
4 Even here, there is a kind of untheorised intimation of this in Weizenbaum's paper. Writing about human conversation in general, he describes how "Responses which

are difficult to so interpret [as consistent] may well result in an enhancement of the image of the partner, in additional rationalizations which then make more complicated interpretations of his responses reasonable. When, however, such rationalizations become too massive and even self-congratulatory, the entire image may crumble and be replaced by another ('He is not, after all, as smart as I thought he was')" (Weizenbaum, 1966, p. 42).

5  We must, of course, also not lose sight of the fact that it is through written language, in the form of text messages back and forth, that a user interacts with a chatbot.
6  Here "presence" is a more useful term than something like the "person" of the analyst, since in the case of AI-driven chatbots, there is no person as such.
7  It is also unclear whether "your worst day" means something like when you feel worst or when you act the worst towards others, etc.
8  Though as I have pointed out elsewhere, in such a scenario the question of judgement might not actually disappear, but *shift*: From personal animus to the kind of structural, algorithmic bias that is often baked in to an AI program's dataset (Holohan and Fiske, 2021).
9  In what seems to be one of the first of its kind in the field of automated psychotherapy, the company Ieso Digital Health is looking to do just this. Ieso currently has a contract with the NHS in the United Kingdom to provide remote CBT therapy, via text-based chat, to patients in the NHS system. The company therefore possesses a vast collection of thousands of saved text conversations between the real CBT therapists and real patients who have used the service. It now intends to utilise this "data" as a dataset "to train artificial intelligence-based computer systems to deliver some of the active or essential ingredients of treatment without humans involved. [...] This isn't science fiction. We are building these technologies right now, and they will enter clinical trials soon" (Blackwell, 2020).

## References

Bickmore, T., Puskar, K., Schlenk, E., Pfeifer, L.M. and Sereika, S.M. (2010). Maintaining reality: relational agents for antipsychotic medication adherence. *Interacting with Computers*, 22 (4), pp. 276–288.

Bickmore, T, Mitchell, S., Jack, B., Paasche-Orlow, M.K., Pfeifer, L.M. and O'Donnell, J. (2010). Response to a relational agent by hospital patients with depressive symptoms. *Interacting with Computers*, 22 (4), pp. 289–298.

Blackwell, A. (2020). *Artificial intelligence meets mental health therapy*. Video. TED Conferences. Available at: https://www.ted.com/talks/andy_blackwell_artificial_intelligence_meets_mental_health_therapy.

Breuer, S., Braun, M., Tigard, D., Buyx, A., and Müller, R. (2023). How engineers' imaginaries of healthcare shape design and user engagement: A case study of a robotics initiative for geriatric healthcare AI applications. ACM Transactions on Computer-Human Interaction, 30 (2), pp. 1–33. Available at: https://dl.acm.org/doi/10.1145/3577010.

Cauwe, J., Vanheule, S., and Desmet, M. (2017). The presence of the analyst in Lacanian treatment. *Journal of the American Psychoanalytic Association*, 65 (4), pp. 609–638. https://doi.org/10.1177/0003065117721163.

Cerf, V. (1973). PARRY encounters the DOCTOR. *RFC 439*. doi:10.17487/RFC0439. https://www.rfc-editor.org/info/rfc439.

Colby, K.M., Watt, J.B., and Gilbert, J.P. (1966). A computer method of psychotherapy: Preliminary communication. *Journal of Nervous and Mental Disease*, 142 (2), pp. 148–152. https://doi.org/10.1097/00005053-196602000-00005.

Cristian, B. (2011). *The most human human: What talking with computers teaches us about what it means to be alive*. New York: Doubleday.

Fink, B. (2007). *Fundamentals of psychoanalytic technique: A Lacanian approach for practitioners*. New York: W.W. Norton & Co.

Fiske, A., Henningsen, P., and Buyx, A. (2019). Your robot therapist will see you now: Ethical implications of embodied Artificial Intelligence in psychiatry, psychology, and psychotherapy. *Journal of Medical Internet Research*, 21 (5), e13216. doi:10.2196/13216.

Fitzpatrick, K.K., Darcy, A., and Vierhile, M. (2017). Delivering cognitive behavior therapy to young adults with symptoms of depression and anxiety using a fully automated conversational agent (Woebot): A randomized controlled trial. *JMIR Mental Health*, 4 (2), e19. doi:10.2196/mental.7785.

Folk, J., Disabato, D., Goodman, F., Carter, S., Dimauro, J., and Riskind, J. (2016). Wise additions bridge the gap between social psychology and clinical practice: Cognitive-behavioral therapy as an exemplar. *Journal of Psychotherapy Integration*, 3. doi:10.1037/int0000038.

Freud, S. (1912/2001). The dynamics of transference. *The Standard Edition of the complete psychological works of Sigmund Freud, Volume XII (1911–1913)*, pp. 97–108.

Fulmer, R., Joerin, A., Gentile, B., Lakerink, L., and Rauws, M. (2018). Using psychological Artificial Intelligence (Tess) to relieve symptoms of depression and anxiety: Randomized controlled trial. *JMIR Mental Health*, 5 (4), e64. doi:10.2196/mental.9782.

Fulmer, R. (2019). Artificial intelligence and counseling: Four levels of implementation. *Theory & Psychology*, 29 (6), pp. 807–819. https://doi.org/10.1177/0959354319853045.

Hofstadter, D.R., and The Fluid Analogies Research Group. (1995). *Fluid concepts and creative analogies: Computer models of the fundamental mechanisms of thought*. New York: Basic Books.

Holohan, M., Fiske, A. (2021). "Like I'm talking to a real person": Exploring the meaning of transference for the use and design of AI-based applications in psychotherapy. *Frontiers in Psychology*, 12, September 27. doi:10.3389/fpsyg.2021.720476.

Howard, G. (2020, April 30). Surviving coronavirus using a free mental health app. Audio podcast transcript. In *Inside Mental Health*. San Francisco, CA: Healthline Media. https://psychcentral.com/blog/podcast-surviving-coronavirus-using-a-free-mental-health-app#1.

Lacan, J. (1988). *The seminar of Jacques Lacan, Book I, Freud's papers on technique (1953–1954)*. Ed. J.-A. Miller; Trans. J. Forrester. New York and London: W.W. Norton.

Lacan, J. *The Logic of Fantasy. Seminar XIV, 1966–67*. Unpublished translation by Cormac Gallagher. Available at: http://www.lacaninireland.com/web/wp-content/uploads/2010/06/14-Logic-of-Phantasy-Complete.pdf.

Lacan, J. (1957/2006). Seminar on the purloined letter. In *Écrits: The first complete edition in English* (pp. 6–48). Trans. B. Fink. New York: W.W. Norton.

Mauldin, M.L. (1994). *CHATTERBOTS, TINYMUDS, and the Turing Test: Entering the Loebner prize competition*. Proceedings of the Twelfth AAAI National Conference on Artificial Intelligence, Vol. 94. AAAI Press, Seattle, Washington, pp. 16–21.

Nobus, D. (2000). *Jacques Lacan and the Freudian practice of psychoanalysis.* New York: Routledge.

Nobus, D. and Quinn, M. (2005). *Knowing nothing, staying stupid: Elements for a psychoanalytic epistemology.* London: Routledge.

Prasko, J., Diveky, T., Grambal, A., Kamaradova, D., Mozny, P., Sigmundova, Z., et al. (2010). Transference and countertransference in cognitive behavioral therapy. *Biomedical papers of the Medical Faculty of the University Palacky, Olomouc, Czech Republic*, 154 (3), pp. 189–197. doi:10.5507/bp.2010.029.

Scholten, M.R., Kelders, S.M., and Van Gemert-Pijnen, J.E. (2017). Self-guided web-based interventions: scoping review on user needs and the potential of embodied conversational agents to address them. *Journal of Medical Internet Research*, 19 (11), e383. https://doi.org/10.2196/jmir.7351.

Turkle, S. (1980). "Computer as Rorschach". 17 Society 2 (January/February 1980):15–24. *Science, Technology, & Human Values*, 5 (4), pp. 74–74. https://doi.org/10.1177/016224398000500449.

Turkle, S. (1995). *Life on the screen: Identity in the age of the internet.* New York: Simon & Schuster.

Weizenbaum, J. (1966). ELIZA: A computer program for the study of natural language communication between man and machine. *Communications of the ACM*, 9 (1), pp. 36–45. https://doi.org/10.1145/365153.365168.

Weizenbaum, J. (1976). *Computer power and human reason: From judgement to calculation.* New York: W.H. Freeman & Co.

Zeavin, H. (2021). *The distance cure: A history of teletherapy.* Cambridge, MA: MIT Press.

Chapter 8

# The Rise of the *Lathouses*
Some consequences for the speaking being and the social bond

*Hilda Fernandez-Alvarez*

## Introduction

It is mid-afternoon and I am sitting on a plane in a position that allows me to discreetly observe two couples, each comprised of a mother and an infant. The babies are roughly the same age, between six to nine months old, and each of them is sitting on their mother's lap. Baby A, to my right, sees me seeing them and smiles with coquetry, redirecting their gaze from me to the mother and excitedly moving their body up and down, confidently touching the mother's mouth and nostrils, pulling her hair and patting her face with joy. The mother distractedly kisses the baby as she seems busy giving orders to two other children travelling with her. I keep playing the gaze game with baby A for a little while. Meanwhile, baby B, on my left, is pleasantly cuddling in their mother's lap, but their eyes are looking at a small TV screen on the rear of the seat in front of them, observing a map with the icon of an airplane moving slowly, representing the movement of the plane in real space. The companions of this couple, a man and a toddler, are seated across the aisle, each in their seats watching the small screen before them, while the mother is deeply focused on touching and swiping the screen of her phone. Shortly after our gaze game has reached its conclusion, baby A is pushing the mother away, appearing frustrated and vocalising loudly, as if trying to move away from the mother's proximity. Dyad B continues to be absorbed by the screen, while the mother sporadically caresses the baby's head softly.

In this chapter, I explore how these mother-infant dyads may illustrate two different paradigms of *jouissance* in our present time. The embodied paradigm of dyad A concerns the social exchanges of the subject's sensual body *among other bodies* – which, while imaginary in nature, presents a surplus, a *je ne sais quoi*. The other paradigm concerns the virtual exchanges of a globalised culture plugged into digital screens, which we could think of as *lathouses* after Lacan's neologism from his seventeenth seminar (Lacan, 1969–70/2007). The term *lathouses* refers to technoscientific objects able to extract enjoyment via gadgets, produced *en masse* for the masses, and resemble the fetishistic aspect of the Marxist commodity form. The *lathouse* plays with the

DOI: 10.4324/9781003272069-9

phonemes "la/the," the Aristotelian *ousia* (substance or being), and the French ventose (suction cup) to suggest significations such as being suctioned. The *lathouse* is a notion that captures very well the manner in which the digital commodity extracts human *jouissance* through a cyborgic mechanism, part human and part technology that feeds on the subject's *jouissance* for the profit of the owners of digital capital and the means of production. (Fernandez-Alvarez, 2019, p. 98).

Technological usage increased significantly during the pandemic lockdown, as the coronavirus engendered distant bodies forced to retreat to intimate spaces. The *lathousian* gadget was a key factor in facilitating social connection during social distancing times, consolidating the already emergent virtual paradigm. The rise of small screen use is of critical concern to psychoanalysis, because the clinic, as a reflection of society, brings about emerging ways of *jouissance*. Increasingly, the cyborgic coupling of a subject attached to the *lathouse* is a generalised libidinal bond, that manifests what Lacan rendered as jouissance of the Other, inside the body and outside language (1974/2019, p. 107).

The posthuman field inquires about the relationship of the speaking subject with digital technologies, and studies the interfacing of humans with technology at present. Posthuman studies have largely engaged with such questions, and Svitlana Matviyenko and Judith Roof frame it critically when they articulate that our current technological era institutes the loss of the human being's exceptionality with regards to other systems or entities (2018, p. 3). An entity that challenges human exceptionality has paradoxically resulted in a generalisation of "the Other's jouissance," which Jacques-Allain Miller has identified as "the posthuman standard" (2005, p. 11), because it renders the subject as "one-all-alone."

According to Flieger, posthumanistic approaches can fall into the categories of "'doomsday', 'celebratory' and 'critical'" (2010, p. 354). In this chapter, I approach the embodied and digital paradigms from a psychoanalytical critical perspective regarding the way in which the *lathouse* hinders subjectivity and social bonds. I propose that the coupling of the subject and their small screen might affect the speaking body by a) impoverishing the Imaginary register; b) intruding on the structuring of *lalangue*; and c) hindering social bonding.

Extensive scientific literature reviews of so-called "digital natives" (Prensky, 2001), born and raised with ubiquitous digital technologies, show that children overexposed to technologies might present with issues such as early myopia, obesity, sleep disorders, anxiety and depression, social and behavioural problems, attention-deficit/hyperactive disorders (ADHD), addiction to videogames, and the pervasive effects of early access to pornographic material (Dresp-Langley, 2020; Canadian Paediatric Society, 2017; Limone and Toto, 2021; D'Alberton and Scardovi, 2021). Joanna Fortune has written about increasing numbers of children being brought into treatment by their parents with "symptoms ranging from anxious withdrawal to aggressive acting out" (2017, p. 226). Most analysts also recognise that the current clinic presents clinical manifestations where the imaginary register appears to be losing its ability to hold the identification of the subject, resulting in the prominence of anxiety rather than inhibition or symptoms. The emerging clinics have been occurring since the epoque of Lacan's teaching, marked by a decline in the symbolic function of the Name-of-the-Father, and this has been named in different ways, such as Freud's actual neurosis (Verhaeghe, 2004, p. 290; Verhaeghe and Vanheule, 2005, p. 493), ordinary psychosis (Miller, 2008, p. 146), or through the symbolically challenged presentations of psychosomatic disorders and addictions. With the rise of the *lathouse*, the clinic has demonstrated that the universal imperative to *jouissance* is affected by the particularity of virtual acceleration. Such a situation renders an imaginary register increasingly disengaged from the symbolic order, a necessary register for an unconscious that can be analysed.

## How the *lathouse* intrudes in the linguistic exchanges of a speaking body

To discuss how linguistic exchanges occur in the virtual paradigm instantiated by dyad B, we first need to clarify what the *lathouse* is and how it works. The *lathouse* is, firstly, a material technological device with a screen; for example: smartphones, computers, laptops, or wrist watches, as well as all related social media and app-based activities. And, secondly, the *lathouse* is a spectral void that makes a semblance of object *a*, occupying a central space with regards to the three registers of human experience. Some analysands have expressed in the clinic how the digital world causes a particular immersion that prevents them from being aware of their surroundings, in stark contrast with other immersive activities such as reading a book, writing, or drawing on paper. Digital absorption can be understood as an effect of the *lathouses*, which are located, as Isabel Millar writes, "on the side of the drive and the body" (2021, p. 64). These technoscientific objects insert themselves through the imaginary register, the field of appearance, for later reconfiguring the real by absorbing the substance of enjoyment through the gadgets we use.

Elsewhere I have claimed that while *we enjoy* the *lathouse* object, engaging with the ever-increasing novelties of our gadgetry, the *lathouse* suctions out part of that enjoyment and transforms it into data that constitutes financial gains for the digital corporation (Fernandez-Alvarez, 2019, p. 94). These objects operate in the *alethosphere*, a Lacanian term inspired by Heidegger's *aletheia* to refer to a truth that unveils within a given space, and which Lacan illustrates through the example of the first astronauts, who survive a potential disaster by having a human voice as support (Lacan, 2007, p. 161). Such a virtual space could be thought of as what Clint Burnham coins as the "Internet's two bodies" (2018, p. 95), which include the virtual elements of software, platforms, or apps, as well as the materiality of hardware, cables, servers, operational installations behind the Cloud. To these two bodies of the

Internet, we must add the body of the subject whose consumption of physical and libidinal energy gives life to the *lathouse*.

Working on the specific paradigm of sexual satisfaction, the basic model for understanding the concept of *jouissance*, Lacan wonders if what one enjoys, itself enjoys? (1966–1967, 31.05.1967). We could ask the same question about the *lathouse*: does my screen, my gadget, my Iphone enjoy? The *lathouse*, qua semblance of object *a*, records the subject's fantasies, desires, and even their metabolism, while the subject constantly aims to find the object lost in the real via an undead repetition of human *jouissance*. *Jouissance* is a cornerstone concept of Lacanian psychoanalysis and at the same time is one of the more elusive notions. The particularity of digital enjoyment has been approached from various vantage points in Lacanian scholarship. Burnham assumes virtual enjoyment occurs through the transgression exercised via "spam mail, malicious memes, LOLcats, and trolls" (2018, p. 31); as a "passionate attachment to the gadget" (p. 47); and as the vicarious enjoyment of the fantasy, as, for example, when one types LMAO or ROFL (p. 49), calling these instances *lolangue* (p. 107). Matthew Flisfeder, focusing mostly on social media, claims that the virtual is constituted by a narcissistic and ideological enjoyment and that the subject must "occupy the terrain and start to use it for purposes of producing class consciousness" (2021, p. 65), a similar claim to that made by Alfie Bown (2017, p. 25). This particular question of enjoyment, however, is best tackled by Millar when she proposes a new paradigm of *jouissance*, the Sexbot, which refers to the *undead* body of the *lathouse* located "between the human and technology, between knowledge and enjoyment and between sex and death" (2021, p. 170). Millar argues that the *lathouse* leads to replication or asexual reproduction (p. 172), which she approaches from the perspective of the artificially-produced baby, the sex robot, or the artificial womb, at core aiming at an "extermination of all otherness, for which the feminine is the metaphor" (p. 173).

Beyond the serious phylogenetic concern of self-replication in the real, of significant political and ontological consequences for the human species, I want to rethink how the sameness and disregard of otherness, an implicit structure in our cyborgic use of the *lathouse*, affects the speaking subject. Because the *lathouse* inserts itself into the subject's experience as a semblance of object *a*, it has important effects on the knotting of the three rings (imaginary, symbolic, and real). I will discuss how the *lathouse* impacts each of these Lacanian registers with a focus on the body, the source of all *jouissance*. In psychoanalysis, the body can be read as a narrated sensual image (imaginary), as a logical rendition of a coded language (symbolic) and as a *sac of organs* or flesh shaped by the drive (real).

## The *lathouse* impoverishes the imaginary register

The imaginary field tends to be theoretically neglected because it is the house of the ego, the source of misrecognition and aggressive narcissism that hinders psychoanalytic discourse. Yet this register needs to be salvaged from the waste bin because the imaginary is essential in creating a body that sustains the embodied real life (IRL) and actualises social bonds. When Lacan explains the unary trait in Seminar XIX as a symbolically-embedded imaginary mark that supports identification, he recognises his own influence in the Manichean reception of his theory by saying: "It occurred to me that people said I used to make value judgements of the type – *imaginary*, poo, *symbolic*, yum-yum" (1971/2018, p. 147, original emphasis). Nothing of that indeed, because, as clarified by Lacan in Seminar XXI, the three registers of the real, symbolic, and imaginary are "three dimensions of the space inhabited by the speaking being (*le parlant*)" (Lacan, 1973, session 11.12.73). These spaces are in no way parallel to the Cartesian ones of width, height, and depth, but rather are *dit-mansions* or dwellings of language that are "strictly equivalent" (Lacan, session 18.12.73). It is such equivalence that provides the consistency or "volume" to the subject's experience through their knotting of the Borromean knot, which results in a certain fate for the subject.

Lacan then deems the Imaginary register to be as important as the others because this dimension constitutes the core of experience even if it relates to a specific form of "*vague enjoyment*" (13.11.1973) that is dominated by the *opsis*, which is appearance or resemblance. The imaginary register corresponds to the Kantian formal principle of aesthetic apprehension, where the subject intuitively and sensually apprehends time and space. Similar to Kant's proposal that empirical experience is grasped by reason only, the imaginary, for Lacan, becomes apprehensible only through its translation into the symbolic. This leads Lacan, in Seminar III, to establish the limits of analysability, a phenomenon whose condition is to represent something other than itself (1997, p. 15). Twenty years later, Lacan renders the imaginary as "always an intuition of what is to be symbolized ... something to chew on, to think" (1973, session 13.11.1973), and this is the reason why the imaginary has always come through the symbolic, which for its part "is always enciphered (*chiffré*)" (1973, session 13.11.1973).

Summing up: albeit an unstable register, the imaginary is fundamental to the granting of a body. By the mediation of the symbolic register, which permits the linguistic operations of meaning, metaphor, metonymy, etc., the flickering condition of the imaginary stabilises, which enables the subject to access processes such as identification, representation, naming, or meaning-making. That is why to engender a body or engage in a psychoanalytic question, the imaginary must be modulated by the symbolic order.

What is the status of the imaginary register in our two paradigms? Although infant observation, a requirement for classical psychoanalytic training, relies on meaning read by the observer, I aim to read these vignettes structurally: that is to say, by locating the places each participant occupies in a relational exchange. The embodied paradigm, illustrated through the interactions of baby A and their mother, is materialised through body-to-body interactions, indicating what Lacan called the "mutual voracity of the mother/child couple" (2006, p. 288), an essential precursor of the imaginary passion that will support future sexual love. Baby A explores the body of the mother as a sensual *object* with a commanding liberty, as if it was an extension of the child's own body (touching, pulling and pushing tissues, inserting fingers in the cavities of mouth and nose), more noticeably so when the mother leans towards the other kids; is baby A demanding the mother's attention only for themself? While dyad A gives us a text of the exchanges that appear to be occurring through their embodied interactions, dyad B presents a true enigma, because the text available to the observer is a mother-child dyad captured and reflected through screens, each engaged in their own absorption with little body-to-body interaction. What exchanges are effectuated between this child and the m(O)ther? Is their perception of the screen marked by the rhythm of the mother's soft caressing? Is the baby perhaps meditating on the representation of real space? Because an infant's thoughts are impossible to grasp, we can only speculate about the circulating objects in these paradigms. Some points of engagement are the mirror stage and the imaginary triangulation of mother-child-phallus, which Lacan speaks of as constitutive of the imaginary relations of a subject with their primordial others.

Both of the observed infants must be on the cusp of what Lacan called "the mirror stage," the process in which a child around the age of six to nine months reaches a "jubilant assumption of his specular image" (2006, p. 76) as a result of producing a constitutive gestalt of their own body, an illusory "'orthopedic' form of its totality" (p. 78), up until then of a fragmented nature, by reflecting such an image in actual and human mirrors. This novel discovery will disappear around 18 months of age when the little subject transitions towards identification by assuming their own body image via the introjection of the human form as other (Leader, 2021, p. 48). How are these infants mirroring themselves in their specific contexts? Although these two paradigms cannot be fully separated because the rise of *lathouses* affects most exchanges among speaking subjects, I will analyse the paradigms in a separate fashion.

The exchanges between baby A and their mother seem to be incited by the child's awareness of being observed. Is the child showing me the extension of their body, stating perhaps that they have a face, mouth, hair, and, yes, eyes to look back to me too? Lacan articulates the gaze as a scopic drive, which refers to an object of desire within the visible realm that jumps out from a certain radiant point in the environment to reflect an image in which the subject finds itself excluded or absent. Being seen is a form of subjective scotoma: "I see only from one point, but in my existence, I am looked at from all sides" (Lacan, 1964/1998, p. 72). The spectrality of the gaze is essential to the constitution of the ego and the body image, and in vignette B the human gaze is absent, which makes us wonder how early linguistic exchanges affect subjectivity via the technological gaze effectuated by the gadget. According to Kaye Cederman, early and repeated use of digital devices hinders the process of identification in young children and is detrimental to the ability for "deep attention" (2017, p. 258), which can cause various attention disorders. Fortune explains that the substitution of the human gaze by the lens of the smartphone leads children to fail in the assumption of the self-image as other, and consequently results in the effect of imaginary misrecognition. The Rimbaudian aphorism, retaken by Lacan, that reads the I as an Other, is not consolidated by the intrusion of the *lathouse* and instead "[t]he child subject becomes fixated on their own image/reflection … and is consumed with their own image" (Fortune, 2017, p. 229). This observation is of great importance because the *lathouse* might impede, in early childhood, the emergence of otherness in the incipient ego, which causes great confusion for the subject, as Miller states: "the world structured by the mirror stage is a world of transitivism. Transitivism means that you don't know if you did it or the other did it" (2008, p. 150). Hence there is bodily confusion with others.

Back to our vignettes. The infant is, in principle, an object for the mother because the little creature is profoundly connected to the mother's narcissism as an extension of the self and as a receptacle for the mother's language, which de facto manifests the signifiers and meanings passed on to her through her own lineage. Adding to the Freudian apparatus, Lacan emphasises that an imaginary third party is always involved in a mother-child relation, and the child's first object is the imaginary phallus or φ, a place the child imagines to be for the mother by turning "himself into the object for the other party" (Lacan, 2020, p. 6). That is why the mother as object, Lacan explains, is never a harmonious object but rather a lost object for which the subject is perpetually in a quest to find, until they indeed *re-find it* in reality via the *imaginary reciprocity* that allows an infant to identify with the third term that supports the dyad and contributes to creating the subject's identification as an object for the Other (2020, p. 19). Although the imaginary phallus is a privileged object it is simultaneously "a labyrinth in which the subject loses his way, and in which he can even wind up being devoured" (Lacan, 2020, p. 183).

The exchanges between mother and child as mutual objects, mediated by the imaginary phallus, are also affected by the fact that the mother possesses the privilege and curse of being the first incarnation of an Other for the child. The exchanges occurring in these vignettes are already linguistically coded through the signifiers that preceded the infants' lives and which determined how the mothers signify what occurs in the dyad and among others. And so, while the exchanges with the mother must occur to satisfy the material needs of nourishment, touch, etc., early interactions with the *lathouse* as an imaginary phallus might indeed reify small screens as an extension of the self and thus fabricate a materiality to such spectrality. For example, due to its absorbing quality, which extracts the physicality and tensions of body-to-body encounters, the screen might substitute for the mother's gaze, short-circuiting the imaginary register from the mother-child-phallus to the mother-child-*lathouse*. Consequently, is it possible that the *lathouse qua* imaginary phallus may obstruct the emergence of castration (−φ), defined by Lacan as a symbolic lack of an imaginary object? As indicated above, the *lathouse* is not only an imaginary element in the constitution of the subject, but it also partakes of the real due to the potential infinite repetition of its indestructible *undeadness* (Millar, 2021; Ivanchikova, 2021). If the *lathouse* is in the real, such location may prevent the creation of a real hole of privation, which is a necessary condition for actualising castration.

## Is the *lathouse* re-configuring *lalangue*?

Beyond the mirror stage, the *parlêtre*, in their upbringing, must learn symbolic ways to help discharge the tension of the insisting drive accumulated in the body. The subject bypasses the fragmented body through the image, but they must find a word to sustain symbolic access to the two Freudian principles: the pleasure principle, which creates somatic homeostasis, and the reality principle, which engenders a minimal somatic boundary, vital for sustaining subjectivity within the social milieu.

Through the Other's code – signifiers, silences, and residues of object *a*, such as gaze or touch – the subject is incarnated by the apparatus of representations that *being sensual is nonsensical*. This is what Lacan understands as *lalangue*, which I read mostly as a cadence of the Real, a babbling response to a lullaby, a language of love, perhaps of hate too, that elicits a certain bodily musicality acquired from "the somatic echoes of the said" (Lacan, session 18.11.1975). This psychosomatic partiture of flesh, letters and silences shows an insistence, or fixity as Miller has it (2008, p. 157), strongly linked to discursive forms that open the subject to *jouissance*. Lalangue is imprinted on our bodies early, and equally mortifies and vitalises the subject through the effects of unconscious language insisting on the subject's flesh.

Lacan renders *lalangue* as an invocatory drive due to the superegoic imperative that inheres this phenomenon, in which the subject is summoned to listen to what emerges from the life and death pulsations of their body of *jouissance*, leading the subject unto unrecognised desires written on their body. Even when *lalangue* cannot be thought of as developmental because it is not subjected to maturation or to any form of evolution, it is primordially nourished by early perceptions and the traumatic events that create the signifier-based enciphered code on the body, inaccessible to epistemological articulation even when the body carries an impossible truth that determines the enjoying ways of a subject. As Freud discovered early in his career, the subject's perceptions are stored and organised by a sensori-perceptual organism through various systems of signs that he conceptualised as the stratification of memory traces (1954, p. 173). Such imprints constitute a first topography or structural topic envisioned by Freud as the conscious/

preconscious/unconscious system. The imaginary register is the first organiser of the environmental impacts the infant faces through their senses, and hence forms the basic imprints of libidinal images that stay in the psychic and somatic apparatus, which provide the first building blocks with which the subject structures the disorganised soma from birth. *Lalangue* is then formed imaginarily by language but is not based on representation, and thus skips the signification constituted by one signifier (S1) representing the subject for another signifier (S2). This is the reason why *lalangue* does not have access to symbolically articulated knowledge, it only gives the possibility of accessing a *savoir-faire* or *know-how*.

*Lalangue*, as a libidinal form of non-sensical enjoyment that codes a signifier in a sensual form, seems to be increasingly mediated by the *lathouse*, as in vignette B. Is it possible to conjecture that *lalangue*, which is the basis of human *jouissance in* and *of* a speaking body, is becoming changed in its configuration as a result of the dominance of the *lathouse*? In my practice, I have encountered various subjective difficulties related to technological use, such as dissatisfying pornography consumption that prevents or hinders sexual activity in real life or the long-term isolating effects of trolling activities on social platforms, a way of fighting others in phantasmatic ways without the real effects of social assertion in their subjectivities. Also, it is common to hear about multiple difficulties with online dating, "so many apps and love nowhere to be found" or compulsive video gaming that obstructs everyday life. The *lathouse* also brings about uncertainties of navigating virtual relationships or digital sex or concerns about the unmanageable absorption of screen time. Some experience anxious dissatisfaction and narcissistic trapping by social media activity or impotence in forming social connections outside of virtual spaces. Lacan expressed disbelief of future domination by the *lathouse* because he argued that "we will not actually succeed in getting to a point where gadgets are not symptoms" (1974/2019, p. 108). Indeed, the *lathouse* is now our shared symptom in the social sense. How does this mechanism occur? The *lathouse* might affect *lalangue* in the following ways:

a   In the imaginary, the *lathouse* captures the body. Lacan reminds us that "the body enters the economy of *jouissance* through the image of the body" (2019, p. 96) and the recording of movement, rhythm, sound and aromas, tactile imprints and images, all sensual and linguistic codes forming the *lalangue*, are reconfigured by the mediation of the *lathouse*. The *lathouse* siphons the subject's sensori-perception and feeds them images of all sorts, videos, memes, or merchandise, impoverishing the imaginary register by extracting the subject's sensual body from their material environment (other humans, animals, nature, etc.).

b   In the symbolic, the *lathouse* supersedes the unconscious. While the signifiers that precede any child's lineage will continue shaping the *lalangue*, the intruding *lathouse* re-ciphers the code of *lalangue*. There is an important distinction to make, however, between the symbolic exchanges that occur within a social-relational context – for example, through Zoom meetings, virtual encounters with acquaintances, friends, or family, videogame playmates, etc. – from those that occur between the subject and the infinite multitude. In the relational context, it seems that symbolic exchanges might maintain their ability to represent the subject with a signifier for another signifier. When the subject relates to the infinite *lathouse*, a signifier is not so much at stake but is the *real* of the material gadget and is a vehicle for the *jouissance* of the Other, impossible to grasp symbolically. The senseless sensed that is shaped by the *lathouse* bypasses the signifier; for example, in vignette A, the m(O)ther leaves a symbolic mark through her discursive and somatic exchanges, while in dyad B the young child is left alone with autoerotic *jouissance*.

c  In the real, the *lathouse* enjoys the subject. The Lacanian aphorism that reads: "just as phallic jouissance is outside of the body, the jouissance of the Other is outside language, outside the symbolic" (Lacan,1974, p. 107) is of great importance in locating the incidence of the *lathouse*. The *jouissance* of the Other, when applied to the context of the posthuman, does not refer to the specific modality of feminine *jouissance*, the not-all, but to that which is outside of language and inside the body, as an analysand voices, in the "dark and alone" experience of the autoerotic senses. Lacan spoke of the difference between having a body and being a body (Miller, 2008, p. 156; Klainer, 2018, p. 8), the first modality implying that there is an imaginary identification, a body image, and a symbolic mediation via the Other, whereas the body as being cannot be regulated by the symbolic order, except with the help of a fourth ring to knot the three registers within what is known as the *sinthome*, a possibility for holding an imaginary consistency to sustain the *parlêtre* together (Klainer, 2018, p. 8; Gillespie, 2018, p. 167). We have known through the later theorisation of Lacan that language indeed enjoys us. The enjoyment coming from the real of the *lathouse* indicates to us a new colonisation of life: the *lathouse* enjoys us as a symbolically unhinged Other.

Because the three registers are affected by the *lathouse*, we could ask if the sexual non-relation is discursively mutating from a passionate embodied exchange to real or metaphoric masturbation on screens? To illustrate how the *lathouse* colonises life and *jouissance*, we can look at a study by D'Alberton and Scardovi, who discuss access to pornographic sites by minors as an increasingly widespread phenomenon: "children nowadays encounter an enormous quantity of images and information that exceeds their elaborative capacity" (2021, p. 135). These authors indicate that the intense sensorial stimulation of the virtual pornographic image, disengaged from symbolic elaboration, can lead to traumatic experiences and unforeseen effects. Theirs is another way of inquiring about the effects of the primal scene when displaced from familiar figures, the parents or caregivers of the flesh, to online images that bring about the proximity of a highly graphic depiction of sexual activity that might imprint a form of enjoyment. Like the young man in my practice whose pornographic consumption has erased any possible pleasure in real-life sex because, he says, his *partenaire* never looks "as hot" or "as daring" as the videos he watches. This example suggests a question that exceeds this chapter: if as Lacan indicated, "the sexual relation is lacking in all forms of society. It is linked to the truth that structures all discourse" (2019, p. 92), what are the consequences of disembodying the sexual non-relation, foundational to subjectivity? Let us turn now to how the social bond might be impacted.

## The *lathouse* disembodies the sensual experience of the subject, impacting social links

In Lacanian psychoanalysis, the study of physical and bodily components in the social is under-theorised, as it is seen as a matter of imaginary intersubjectivity that leads, once again, to misrecognition. The symbolic and the real have been the more developed theoretical fields within psychoanalysis, rightfully so, as they are the sites where most clinical interventions occur; however, with the so-called decline of the Name-of-the-Father, the order which sustains symbolic stability, alongside the rise of *lathouses*, thinking embodied intersubjectivity is crucial in understanding how the de-materialisation of social relationships affects social bonds.

The digital world offers the endless enjoyment of a multiplicity of virtual experiences. The epistemological, aesthetic, cultural, historical, and socio-political access to the virtual world appears infinite. The opportunity to gather solidarities and create virtual communities is indeed a fact due to digital anonymity, availability, and also affordability, as long as the *lathouse* works within a symbolic frame – when a subject is represented by a signifier for another signifier. That is why *lathouses* provide viable social bonding only for those who are *already* connected to the social because, as shown in the clinic, the addictions to videogames, pornography, or social media often indicate a lack of meaningful social bonding. Consequently, the real of the *lathouse, qua* mere enjoyment, seems to hinder social bonding, and if unmediated by the symbolic it leads to isolation and difficulties in navigating social reality.

Social bonding, as per the common signified of the signifier "bond" (gathering, link, relation), might erroneously suggest the necessity for a subject to belong de facto to a community or group. Social bonding is better understood by the term discourse, as a mechanism that establishes linguistic connections that allow a subject to knot the three registers of experience in such a way that permits them to count themself as one of value among others. In what way is the sensual body important to *naming the subject*?

Social bonding is equally nourished and simultaneously hindered by the sensual body; its absence causes a deleterious devitalisation of the subject's body, as occurs in social isolation, which subsumes the subject into toxic or deadly *jouissance*, a consequence of the fact that the sensual experience cannot but invest libido in their own body rather than in body-to-body exchanges. But human experiences with others can also hinder social bonding, as dyad A indicates: a push and pull from significant or beloved others is always ambivalent even if, as Stephanie Swales and Carol Owens state, "in our time ambivalence is increasingly foreclosed from the social bond, there is nowhere for the normal, natural antagonism that accompanies human relations to go" (2019, p. 4).

When analysands complain or are amazed by the different effects of their virtual experiences compared to socially embodied ones, they struggle to find a readily available answer. It seems that sensuality facilitates social bonding because the presence of other material bodies, human or nonhuman, mirrors enjoyment in a way that creates a sense of vitality, belonging, identity, or meaningfulness, whose epitome can be found in the experience of nature, the performative arts, or in the joyful celebration or *fiesta*. Yet sensual experience among others is not synonymous with social connection as it can also obstruct the social link, because the material presence of others can become unpleasant as a result of others' overproximity or the subject's inability to negotiate affects and emotions around other bodies, morphing the sensual experience among others into *jouissance*, which brings anguish to the subject's body.

Embodiment is a phenomenon of an imaginary and real nature but has access to analysis only through the symbolic order. The study of embodiment has been widely explored by other epistemologies and discourses, referring to how a subject obtains information via their body while around other material beings. For example, attachment theory explores the embodied conditions that create safety, security, and protection within the dyad of mother – or early care provider – and child (Benoit, 2004, p. 541). Attunement theories explore how early attachment is affected by how people "tune to" physical signs and subtle facial expressions to calm each other when distressed, and these regulate early responses to fear and danger (Van der Kolk, 2014, p. 112). The sociality of embodiment has been approached by Stephen Porges through the theory of the polyvagal nerve, which refers to stress-related human responses to others while in social engagement (2001, p. 185). Also, neuro-psychoanalysis studies mirroring mechanisms, mimetic functions, imitation, or simulation, mechanisms that support the embodiment of language (Weigel and Scharbert, 2016, p. 48) and shared interpersonal space. Generally speaking, those studies nuance the great importance of embodied intersubjective exchanges that are relevant to what Lacanian theorists would refer to as the study of the imaginary elements of the social knot or link. In the Lacanian theory of the Borromean knot, a subject can tie together the three registers of human experience – real, imaginary, and symbolic – with a fourth ring that is known as the signifier Name-of-the-Father (Lacan, session 21.01.75). These rings are equivalent and only their spatial position establishes a distinction, whether the rings are crossing over or undercrossing, providing distinct clinical values. The Freudian triad of anxiety, inhibition, and symptom (1926/1973, p. 88) is retaken by Lacan in Seminar XXII (1974–75), who correlates each register with clinical manifestations: anxiety is primordially real, inhibition is mainly imaginary, and the symptom is of a symbolic nature (Lacan, session 21.01.75). The inability to fasten the imaginary under the symbolic, as it occurs in inhibition or the symptom, leads to a knotting where anxiety becomes the primordial attempt at forging a social link. Anxiety is a precarious form of nomination, demonstrated by the clinic of addictions, anxiety, or ordinary psychosis, because it does not prevent the invasion of the real into the imaginary register. According to Miller, ordinary psychosis is characterised by a social, bodily, and subjective externality which shows a subject to be "unable to assume a social function" (2008, p. 155), who presents the non-dialectical fixity of a "void, emptiness, or vagueness" (p. 157) and who must "invent some artificial bond to re-appropriate his body, to tie his body to himself" (p. 156).

The ubiquitous mediation of the *lathouse* and its infinite undeadness hinders possibilities for connecting to the vital pleasures of the physical or material world. The human subject voluntarily submits their enjoyment into the *lathouses* with their proliferative surveillance, tracking, and commercialisation of the most intimate spaces we inhabit, thanks to the algorithms we feed daily in our digital trajectories. In the clinic, symbolic interventions with subjects with *lathouse*-related symptoms exert effects towards an embodied shift that, while not excluding the virtual, allows the subject to move from the dominant spaces of the *lathouse* to embodying themselves in their environment. Some might connect to the aroma and pleasure of a forest bath or a strenuous hike on the mountain; others might encounter dogs or cats, birds, rocks, or musical instruments; some others might write and read in or outside of the screen, which allows the subject to feel a calming vitalisation of the body and a sense of connection to the social – the world or environment – in a meaningful way. When embodiment among others occurs as a symbolic intervention of the analysis, the subject might reduce their psychosomatic symptoms, such as a lack of energy, the occurrence of illnesses, a sense of confusion, or a lack of worth caused by social isolation. These improvements could be understood as effects of the sublimation of *das Ding* or The Thing, a concept Lacan takes from Freud to delineate the primordial object to which we aspire, but if reached would lead us to the field of destruction (Lacan, 1992, p. 71). That is how the embodiment of the sensual body in pleasure, against the entropic mechanism of the enjoyment of the drive, contributes to the social link, as the sublimation of *das Ding* imparts vitality to the body by connecting to other bodies, these being others, human or non-human.

## Conclusion: Does the *lathouse* allow for the analytical act?

Soler states that psychoanalytic practice has always worked "in circumstances that were always adverse" (2014, p. 200), and the pandemic has been one instance of adversity. As Nestor Braunstein indicates, with the pandemic, psychoanalysis changed unwillingly as it was submitted to known concerns of the *lathouse*: tracking, surveillance, and data mining from the very practice itself (Braunstein, 2020, n.p).

From psychoanalysis, we learn that the unconscious is a force and that "it speaks;" speaking requires a body, and the analyst is certainly not concerned so much with the imaginary sensual body but with the body of *lalangue*. Although it is crucial to listen to the materiality of the speaking body, the physical body does not constitute a *sine qua non* condition for psychoanalysis to take place, for what is important is the function and presence of the analyst, and thus an analysis can be conducted remotely, as has become common practice during the pandemic. The function of the analyst is an effect of their listening position, encouraging the observance of free association, maintaining the *evenly suspended attention* to the analysand's free associative speech, and focusing on the materiality of the signifier. The presence of the analyst refers to how they actualise the contingencies of the real, and thus the analyst's presence is mostly what "destabilizes significations and incessantly provokes a restructuring of symbolic and imaginary material" (Cauwe, Vanheule and Desmett, 2017, p. 21).

Discussions in psychoanalytic fora indicate that most Lacanian psychoanalysts returned to work in person, with a certain hybrid flexibility. Some observations from my practice show that the *lathouse* tends to accentuate gaze and voice as semblances of object *a*, which is similar to what indeed occurs most often in embodied sessions. Other important considerations emerging in digital analysis relate to how the residue of the cybernetic traumatic (Pasquinelli, 2015, p. 7) is negotiated between the analyst and the analysand, for example, how losses constituted by glitches and technical difficulties are distributed to account for it. Finally, gauging the logical moment of the analysis and the singular circumstances of the symptom involved are crucial dimensions to determine if the *lathouse* hinders or supports analytic work, such as the difficulties of remote work in post-traumatic suffering, paranoia, etc.

In my practice, an analysand, knowledgeable about machine learning and AI, wonders if increasing automation might impact psychoanalysis and if the future could create a Siri-like analyst, an ominous idea in their view, but then adds that "Siri could not replicate the spontaneity and the desire of the analyst to listen." I have said that *lathouses* are on the side of the real and make a semblance of object *a*, and Lacan cautioned us that "[t]he future of psychoanalysis depends on what becomes of the real" (Lacan, 1974/2019, p. 108). If that is true, the analyst must assume their role with regards to the *lathouse*, taking into consideration the crucial dimensions of the universality of language, the particularity of the virtual paradigm, and the singularity of the subject's speech to establish the viability of analysis via the *lathouse*.

## References

Benoit, D. (2004, October). Infant-parent attachment: Definition, types, antecedents, measurement and outcome. *Paediatrics & Child Health*, 9(8), pp. 541–545. doi:10.1093/pch/9.8.541.

Bown, A. (2017). *The playstation dreamworld*. Cambridge: Polity Press.

Braunstein, N. (2020). Tampoco el psicoanálisis volverá a ser lo que era. Personal blog, 20 September. Available at: http://nestorbraunstein.com/?p=687.

Burnham, C. (2018). *Does the internet have an unconscious? Slavoj Žižek and digital culture*. New York and London: Bloomsbury.

Canadian Paediatric Society. (2017). Screen time and young children: Promoting health and development in a digital world [Position statement]. *Paediatric & Child Health*, 22(8), pp. 461–468.

Cauwe, J., Vanheule, S., and Desmet, M. (2017). The presence of the analyst in Lacanian treatment. *Journal of the American Psychoanalytic Association*, 65(4), pp. 609–638. doi:10.1177/0003065117721163.

Cederman, K. (2017). Left to their own devices? Child analysis and the psycho-technologies of consumer capitalism. In C. Owens and S. F. Quinn (Eds.), *Lacanian psychoanalysis with babies, children, and adolescents. Further notes on the child*, pp. 251–264. London: Karnac.

D'Alberton, F. and Scardovi, A. (2021). Children exposed to pornographic images on the Internet: General and specific aspects in a psychoanalytic perspective. *The Psychoanalytic Study of the Child*, 74(1), pp. 131–144. doi:10.1080/00797308.2020.1859277.

Dresp-Langley, B. (2020). Children's health in the digital age. *International Journal of Environmental Research and Public Health*, 17(9), 3240. doi:10.3390/ijerph17093240.

Fernandez-Alvarez, H. (2019). Will a cyborg steal my jouissance? Unconscious labour and the enjoying body of the virtual. *Lacunae APPI International Journal for Lacanian Psychoanalysis*, 18, pp. 94–118.

Flieger, J.A. (2010). Is there a doctor in the house? Psychoanalysis and the discourse of the posthuman. *Paragraph*, 33(3), pp. 354–375. doi:10.3366/E0264833410000957.

Flisfeder, M. (2021). *Algorithmic desire: Toward a new structuralist theory of social media*. Evanston, Il: Northwestern University Press

Fortune, J. (2017). The "iMirror Stage": Not-so-smartphones and the pre-schooler—some clinical observations. In C. Owens and S.F. Quinn (Eds.), *Lacanian psychoanalysis with babies, children, and adolescents. Further notes on the child*, pp. 225–234. London: Karnac.

Freud, S. (1926/1973). Inhibition, symptom and anxiety. In J. T. Strachey (Ed.), *The standard edition of the complete psychological works of Sigmund Freud: Vol XX*. London: Hogarth Press.

Freud, S. (1954). Letter 52 (M. Bonaparte, A. Freud, and E. Kris, Trans.). In E. Mosbacher and J. Strachey (Eds.), *The origins of psychoanalysis: Letters to Wilhelm Fliess, drafts and notes: 1887–1902*, pp. 173–181. New York: Basic Books.

Gillespie, N. (2018) Posthuman desire: The one-all-alone in *Her, Ex Machina*, and *Lars and the Real Girl*. In S. Matviyenko and J. Roof (Eds.), *Lacan and the posthuman*, pp. 153–169. London: Palgrave.

Ivanchikova, A. (2021). The fantasy of technoimmortality and the psychoanalytic Infinite. *The Comparatist*, 45, pp. 64–89.

Klainer, E. (2018). Having a body: Some clinical consequences of Lacan's late teaching. *Lapso*, 3, August.
Lacan, J. (1955–56/1997). *The seminar of Jacques Lacan: Book III: The psychoses* (Ed. J. A. Miller; Trans. R. Grigg). New York: W.W. Norton.
Lacan, J. (1956–57/2020). *The seminar of Jacques Lacan: Book IV: The object relation* (Ed. J. A. Miller; Trans. A. R. Price). Cambridge: Polity Press.
Lacan, J. (1959–60/1992). *The seminar of Jacques Lacan: Book VII: The ethics of psychoanalysis* (Ed. J. A. Miller; Trans. D. Porter). New York: W.W. Norton.
Lacan, J. (1964/1998). *The seminar of Jacques Lacan: Book XI: The four fundamental concepts of psychoanalysis* (Ed. J. A. Miller; Trans. A. Sheridan). New York: W.W. Norton.
Lacan, J. (1966–1967). *The seminar of Jacques Lacan: Book XIV: The logic of phantasy* (Trans. C. Gallagher). http://www.lacaninireland.com/web/wp-content/uploads/2010/06/14-Logic-of-Phantasy-Complete.pdf.
Lacan, J. (1969–70/2007). *The seminar of Jacques Lacan: Book XVII: The other side of psychoanalysis* (Trans. R. Grigg). New York: W.W. Norton.
Lacan, J. (1971–72/2018). *The seminar of Jacques Lacan: Book XIX: … or worse* (Ed. J. A. Miller; Trans. A. R. Price). New York: W.W. Norton.
Lacan, J. (1973–74). *The seminar of Jacques Lacan: Book XXI: Les non-dupes errent* [Part 1] (Trans. C. Gallagher). Available at: http://www.lacaninireland.com/web/wp-content/uploads/2010/06/Book-21-Les-Non-Dupes-Errent-Part-1.pdf.
Lacan, J. (1974–1975) *The seminar of Jacques Lacan: Book XXII: RSI* (Trans. C. Gallagher). Available at: http://www.lacaninireland.com/web/wp-content/uploads/2010/06/RSI-Complete-With-Diagrams.pdf.
Lacan, J. (1974/2019). The Third. *The Lacanian Review*, Spring Issue 7.
Lacan, J. (2006). *Écrits: The First Complete Edition in English* (Trans. B. Fink). New York: W. W. Norton & Company.
Leader, D. (2021). *Jouissance: Sexuality, suffering and satisfaction*. Cambridge: Polity Press.
Limone, P. and Toto, G.A. (2021). Psychological and emotional effects of digital technology on children in COVID-19 pandemic. *Brain Sciences*, 11(9), p. 1126. doi:10.3390/brainsci11091126.
Matviyenko, S. and Roof, J. (2018). Introduction. In S. Matviyenko and J. Roof (Eds.), *Lacan and the posthuman*, pp. 1–13. London: Palgrave.
Millar, I. (2021). *The psychoanalysis of artificial intelligence*. London: Palgrave.
Miller, J.A. (2005). A Fantasy. *Lacanian Praxis: International Quarterly of Applied Psychoanalysis*, 1, pp. 5–16.
Miller, J.A. (2008). Ordinary psychosis revisited. *Psychoanalytical Notebooks*, 19, pp. 139–167.
Pasquinelli, M. (Ed). (2015). Introduction. In *Alleys of your mind: Augmented intelligence and its traumas*, pp. 7–18. Lüneburg: Meson Press.
Porges, S. (2001). The polyvagal theory: Phylogenetic substrates of a social nervous system. *International Journal of Psychophysiology*, 42(2), pp. 123–146.
Prensky, M. (2001). Digital natives, digital immigrants part 1. *On the Horizon*, 9(5), pp. 1–6. doi:10.1108/10748120110424816.
Soler, C. (2014). *Lacan: The unconscious reinvented*. London: Karnac.
Swales, S., and Owens, C. (2019). *Psychoanalysing ambivalence with Freud and Lacan: On and off the couch* (1st ed.). Oxford: Routledge. doi:10.4324/9780429448652.

Van Der Kolk, B. (2014). *The body keeps the score: Brain, mind, and body in the healing of trauma*. London: Penguin.
Verhaeghe, P. (2004). *On being normal and other disorders: A manual for clinical psychodiagnostics* (Trans. S. Jottkandt). London: Karnac.
Verhaeghe, P. and Vanheule, S. (2005). Actual neurosis and PTSD: The impact of the Other. *Psychoanalytic Psychology*, 22(4), pp. 493–507.
Weigel, S. and Scharbert, G. (Eds) (2016). *A neuro-psychoanalytical dialogue for bridging Freud and the neurosciences*. Berlin: Springer. doi:10.1007/978-3-319-17605-5.

Chapter 9

# Lacan on the "Telly"

Psychoanalysis on the Small Screen

*Carol Owens and Eve Watson*

*Our chapter here is comprised of the material of the actual paper that we delivered at the Irish Psychoanalytic Film Festival event in 2021 with a subsequent expansion of some of our original ideas. The paper we presented was the outcome in fact of a number of conversations we had at the time. Typically, we found ourselves having a two-layered conversation: the first, taking our lead from the theme of the 2021 Film Festival event, thinking and talking about the shift from big to small screen(s), considering in fact the big and then the small screen representations of psychoanalysis; the second, a wormhole of the first layer, the whole business of psychoanalysis – not merely represented on multiple screens – but in fact conducted on (the) small one(s). We worried about the buffoonery in representations of psychoanalysis on the screen and then we wondered if such buffoonery managed to slide into the actual work of psychoanalysis via the screen. In part, this slippage from one screening of psychoanalysis to the other – that is, not the shift (of the current volume's title) from large to small but rather from the screen which relies upon a spectator to the screen which relies upon an analysand – derives from our deliberate misreading of the title of Lacan's book which contains the transcript of his Television lecture (from 1973), but also a paper entitled "A Challenge to the Psychoanalytic Establishment." Misread thus, we playfully rendered our own talk and thoughts as "Television: A Challenge to the Psychoanalytic Establishment" rather than, "Television," and "A Challenge to the P E". (Well, we thought it was funny.) Since the paper began as a series of conversations, we attempted to represent that in our paper by preserving the style of a conversation, albeit, a conversation performed for the event. Somewhat expanded upon now, we have preferred to maintain what follows in the style of a dialogue.*

Carol Owens (CO): There are two interconnected motifs that we are interested in teasing out in our conversation today, but the title for our presentation is a bit more than a double entendre. On the one hand, it is an opportunity for us to explore some of the challenges that have attended the screenings of psychoanalysis as a highly unusual practice, governed by a theoretical orientation and operating in its conceptual fundaments unlike any

DOI: 10.4324/9781003272069-10

other human encounter, and on the other hand, it allows us to say something about the practice of doing psychoanalysis mediated by a screen. It is all about the screen in other words; why psychoanalysis resists or escapes representation on screen in certain fundamental ways, and then, how nowadays the screen in various shapes and sizes, mostly small, has mediated psychoanalytic work. The two screen aspects are related, we think, interrelated; since the portrayal of psychoanalysis on screen somehow always misses the mark, or produces absurdities. Perhaps indeed, the move to working psychoanalytically with screens rehearses what we find to be an anxiety conditioned more by what is screened in terms of *what is included* rather than screened in terms *of excluded or censored*.

Eve Watson (EW): Yes, indeed, we can be thinking psychoanalysis on screen, as a screen, and not a screen! We agree, the portrayal of psychoanalysts on screen is abysmal. On television, from *Frasier* to *In Treatment*, and in films such as *Spellbound* (1945), *Shrink* (2010), and *A Dangerous Method* (2011) psychoanalysts have been made to look absurd, unprofessional; they exude neurosis, buffoonery and downright quackary. So the scene has not exactly been well set for the actual movement of psychoanalysts to working on the small screen of computers, phones, and laptops during the ongoing pandemic. I would venture to guess that some analysts may well have carried this denigrating stigma with them in moving to working in the frame of the small screen, what Dany Nobus called "computer-mediated analysis" (CMA) during a Freud Lacan institute webinar in May 2020 that explored changes in psychoanalytic work during the pandemic. It's not easy to lay aside decades of negative stereotyping. Another factor playing into the denigration of psychoanalysis often playing out on screen is the fact that psychoanalysis offends against well-guarded sensibilities, moral and rational, by posing infantile sexuality and the unconscious, which Freud correctly predicted would contribute to its cultural deprecation (1916 [1915], p. 21). Freud reflected the position of psychoanalysis would be challenged by all of the resistances the psyche could muster "...the whole trend of your previous education and all your habits of thought are inevitably bound to make you into opponents of psychoanalysis" (1916 [1915], p. 15). The cultural transference to psychoanalysis is broadly negative with even some insiders taking up a cause against it (Masson 1991, Schneiderman 2014). Lacan did not help the case of psychoanalysis on screen by calling his viewers idiots during his Television presentation! (1973, p. 3).

CO: When we began to talk about these ideas, in fact we followed a trail of this buffoonery and the idea of what is representable and what is not representable of psychoanalysis first on the big screen, then on the smaller one, i.e., the television. From there we started to reflect that something of what is not representable of the work finds its way into what intrudes into the work with small screens. We conjectured that CMA and the shift to working on small screens foregrounds Lacan's assertion that psychoanalysis is nothing more than an artifice. If psychoanalysis is an artifice, a trick, a cunning deception, then it is not merely a trick of the eye, although the notion of gaze, specifically the Lacanian gaze, is what seems to be at the heart of the failures of psychoanalysis to be convincingly represented first on the big screen and later on the small screen. Cinema and TV catch/trap the spectator through the use of images, while the relation of psychoanalysis to images is that it relates them to the signifying chain. This begs the inevitable question: What characteristics must a psychoanalytic film have if psychoanalysis constantly resists representation? This was first of all a question for Sigmund Freud when Karl Abraham approached him with the exciting prospect of making a movie about psychoanalysis back in 1925 (Abraham, 7 June 1925; Abraham and Freud 1965). A heated and quite sad exchange of opposing views is detailed in the letters between Freud and Abraham about the production of the film that was called *Secrets of a Soul,* especially poignant since Abraham's last letter from Freud before his death in January 1926 is still occupied with their disagreement about what they referred to as the "film affair". From the very beginning and despite Abraham's cautious interest in it, Freud had no enthusiasm for any involvement with it, arguing that: "I do not believe that satisfactory representations of our psychoanalytic abstractions is at all possible" (Freud, 9 June 1925). This strong position of Freud's – about what is and is not representable of psychoanalysis – seems to have been a pivotal theme of discussion between Abraham and Sachs, with Abraham following up in his letter to Freud of 18 July 1925 that Sachs and he believed that they had every guarantee that the film would be completed in a thoroughly serious manner and that above all, that they had succeeded in making the most abstract matters "representable". Now while it may be true, and as Glover and Lowenstein both apparently suggested, Freud's reservations about making the film were perhaps the result of his lack of awareness about what film technique could achieve, it is also interesting however to consider that Freud was spooked in another way. What if Freud's own *secret of the soul* was really a worry, perhaps unconscious, that the non-representability of psychoanalysis might reveal or expose the absence of the psychoanalytic signified; not, in other words, some function of cinema's failure to adequately signify the practice of psychoanalysis. The horror then was the risk that what does not have meaning capturable on screen might end up being judged to be meaningless off screen. Here we can be reminded of Lacan's notion in relation to the concept of gaze that the veil of representation conceals nothing other than beyond the visual field there is nothing at all. This idea is made use of in much film theory and according to Shoshanna Felman is at work in Lacan's parodic self-presentation in his own TV appearance (Felman 1988). He shouts and prances like a showman on a stage, and pronounces at the start that there's no difference between the television and the audience of his seminar: there being what he calls but "a single gaze" (Felman 1988, p. 100).

For Lacan on the telly, there is not so much the question of what cannot of psychoanalysis be represented in the visual field but rather that of what cannot be fully said, "saying the whole truth is materially impossible: words miss it" (Lacan 1973, p. 3). But for Lacan this impossibility isn't a deal breaker, nor is it due to some incapacity of his own that words fail him; rather it is that through this very impossibility the truth holds onto the real.

EW: ...And so perhaps another reason for the denigrating representation of analysts on the screen is the eternal problem of representing what an analysis actually is and how a case proceeds. It can only be half-said, a case study is an impossibility of representation. As Parker, notes, an analysis is a place where the truth is said but it is quickly covered over again; an analysis is framed by a dialectic of deconstruction, construction and reconstruction and an interplay between rationality and irrationality (Parker 2018, pp. 14–16). How can this be re-produced? Think of how the substantial and significant realisations and epiphanies in an analysis occur in the most banal of ways, in moments that in the telling can perhaps only be parodied. Real effect or *tuchic* encounter cannot be reproduced as to tell it returns it to the automaton of the signifying system and it is lost, swallowed up in its everydayness. In our preliminary discussions, we thought of the Freud Museum London's videos which we think present this problem built in, brilliantly. The video, for example, "Is Psychoanalysis Weird?" makes no effort to "de-weird" psychoanalysis (Freud Museum London 2015). In fact, the video asserts its weirdness, with speakers describing psychoanalysis as weird because it addresses human nature and "stuff that goes on outside of the daylight, it's a night-time activity, it's dreams, it's sexuality, and so on". With strange, creepy, disturbing sound effects, distorted images, and shaky screens, stilted, clipped video and disturbing images, the video cleverly presents psychoanalysis as a parody of its own oddball or fringe status and in doing so derails parodic reactions in the viewer by simply putting its parodic status to work. In the video, the London-based psychoanalyst, Astrid Gessert, relates a little clinical vignette about a red rose and the power of its telling is, in fact, its banality, its ordinariness in how the analyst invited the analysand to associate to her use of the words "red rose" and this led to an association and a repressed memory. She concludes with stating, "it's just like that, that's how psychoanalysis works". No magic, no hypnosis, no crazy talk by the analyst, just the work of free association to the "red rose" led the analysand to the lifting of a repression. And the viewer is left with the sense of the vignette being only half-told, which it can only ever be. A Hollywood blockbuster (when writing this I actually typed "blockbluster"!) this will never be, but this video has proven to be successful with new viewers and is popular.

CO: In fact, the Freud Museum London videos take Lacan's performance on the Telly further than he did! He was *very weird*. He was *very strange*...to answer the questions the Freud Museum's first video asks. Perhaps then we can think of Lacan's performance on the telly as a sort of satirical comedy aimed at setting a trap for the spectator's gaze, not the trap of representation but rather, the trap that is not so different to what happens in psychoanalysis in the process of the transference. And, that, at the end of the day, is perhaps the most radically unrepresentable aspect of the work of psychoanalysis, while at the same time, what is fundamental to it. When we started to reflect on how the troubles of representability of psychoanalysis have leaked into the practice of computer mediated analysis – CMA – the phrase coined by Dany Nobus, we playfully borrowed the other title of Lacan's book *Television: A Challenge to the Psychoanalytic Establishment*, in order to ask, well, how big then a challenge is television or other small screenings to psychoanalysis. Is this way of working in our era of supreme dominance of the image a problem for psychoanalysis?

From early on in the pandemic, various psychoanalytic events and fora have met on Zoom to facilitate analysts and psychoanalytic therapists to talk about their changing practices, and how they have been managing them working as they are on various devices, apps, and so on. And from the beginning it was clear that the practice of working with clients on the phone or other device was haunted by older debates about what constitutes psychoanalysis as a practice, whether a conversation between the one who calls herself an analyst and the one who attends the analyst for what is called a psychoanalytic session, can in fact take place anywhere except in one room. But now, in 2021 (at the time of preparing this paper for the Film Festival event), more than a year later, we know that for the majority of practitioners, the work has taken place outside that one room, even though the work itself seems very different at times, and poses new challenges, and new technical issues. The move to computer-mediated analysis has been challenging because it has meant breaking with not just the practice of almost a century of tradition of two people sharing a room and space, but the disturbance of the representation of the practice of two-bodies in that space. The challenge introduced to the work mediated by screens is how the screen itself interlopes as a certain kind of object. As a lens, it reflects both analyst and analysand in the same frame; and as a screening of the work it disturbs the representation of the work that both analyst and analysand have internalised. But there are other challenges too.

EW: Dany Nobus, in his discussion of CMA (May 2020), referenced analysts' experience of working with computer-mediated technology and noted the significance of the sound and image falling away due to problems of technology, broadband connection or the phone line, specifying the anxiety it produces in the analysand. We need to remember that anxiety is for the psychoanalyst "a crucial term of reference, because in effect anxiety is that which does not deceive" (Lacan 1964, p. 41). The anxiety at stake brings us to the gaze and the territory of the stain where the real looks on, in addition to the object-voice, which is the aural *object* a in the voice as a haunting "nothing" made manifest. The tinny voice, the crackling line, and the freezing of the screen are haunting reminders of the gaze and voice as *objects a*. When the screen freezes, it's as if the screen in that moment is looking at the viewer and not the other way around. It is a strange instantiation of lack made momentarily manifest – the screen as a looking Other – and the subject is disturbed from their position. Sometimes a reflection can appear on the screen in which the viewer sees themselves seeing themselves, a moment in which a consciousness of looking is revealed. This is a disturbance of reflexive consciousness and opens out to an Other that is looking, a dimension of the gaze beyond the screen-image.

Lacan himself noted cultural, scientific, and media changes back in 1964 that he did not think would preclude the gaze or voice:

> Perhaps the features that appear in our time so strikingly in the form of what can more or less be correctly called the mass media, perhaps our very relation to the science that ever increasingly invades our field, perhaps all of this is illuminated by the reference to those two objects, whose place I have indicated for you in a fundamental tetrad, namely, the voice – partly planeterized, even stratospherized, by our machinery – and the gaze, whose ever-encroaching character is no less suggestive, for, by so many spectacles, so many phantasies, it is not so much our vision that is solicited, as our gaze that is aroused.
>
> (1964, p. 274)

Remote work during the pandemic worked because analysts figured it out and made it work although, it has to be said, not without their own anxiety as well as trepidation and downright worry. This raises the question: is psychoanalysis mediated by the small screen a virtual version of the real thing? This answer is no if we bear in mind that reality is structured by the ego and it is the unconscious structuring of the subject that permits the ego "its apparently natural relationship to an already-out-there real world" (Gallagher 1994). It would therefore be more accurate to say the virtual session is a version of relating to the world that is already virtual. Dreams, terrors, phantasies, inspired by the pandemic but not necessarily about the pandemic become vehicles of the object a as both loss and presence. In this, the split between the eye and the gaze is made manifest. Let's consider this more closely.

In "The Line and the Light" chapter in *The Four Fundamental Concepts*, Lacan highlights the importance of the screen in refracting both reality and the real. The screen operates as a kind of defence against the real by forming a shield against it, and at the same time, reality is the reflection of a scene, as Lacan put it, a picture that has already been painted (1964, p. 96), in effect a reproduction of an impression already made and only an obscure trace remains. This trace is the gaze and just as the screen can obscure the gaze, it can also appear and address the subject. This usually happens by surprise, as a startling and sometimes disturbing *tuche*. This is well represented in the famous mirror scene from the Marx Brother's film, *Duck Soup* (1933), in which Groucho suspects his mirror image is "off" doesn't properly correspond and he tries to catch out the alter ego, in a kind of frantic mimicry, and eventually succeeds. The audience laughs at the moments the alter ego doesn't match, a hilarity that corresponds to anxiety as more typically, the image that looks back or fails to mirror is the stuff of nightmares because it means identification with the image which coheres and sustains the subject's ego has fallen away. The subject is momentarily left stranded without a symbolically-mediated-image as support against impingements of the real and this can more seriously take the form of hallucination, delusion, and the collapse of the self into an exteriorised vituperative field of others. It is notable that this mirror scene in the film ends with the arrival of a second alter ego and combative chaos descends, a dominion of imaginary battles ensues. Thus, working with a small "screen" can augment defences against impingements of the real and whether this takes on a necessary or contingent function is structural. In psychosis, the screen may take on a more fundamental imaginary support while in neurosis the screen can support a glimpse of the Other's look without necessarily fragmenting the subject.

The screen is the analytic frame, and a session, including a computer-mediated one, works to the extent that it establishes and maintains the analytic frame. The analytic frame, again, does not privilege the visual field but seeks ways to support speech that escapes capture by egoic notions of being seen and heard, often demanded at once. That is why the couch is important as it downplays the structuring and imaginary function of the visual with its "geometrical perspective," as Lacan (1964) called it. When the ordinary specular and aural fields, in other words, what we typically see and hear, which simultaneously conceal and proffer an opening to an encounter with the gaze and the voice as *objects a*, are downplayed, this can inspire as much as it can silence. These drive objects are "real" properties of being; we are spoken and looked into existence and these phenomenological fundamentals elude capture by what is typically "seen" and "heard". Rather, they emerge in instances of not-seeing and not-hearing, or in hearing and seeing something strange, unexpected, and inexplicable. The frozen screen, for example, can suddenly render an unrecognised trait in the subject, or the strange tinny voice can elicit a sense of "call" or superegoic demand the subject was unaware of.

Lacan helpfully reminds us that the psychoanalytic discourse is as artificial as any other discourse (1973, p. 37) and if we pause to consider some of Freud and Lacan's methods, they were indeed masters of adaptability, from Freud's "constructions in analysis" to Lacan's famous five-minute sessions near the end of his life.

The effects of the pandemic have led to a renewal of interest in and consideration of technique and the direction of the treatment and this has led to some important work and interrogation of what a psychoanalytic practice is in the twenty-first century. I think these computer- and technologically-mediated ways of working have had the effect not only of refining and honing the analyst's listening but also encouraging the analysand to speak about how they are seen by others because it is an immediate concern. Questions such as "can you see me?", "how is the screen?", "how do I sound?", while initially posed as supposedly technological issues, echo with ego-ideal, ideal ego, and sometimes the superego. For some analysands, however, moving to "remote" analysis and the loss of the clinic room and the traditional two-body-presence in analytic work was too much to bear and a loss too many: a "presence" of mind is a necessity for them. They waited to return to the clinic room and practiced a silent living as a response to the passivity of being subjected to the pandemic's trauma. In effect, free association for some does not respond to being called forth through a small screen. For others, working from distance is not a problem and this has to do with the status of scopic and invocatory drives for them and how those drives interact with their structural organisation.

CO: This whole business of speaking at a distance, and whether that speech is somehow less authentic, less "real" than a virtual conversation has pervaded the experiences – long preceding any pandemic – of the ways human beings stay in touch with each other when they cannot meet. So in some ways, our focus on what happens to psychoanalysis – outside of the traditional frame, as a specific kind of conversation – could be thought of as a kind of sub-set of all the kinds of conversations people have with one another when they are not actually together in the same room. Considering what makes psychoanalysis different and how it becomes challenged when it is conducted over the phone, or on a screen, is in some ways to rehearse an old trope common among psychoanalysts for a good number of years. I'm not interested in bringing up these old arguments about "phone analysis," but we do need to reflect that for some analysts discussions about the operations of the drives, as well as thoughts about the presence/absence of the analyst in the room in remote work practices are a bit old hat. (Though I have to admit to smiling to myself when I heard how well those practitioners who had forever condemned that practice of remote work as "not psychoanalysis" had nonetheless adapted their clinical practices to the requirements of the pandemic quite niftily!). Bruce Fink's essay on phone analysis was published way back in 2007 and in many ways can almost be read as a guide for pandemic practitioners covering as he does the standard objections that might arise but also some very practical as well as theoretical aspects to working on the phone. This quote from that work seems particularly apropos for our times: "Virtually every analyst is led, at one point or another, to talk at some length with an analysand by phone, whether due to an emergency hospitalization, panic attack, deep depression, or *some other unexpected, unusual situation*" (2007, p. 204, my emphasis)! Fink's discussions are limited to the phone of course and naturally he quotes Freud from his "Recommendations to Physicians Practicing psycho-analysis", on what is required of an analyst: He must adjust himself to the patient as a telephone receiver to a transmitting microphone (2007, p.

191). But what Fink omits from the beginning of the quote is just as telling. Freud actually says: "he must turn his own unconscious like a receptive organ towards the transmitting unconscious of the patient" (Freud 1912b, p. 115). In other words, it's all about the listening. This is a point that Lacan emphasises many years later in his *Direction of the Treatment* paper: "it may be objected that the analyst nevertheless gives his presence, but I believe that his presence is implied simply by his listening, and that this listening is simply the condition of speech" (Lacan 1958, p. 516). In other words, it's all about the speech. Still though, probably Freud could not have imagined that the telephone metaphor would become a method; no more in fact that Lacan could have imagined the inclusion in the analyst's and analysand's visual field of their own image on a screen.

EW: But psychoanalysts don't work with the specular field in an analysis even when there is a screen like a phone or computer except to eliminate it as a point of analytic focus. Can the presence of a screen impede a focus on unconscious formations and the dialectic of free association? The virtual screen can materialise an already existing screen, the imaginary-symbolic field which "frames" the real and has unconscious effects. This can inhibit the speaking-subject just as much as it can support the transference to the Other. Let's take a scene from *The Sopranos* (2007) to consider this.

This is a scene in which Tony, the main protagonist, speaks to his therapist, Dr. Melfi, about his son. The scene begins with Tony staring at a statue of a naked woman in the waiting room. The statue's symbolism, on one level, seems to indicate "woman-trouble" and Tony's phallicism as sexual appetite which inflects his sessions with Dr. Melfi. Troublingly, as he sits there, it is as if the statue for an instant looks at him. We are left to conclude there is more going on than meets the eye and in fact, the look does presage the appearance of new material in the session. While it is not a statue that comes anywhere close to Bernini's ecstatic St. Teresa, it does evoke something of an Other non-phallic *jouissance* (*The Sopranos* 2007). Having planned to leave his therapy that day, Tony goes on to speak of his frustration and terror that his son might commit suicide as a result of his devastation at breaking-up with his girlfriend. Tony concludes that he has given his son his own miserable genes and frames his despondency as a terrified plea, "Is this all there is?" What can't be concealed in this moment is his sense of failure as a father and his helplessness and anxiety. His "failure" looks at him and the statue's "look" can be reconsidered as one that saw right through his tough guy and womanising veneer to a nothing, a "stain" of failure that screws with his self-identity. The silent statue also evokes the object-voice, a voice without a bearer, a pervasive but absent sonority that threatened to call him to the place of the dead, as his son, where nothing "is". The threat latent in this scene subversively lurks everywhere for, as a mobster, Tony lives under the constant threat of assassination and death. The final scene of the entire series, as those who have seen it will know, brings this threat to this logical conclusion.

In "Television," Lacan denounces psychologists, psychotherapists, psychiatrists, and all the mental health workers whom he describes as "psycho-so-and-sos" in their servility to dominant do-good discourses and worse, capitalistic discourse. He offers psychoanalysis as that which is oriented to the unconscious which ex-ists and the objects a (1973, pp. 13–14). The psychoanalyst instead "acts as trash," as a kind of "refuse of *jouissance*" (p. 16) in order to temporarily serve as cause of the subject's own desire. This he addresses to the "few ears glued to this TV" (p. 15). This mixed metaphor gives pause for thought about the screen and is a reminder of the intersection of the gaze and voice at work in subjective desire and in the organisation of *jouissance*. The screen, as analytic frame, can facilitate the experience of the nullity of reality and the dissolution of fixed meanings and an encounter with the objects around which desire and *jouissance* circulate. Or it can provide a protective cover against them. All that requires is sometimes switching on the mute button and switching off the video.

CO: …. And this, what you are calling a "protective cover" can work both ways, indeed this "switching off" actually calls to my mind the reason why Freud put patients on the couch back in the day – as he put it quite bluntly: "I cannot put up with being stared at by other people for eight hours a day (or more)" (Freud 1913c, p. 134). Freud, then, also surmised that he was not alone in feeling that discomfort. Honestly, I admit that I also have invited the occasional patient to take to the couch for that very reason; something in the intensity of that encounter felt necessary to interrupt, and reminds me how the eye functions both as the mediator of the gaze and as potential screen. Notwithstanding Freud's insistence that breaking the gaze, interrupting the stare, also had an effect on the way that the patient went on to speak, and in particular to "isolate the transference" (ibid.), the functions of "keeping the screen on", *keeping the eyes open,* was brought home in another unexpected way very clearly to me (and judging by the millions of comments on the internet in some form or another, to many others too) early on in the pandemic, during the first lockdown in fact. The TV series *Normal People* early on in the first lockdown here in Ireland (and the UK in fact) – as an instance of almost Aristotelian catharsis – gathered together, and commented upon the themes of distance and proximity via the screen (skype) and the lack at the heart of the human condition which makes it impossible for even so-called "free" association to allow us – as speaking beings, divided by language – to say it all. The TV adaptation of the book *Normal People* by Irish author Sally Rooney, directed by Lenny Abrahamson and Hettie McDonald, was aired two nights apart on RTE1 and BBC3 six weeks into the Irish lockdown (see Galioto, this volume for a deeply-detailed reading of *Normal People*). In his book of the pandemic, "Pandemic!" Slavoj Žižek advocated that the lockdown was the right time to gladly succumb to all our guilty movie and TV pleasures, himself confessing a preference for dark Scandinavian – preferably Icelandic – crime series. But actually, here in Ireland, not only were we holding our breath for the next episode of *Normal People*, we were also writing about it in the Newspapers, on Twitter, Facebook, and Instagram, and talking about it on the radio, on zoom calls with friends and loved ones in forbidden zones, and on the couch (on the phone, zoom, Facetime, WhatsApp, etc.) in psychoanalytic sessions. The story follows Conor and Marianne in their last few months of secondary school in rural Sligo, and their college years at Trinity College in Dublin following the curves and contours of what Lacan would call the non-sexual rapport of their relationship, the many misunderstandings, the awkward and funny encounters where something very special takes place, the long explicit sex scenes, the times spent apart, etc.

The newspaper headlines punctuated the lockdown in the style of Lacanian equivoques about the Irish psyche/society/political situation: "Longest sex scene ever to air on Irish television"; "Its Marianne's fault we can't get a government to satisfy *Normal People*"; "Why *Normal People*'s depiction of depression is so ground-breaking". So first there was the sex, or better said, first there was the intimacy. Yes, the bishops were fainting, and the teenagers were cringing, and the sex scenes got posted on Pornhub, and yes, amazingly it was the first time on Irish TV that a post-coital full-frontal naked man was on view. But the real intimacy that was captured and that captivated the hearts of the locked down Irish was in the scenes where Conor and Marianne are together, but, *only* virtually, where Conor, unable to sleep because of anxiety, is kept company by Marianne on skype, where he goes to bed with Marianne's face on the laptop screen beside him. Although this was a pre-COVID production, not then deliberately tying in to a "new normal", of course it spoke to millions of viewers who, separated from their loved ones, could only, like Conor and Marianne, "keep the skype on".[1] It spoke too to the many clients and analysands who chose to continue their therapies and analyses on screen, laptop, smartphone, and to speak about just that moment of peculiar serendipity in their sessions feeling like Marianne, keeping the skype on! So, together with some of the other three million viewers in Ireland, I was interpellated myself as someone who was *keeping the skype on*. I was a "normal person", staying home, working on screens and all manner of apps. I was a psychoanalyst giving talks at conferences on my computer, at home, on Zoom. My new normal, like that of many of my colleagues, consisted of a deep dive into technology, and like that of many of my colleagues, consisted of the questioning of technique and transference, ethics, and responsibility working in these new normal ways with patients. What constituted the radically "adverse conditions" – from the title of the 2020 CP-UK conference I was invited to speak at, turned out to be details…making sure the Wi-Fi was good, the background credible, facilitating alternative methods of payment, and so on.[2] If we asked – if I asked – What are we doing? Where is my being? What are we changing in the work of psychoanalysis with these new methods? Is it even weirder now?! – I don't remember. Or rather I do, or I did when I saw *Sibyl*.

*Sibyl* is a French film directed by Justine Triet released in April 2019. I saw it towards the end of 2021 on the MUBI app on my iPad. Sibyl is a psychoanalyst who breaks all the rules; in the words of reviewer Alice Blackhurst she represents the multi-faceted norm of neo-liberal identity-choice (Blackhurst 2019). That is to say, the choice not of an either/or, but rather of the many/all. Sibyl used to be a writer of fiction before training and working as an analyst. At the start of the film she is trying to get back into writing and is busy discharging her patients. But then she gets a call from a desperate woman called Margot who manages to convince Sibyl to agree to see her. Sibyl is at once representative of let us say the albeit old-school notion of the psychoanalyst as oracle (it's all in the name), called upon to give advice to her patient Margot (should she have an abortion or not), even direction as it turns out (called upon to step in and even – comically – direct a film that Margot is acting in). At the same time, she is representative of the challenges that psychoanalysis faces as a profession and as a method. We see this, most interestingly, in the gradual slippage from Sibyl working with patients in her consulting room at the beginning of the film to her working mainly with Margot on the phone, on Skype, in text, and by email. Blackhurst makes the beautifully observed point that the film's conspicuous dismantling of psychoanalysis's formal choreographies (the consulting room, the couch etc.,) follows the gradual dismantling of the psychoanalytic experience, under mounting pressure to bend and fold to the demands and pressures of what she calls "the current moment". And is it coincidence then that we see Sibyl transgress the rules of psychoanalysis by recording on her mobile phone the sessions with Margot which we then see her transcribe onto her laptop – providing the material for her new work of "fiction"? In other words, is it a logical ultimate switch that if psychoanalysis moves out of the consulting room then the psychoanalyst must move away from her ethical position?

## Conclusions

CO: Psychoanalysis in its non-representability is troubling and troublesome, it creates transference effects which condition an anxiety about doing psychoanalysis differently, even when – as Bruce Fink euphemistically puts it – the "situation" demands it. Our work involves a bearing testimony to that challenge and a working-through.

EW: The small screen, whether as support to an analysis or as a representation of an analysis, poses questions about the specificity of psychoanalysis and the conditions for free association, the emergence of unconscious formations, the difficult to say, and the impossible to say. Those challenges are themselves framed by the psychoanalyst's commitment to psychoanalytic technique and what the analysand's text reveals and conceals. The screen reveals not hyper-reality but the imaginary, symbolic, and real supports of our so-called reality.

## Notes

1 In an alternative framing of my thoughts on *Normal People* I focused on the performative and demonstrative aspects of the motif "normal" together with, and against the increasing usage of the newly minted pandemic signifier—"new normal" (Owens 2022).
2 See https://psychoanalysis-cpuk.org/international-conference-on-psychoanalytic-work-in-adverse-conditions

## References

Abraham, H. and Freud, S. (eds.). (1965). *A Psycho-Analytical Dialogue: The Letters of Sigmund Freud and Karl Abraham*. London: Hogarth Press.
Blackhurst, A. (2019). The Impossible Profession: On Justine Triet's 'Sibyl'. *Another Gaze*, 25 October. Available at: https://www.anothergaze.com/impossible-profession-justine-triets-sibyl/.
Felman, S. (1988). Lacan's Psychoanalysis, or The Figure in the Screen. *October*, 45, pp. 97–108.
Fink, B. (2007). *Fundamentals of Psychoanalytic Technique: A Lacanian Approach for Practitioners*. New York and London: W.W. Norton & Co.
Freud, S. (1912b). Recommendations to Physicians Practising Psycho-Analysis. *Standard Edition of the Complete Psychological Works of Sigmund Freud*, edited by J. Strachey. London: Vintage, 2001.
Freud, S. (1913c). On Beginning the Treatment (Further Recommendations on the Technique of Psycho-Analysis 1). *S.E., XII*, pp. 121–144. London: Vintage.
Freud, S. (1916 [1915]). "Parapraxes". Introductory Lectures on Psycho-Analysis. *S.E., XV*. London: Vintage, 2001.
Gallagher, C. (1994). The Historical Development and Clinical Implications of Jacques Lacan's 'Optical Schema'. *The Letter: Irish Journal for Lacanian Psychoanalysis*, 2, pp. 87–111.
Lacan, J. (1958). The Direction of the Treatment and the Principles of its Power. In J. Lacan. *Écrits. The First Complete Edition in English*. Trans. B. Fink. New York and London: W.W. Norton. 1966, pp. 489–542.
Lacan, J. (1964). *The Four Fundamental Concepts of Psycho-Analysis*. London: Penguin Books, 2004.
Lacan, J. (1973). *Television: A Challenge to the Psychoanalytic Establishment*. Trans. J. Mehlman. London and New York: W.W. Norton & Co., 1990.
Masson, J. (1991). *Against Therapy: Emotional Tyranny and the Myth of Psychological Healing*. New York: Harper Collins.
Owens, C. (2022). Normal People in Abnormal Times: How a TV show rocked the Irish pandemic lockdown… and other fantasies. *Analytic Agora*, 1, pp. 182–199.
Parker, I. (2018). Psychoanalytic Clinical Case Presentations, The Case Against. *Lacunae*, 17, pp. 6–36.
Schneiderman, S. (2014). *The Last Psychoanalyst*. Scotts Valley, CA: Createspace Independent Publishing Platform.
Žižek, S. (2020). *Pandemic! COVID-19 Shakes the World*. London: Polity Press.

### Video/Film/TV

*Duck Soup.* (1933). Film, directed by L. McCarey. Los Angeles: Paramount Pictures.
Freud Museum London. (2015). *What is Psychoanalysis? Part 1: Is it Weird?* See: https://www.youtube.com/watch?v=pxaFeP9Ls5c.
*Normal People.* (2020). TV Series, 12 episodes, directed by L. Abrahamson and H. McDonald. Dublin: Element Pictures.
*Secrets of a Soul.* (1926). Film, directed by G.W. Pabst. See: https://www.youtube.com/watch?v=aYoXy3bYD1k.
*Sibyl.* (2019). Film, directed by J. Triet. Chicago, IL: Music Box Films.
*The Sopranos.* (2007). "Tony Talks to Dr. Melfi about his Son." TV series, directed by T. Winter. Season 6, Episode 17. See: https://www.youtube.com/watch?v=2QPxZdCMyUc.

Chapter 10

# Power and Politics in Adam Curtis' *Can't Get You Out Of My Head*

## An Emotional History of the Modern World

*Isabel Millar, Brett Nicholls, Rosemary Overell and Daniel Tutt*

### Introduction

Adam Curtis is one of the pre-eminent documentary film-makers of our time. His films tackle the complexity of historical and contemporary culture with an eye to critique of a nebulous and mobile form of power. Unlike other documentarians, the bulk of Curtis' work has always been within the 'small screen' space of the televisual; with the BBC funding his work over four decades. Further, in the last ten years, Curtis has insisted on releasing his work online, on YouTube, almost synchronous with the BBC airdate. This ensures a global audience for his films, but also constitutes a form of small-screen viewing which engages something quite different from consuming a documentary in a cinema, or at a film festival. Streamed on laptops, smartphones or looped through HDMI cables to monitors, Curtis's work functions in domestic spaces. This form of screening Curtis intensified during the pandemic with the 2021 release of *Can't Get You Out of My Head: An Emotional History of the Modern World* (*CGYOOMH*). The documentary was swiftly circulated and, as they say, was 'extremely online'. Memes, mashups and 'hot takes' abounded on twitter, Instagram and Discord communities. *CGYOOMH* offered a formidable intervention into public debates around the apparent failure of progressive, and radical, social movements post-War and the politics of mediation in the constitution and reproduction of hegemonic forces. COVID was absent from the film – perhaps, despite the material onscreen – it offered some odd respite from the daily broadcasting of death tolls; tips on how to best be productive while 'bubbled' inside; and endless 'work from home' Teams meetings. Whilst the current disaster of the pandemic was not there, onscreen, the film's content worked as an *almost-there*. It included footage from the 6 January 2021 riot on the White House – a carnivalesque moment which, viewed from within our enforced isolations perhaps resonated as a strange warning of a coming Apocalypse.

The documentary's reception came with a sense of urgency. While viewing might provide some break from the bleakness of the Plague; it also functioned

DOI: 10.4324/9781003272069-11

as an enjoyable spectacle. Most audience members 'binged' the 6 parts and quickly moved online to discuss the complex threads the film presented. Within the COVID chaos and concurrent sense of hopelessness in the face of global flows of disease, we were presented with a complex, chaotic, social history on screen. Being able to explore and articulate this chaos – and an odd sense of malaise – through *CGYOOMH* brought its own kind of solace. With Curtis' narration we are granted a vocabulary for the affect of paralysis in the face of apparently insurmountable confusion.

We – the authors – were also caught by the swift, intense need to *respond* to *CGYOOMH*. Plague conditions also enable new ways of connecting through a shift to the small screens on our work desks. Avidly following the tweets and takes offered by her far flung colleagues online, Rosemary proposed a pop up: a Zoom event to discuss 'Power, Politics & the Films of Adam Curtis'. It was held in March 2021, soon after the documentary's release (Media, Film and Communications Programme 2021). What follows are our responses to how power and politics works in and through Curtis' most recent film. We discuss how Curtis might parry with the documentary form to constitute a progressive politics … or not.

With the present collection's theme in mind, we fold our discussion through psychoanalysis. In particular, we consider how Curtis' mode of documentary might work discursively – both in the film form, but also in its reception – how it might work to forge social bonds. Building on this, we take up some of the recurring discussions, in both the popular and the academic sphere, which position Curtis as a mediator and co-constitutor of a form of ethical public discourse and, potentially, politics. We also account for the critiques which the expectation of arbitration of ethical publics generates – that is those who lament Curtis as a conspiracy theorist at worst, and a 'depressed hippy' at best. Our reflections below tackle these tensions but add some of the novel ways of reading Curtis' work drawing on Jacques Lacan, as well as Jean Baudrillard, Gilles Deleuze, and Michel Foucault. *CGYOOMH*, and Curtis' *oeuvre* more generally, present us with a tension in the form of its compilatory, mashed up, aesthetic, which, we think, is a fruitful starting point to tease out the socio-political as a site of struggle flashpoints which are, again and again 'revealed' to the audience. We wonder at this movement between the cut up and obscured, to the reveal of the machinations of what Curtis labels 'power'. Curtis *is* a small-screen documentarian, but we feel that an application of the critical insights of these thinkers adds to an understanding of what big 'power', and, indeed, 'politics' means in *CGYOOMH*.

This collection points to the idea of the screen teaching us to desire, the small screen in this case. You could say that our discussion takes up this point in a couple of ways. 1) Curtis offers a viewpoint on the world even if this viewpoint is that the world is in a chaos of sorts. Being able to explore and articulate this chaos and its paralysis effect is a kind of solace. 2) We explore how the small documentary screen connects to and articulates a political view of the world.

This chapter is divided into two parts, the first presents a write up of each of our symposium presentations. The second section will focus on the lively discussion which followed our presentations, in the form of a 'Question and Answer'. This discussion paper is intended as a timely response to *CGYOOMH* which opens up dialogue and generates provocations around Curtis' work.

## Che Vuoi, Curtis?

### Isabel Millar

As Alberto Toscano (2021) recently noted, in Adam Curtis' latest series of films the figure of Abu Zubaydah, the alleged Al Qaeda operative detained without charge and tortured by US authorities for close to two decades is 'something like an allegorical figure conscripted to embody a collective condition', since as Curtis puts it 'there was no story that made sense to Zubaydah anymore, he was trapped in a perpetual now, haunted by fragments of memory with no way of moving into the future'.

Zubaydah's predicament arguably stands in for the conceptual nexus that Curtis has been working up to in various ways over the last 30 years of his career: the impossibility of ever creating anything new, trapped as we are inside a system of pre-emptive capitalist realism, a psychological and cultural situation that the late Mark Fisher might have otherwise diagnosed as hauntological.

Apart from his characteristic stitching of archive footage along with his inimitable selection of eclectic and haunting music, now so recognizable as to verge on parody (cf. Woodhams 2018), the films of Adam Curtis all share another important distinguishing feature. That is his technique of showing how the media make complex things appear simple in order to fit a coherent narrative. Curtis sees this as reaching its peak after the Cold War and finally crumbling into absurdity with the atrocities of the Rwandan civil war in 1994, where no one could decide anymore who were the good guys, hence dissolving into what he termed 'Oh dearism'; a pervasive helpless despair at the 'mindless cruelty' of human beings, which he says following Charlie Brooker's *Newswipe* intro is like 'living in the mind of a depressed hippy' (Brooker 2009). His contention is usually that this resignation stops us from problematising political conflict, and by simplifying these stories we lose their 'true meaning'.

The paradox is that overlaying Curtis' labyrinthine tales and montages of disparate images, there is always his own school-masterly and patrician narrative, telling you exactly what you are supposed to think about the otherwise ambiguous imagery and soundscapes he presents. This combined with his other method, the logic of the perpetual reveal – a situation in the present is found to have its roots in the past and its meaning is never as it seems – results in a hypnotically entertaining form of social critique. But as many critics have noted, Curtis himself often appears to be either making unsubstantiated claims and wild connections or simply contradicting himself about the meanings of these connections within a single narrative; the reveal keeps on revealing.

In *Can't Get You Out of My Head*, Curtis' main thrust is the apparent incommensurability of the individual with the collective and how all revolutionary movements are eventually thwarted by the bursting through of the individual's incompatible and often catastrophic desires. However, he consistently seems to bump up against the same fundamental issue; that is the 'problem' of subjectivity and furthermore his own implication in the telling of his stories.

Curtis goes to great lengths to tell the story of how we came to conceive of the concept of the 'individual', one of his abiding tropes and undeniably the star of *CGYOOMH*. He draws out the connecting thread from early post-Freudians in the American tradition of ego psychology and its development into cognitive behavioural science and rightly sees it as complicit with the bureaucratisation of the cultural sphere. Curtis mounts an attack on positive psychology as a deeply conservative discourse. This he argues finds its ultimate expression in the total datafication of the social bond and the way in which algorithms have now taken over as the acephalic diffuse network of power which in their supposedly benign and purely rational processes have the potential to create terrible forms of instrumental tyranny.

The critique of psychology is of course common currency for the psychoanalytically savvy (which one would think Curtis was), we know only too well how the pseudo-science of psychology reduces the complexity of subjectivity to a set of measurable norms which are inherently ideological and oppressive, and which now proliferate in endless iterations of the DSM (*The Diagnostic and Statistical Manual of Mental Disorders*).

Curtis has eight hours to play with his main concepts 'the individual' and 'power' but refrains from engaging with two of the main problematising strands in theories of subjectivity; on the one hand Marxist or Foucauldian analytics of power and on the other psychoanalysis. Why does he make reference constantly to the idea that 'we are all inside our heads' that 'we believe that our feelings come from inside' and that had we consulted 'earlier sociological notions of selfhood' we would know, is a modern myth?

Does he really want us to believe that he has no truck with Freudian or even Lacanian notions of the unconscious or the idea of the Marxian, Foucauldian Power / Knowledge structures? Perhaps this evasion can be attributed to what Owen Hatherley (2017) calls his 'Reithianism' a tradition of mass audience accessibility inaugurated by the BBC's founder John Reith. Which maybe would explain why in a recent interview with Jacob Sugarman (2021) for *In These Times*, when asked what he considers an authentically radical movement today Curtis refers to Black Lives Matter. What's striking about his response is that Curtis seems to believe that BLM emerged out of nowhere due to a renewed engagement with the idea of structural inequality.

The ideas and frameworks that underpin BLM; the notions of subjection and structural inequality, post-coloniality, antiblackness and the necessity for black socio-economic empowerment are clearly *not new* ideas. This is perhaps where Curtis' standpoint may influence his approach. Paradoxically what Curtis seems to overlook is that ideas do not just spring fully formed from either the individual mind, nor even from the intellectual labour of the well organised group but rather they occur as the convergence of historical forces which sit within a given regime of truth, a fact that his own film making attests to.

But perhaps the old fantasy of the individual sitting in his study making a discovery or coming up with an idea that 'changes the world' is not so outlandish for Curtis. After all, for some people the world really is like that. This is not an *ad hominem* attack, white men from Oxford and Cambridge don't just see the world differently because they are 'privileged' but because their discourses have the power to materially shape the world to a much greater degree than most people. Ultimately Curtis can literally set the agenda of his immediate environment because of the body which he inhabits, and it seems like that is very much how he approaches his idea of historical change because that's how it works for him. Curtis is his own blind spot in discourse, his own stain on reality.

What is also noticeably lacking in Curtis' work is an acknowledgement of the context in which he is producing these cultural artifacts, namely as a household name at the BBC. Could Curtis' reluctance to coin the term 'neoliberalism' (or the 'n-word' as he has problematically and jarringly referred to it), his omission of any reference to such figures as Jeremy Corbyn or Bernie Sanders and his consistent refusal to nail his politics to any mast in the name of journalistic impartiality, perhaps be more to do with which side his own bread is buttered?

The other obvious blind spot which Curtis inhabits, becomes apparent in his reference to Julia Grant, Britain's first operative transgender woman who we witness quietly suffering in the stuffy consulting rooms of a patronising, callous and misogynist medical establishment. Curtis' take on this is to condescendingly commiserate with Julia but nonetheless put her struggle down to the emergence of the kind of identity politics that eschews more important structural questions of class and power, 'a type of individualism' that had 'given up on changing society' as he puts it. This relegation of trans issues to the ranks of mere identity politics is not just politically conservative but philosophical naïve. The experience of trans people is one which strikes at the heart of the relationship between the social, the political and the psychical and implicates us all – male, female, cis, trans, non-binary – in its very irreconcilability. To use the much overused (and misunderstood) Lacanian dictum, it exemplifies precisely that, ontologically speaking *there is no sexual relationship* and that is a problem that must be addressed by all speaking beings.

Beyond arguments that the BBC have limited their output of critical engagements with questions of subjectivity, power and politics to one (or two) middle-aged Oxbridge educated white men with a grammar school accent, there is a conceptual issue with Curtis' *oeuvre* and where it sits in relation to critical thinking in general. Ultimately for all his apparent Oxfordian libertarianism Curtis seems to have no theory of the subject of history or even of power. Clearly, he is concerned with the play of signifiers, the exchange of objects, the loss of meaning and the hyperreal in its most mediatised sense. But perhaps it would be too obvious to call his work Baudrillardian. In a way, it's as if Curtis himself is a Baudrillardian subject created by the code, he himself is hyperreal. In *Forget Foucault* Baudrillard (2007) argues that the only reason Foucault can critique power in the way that he did is because that system is already gone. Foucault gave precise details of the mechanics of power in discourse and in that gesture was exercising that very same power and demonstrating its transparency and hence its obsolescence. According to Baudrillard, Foucault could only ever be a historian of power since he was always one step behind it, a product of it himself hoisted by his own conceptual petard. Could it be that like Foucault, Curtis is already part and parcel of that very same operation of power? Maybe that's because he is talking about a world that is already dead?

It is ironic as Toscano (2021) has pointed out that 'there is a short-circuit between Curtis' methods – scanning through hard drive upon hard drive of disparate digitised BBC footage – and the myriad projects of pattern recognition that populate this series'. Nevertheless these 'fragments of our own political memory – as sampled, remixed and collaged by Curtis – are poorly contained by such a monotonous diagnosis, and are more compellingly experienced, especially through the mediation of Curtis' compellingly curated soundtrack, as historical *moods*' (ibid).

One of the most effective ways to engage with Curtis then, is to listen to him as if he were a fully Lacanian split subject. The narration functions as the super-egoic or perverse injunction, the voice guiding us morally to make the right decisions, meanwhile the visuals are telling a whole other story. A stream of consciousness, the sliding of signifiers, and crucially a constant reveal of the supposed 'moment of truth'. Whilst Curtis tells us the truth has been found, the scopic drive continues to search for that elusive object a in the morass of seductive images. We *could* ask the question, what does Curtis want, what is his desire? Is he the arch-neoliberal? Libertarian lefty? Product of his time? Neutral documentary maker? Agent of the simulation? But maybe his most important role is to just hystericise *us*.

## Paralysis as the order of the day

### Brett Nicholls

I agree with Isabel that Curtis is a Baudrillardian of sorts, particularly in how he suggests the West is imploding as it attempts to control economic and security threats from without and within. I like to think of Curtis as a filmmaker from the British Grierson tradition, which, given his lack of commitment to documentary realism, might sound strange. However, Curtis works from a journalistic position, perhaps even in terms of the fantasy of the heroic journalist. He can also be approached as a baroque novelist of sorts, writing the story of various characters caught up in complex historical forces. At any rate, his employment of an authoritative patrician didactic voice, as Isabel describes it, to explain the seemingly disparate images and sounds that erupt on screen indeed suggests he speaks from a journalistic position. His films are trying to explain what is going on in the political upheavals of today, what Curtis in *CGYOOMH* calls 'strange days across Europe, Britain, and America'.

Are these explanations adequate and convincing? Well, not for everyone. Reviews of Curtis in general tend to split into two stances. The first stance celebrates him as a provocative filmmaker raising critical political questions. This celebration, however, tends to be qualified. Curtis is tackling significant issues. Very few journalists do this, particularly in an accessible medium such as television, *but* what Curtis marshals to demonstrate these issues is perplexing. We might call this first stance the 'Curtis is a virtuoso but-' view. The second stance denounces Curtis as a crackpot conspiracist. His films bear no relationship to the actual state of affairs; they are nothing more than the retrograde musings of a 1960s hippy, lamenting the failure of his generation's decadent counterculture. Reproducing shoddy sociological categories such as 'boomer', which should be disavowed, this second stance is the 'Curtis as unreformed 60s rebel' view (for a fuller account see Nicholls 2017).

For my part, I try to think carefully about the kinds of descriptions Curtis employs to chart these strange days. And I don't want to limit how we might understand the term 'description' to something like realist illustration. So, what sort of descriptions do we see in his films? Apposite the narrator's voice, the films consist of fragments: direct statements such as vox pops and historical footage, as well as a metaphorical and ironic use of images, film, sounds and music (see Michael MacDonald's, Nd, Spotify playlist, 2021). But what I find fascinating about Curtis as a filmmaker is how he describes the mood of a particular historical context. For example, Curtis often punctuates his films with so many images of dancing (he also seems to have a fascination with corridors). In the narrative, dancing reveals the mood of the time. What I mean by mood here is akin to Raymond Williams' structure of feeling (1972). That is the general feelings or emotions that precede thinking and orient our commitment to particular ways of living. The structure of feeling marks out the stakes in our sense of social reality, what Rosemary refers to as 'what feels real'. The 'descriptions' of mood reveal the time as optimistic (the 'hop'), or archaic (the school waltzing lesson), or angry (skinheads body slamming erupting into violent mayhem), or revolutionary (the idealisation of working-class figures in Jiang Qing's plays), and so on. However, one mood is foregrounded in his films, particularly in *CGYOOMH*: "paralysis". Curtis' precise position on what marks these strange days is that Europe, Britain, and America are now in the grip of political paralysis. This paralysis is fuelled by a strange anti-ideology ideology in which the most incorruptible position is to have no political commitment. As Curtis ironically puts it in *CGYOOMH*, 'the only way to escape the horror of the consequences of trying to change the world is to stop trying to change it [...] the safest thing is to believe in nothing'. This anti-ideology ideology, however, does little to stem what Curtis calls 'old forms of power'.

For Curtis, the social world is historically marked by the conflict between old and new forms of power. *CGYOOMH* makes three interrelated points across the six episodes. First, it traces how so many revolutions (new forms of power) attempt to overthrow old forms of power and create a new social reality have failed. As revealed in the film's baroque organisation of socially positioned individual characters, the reasons for these failures are complex. The driving point is despite the forces of change, whether it be through postcolonial struggle in Britain, Mao's Long March in China, or anti-racism in America, old forms of power – British empire hierarchy, China's dynastic order, German Nazism, and American settler paranoia (as per Hofstadter, 1965) – are impossible to overcome. Revolutions failed to eliminate old inequalities, and as a consequence, they re-emerge today but in an even more sinister form.

Second, the film charts three seemingly disparate geo-political developments that intensify the more sinister re-emergence of old forms of power. Oil displaces coal as the primary energy source. As coal mines closed in the late 1970s, Curtis maintains that workers' union power to challenge corporations and politicians weakened. With its vast oil fields, Saudi Arabia took the symbolic place occupied by the workers and began pressuring the West to cut its support of Israel. In a parallel development, the Nixon government unlinked the US dollar from the gold standard and unwittingly gave rise to the reconfiguration of global banking and financial systems. This results in the continuation of the West's exploitation of the former colonies. And as these aforementioned developments unfolded, the rise of computer technologies and artificial intelligence reconfigure older ideological forms of power. Rational management is undertaken to solve the problem of political commitment and its wretched consequences to make the world a better place. This reconfiguration, however, fails to overturn old inequalities and rather liberate from the burden of political judgement, populations are subjected to more granular forms of control.

Third, alongside the aforementioned disparate developments, climate science modelling began to reveal the complexities and instability of the planet's climate. Instead of the previously held view of climate as a self-correcting and stable system, Lorenz discovered small changes within the system could lead to rapid and catastrophic change. This leads to the prevailing view, Curtis maintains, that the world is inherently unstable and any attempt to control it is doomed to fail. At the same time, psychologists discover the complexities of the human brain and conclude human behaviour is inherently irrational, uncertain and difficult to manage. The instability of the climate system and the uncertainty of human behaviour lead, Curtis asserts, to the positivist conclusion that the only way to understand the world is to look for patterns. In this way of thinking, there is no place for political judgement, or the human agent at the heart of liberalism. We cannot be trusted. Instead, statistical inferences produced by calculating technologies will make political decisions for us. The only thing individuals get to decide is what to wear, what commodities to buy (Isabel and Daniel have more to say about individualism). 'We cannot be trusted' means political institutions no longer trust the people.

The upshot of these developments is a savage picture of a world paralysed under the weight of its tumultuous political history. And, strikingly, Curtis is not tempted by the journalistic impulse to reassure audiences that there is hope on the horizon despite this grim picture. There are no metaphysical reasons why there should be hope, and history, at least as Curtis constructs it, suggests this is not the case. His diagnosis is that, given the hegemony of anti-ideology ideology, the social world continues to spiral out of control, vulnerable to any old form of power – the colonial imagination, nationalism, paranoia, fascism – that emerges and takes hold.

There is one compelling moment in the film, for me at least, which presents this paralysis in condensed form. Here, the feeling of political paralysis is as striking as it is disquieting. This is a sequence from Soviet television ('Money changes everything', 35:30), most likely a splicing together of excerpts from the Brezhnev era. Singers in studio settings mock saccharine romance to the tune of the Beatles hit song, 'Let it be'. In this Soviet version of the song, the phrase 'let it be' is translated as *'budet tak'* (будет так), literally 'it will be thus'. This short mocking sequence is linked, in the film, to footage detailing how dissident poet, Eduard Limonov, remained trapped in Soviet ideology despite his resistance, and a reference to Solzhenitsyn's *The Gulag Archipelago*. As Curtis reads this text, Solzhenitsyn argues that political atrocities result from political ideology. Therefore, to avoid the inverse consequences of attempting to make the world a better place, we should abandon ideology and believe in nothing. For Curtis, Solzhenitsyn is foundational for the 'counter-ideology that dominates the world today'. Alongside Limonov and Solzhenitsyn, in this mocking TV sequence, *Budet tak* points to political paralysis. The world is as it is; we can make no difference.

It is hard to know if the film is a ringing endorsement or a cruel parody of the film's opening quote from the late David Graeber, the 'ultimate hidden truth of the world is that it is something we make and could just as easily make differently'. Curtis seems to be maintaining that the world has ended up in a difficult and strange place, and, absurdly, has cut off any political means for change. The direction that Curtis' points to, I think, is the rediscovery of the political. Despite the failure of revolutions, if Curtis is to be accepted, the more alarming and perilous development is abandoning political judgement, *budet tak*, and believing in nothing.

## The People Are Missing

### *Daniel Tutt*

The rise of intense social atomisation in contemporary society must be traced back to the gradual collapse of the masses in political life. This is a theme Adam Curtis has tackled in *Century of the Self* (2002) and *HyperNormalization* (2016) and arguably all of his films touch on the idea. Perhaps taken together each of Curtis' films can be read as variations on the rise of uncontrollable technologies: psychoanalysis applied to marketing and consumerism birthed a Frankenstein of unimaginable mind control. The gradual collapse of collective political liberation throughout the 1970s led to a defeatism on behalf of an entire generation of radicals in the west. In Curtis' political cosmos, people are subject to powerful ideas which infect them like a virus and these ideas work like a virus and latch onto the social body and they grow to outsized proportions. These ideas are funnelled down into systems of control wherein the elites struggle to manage the chaotic system they oversee.

In *CGYOOMH*, Curtis offers a slightly new perspective on this theme, but he works with his same dark and more pessimistic premise that has become his hallmark. He presents a dystopia of the present; a society of alienated technological capture and total control. The very desire for collective liberation has disappeared, replaced by a more pernicious hyper-individualism. The film is an attempt to offer up a historical account for where this virus of hyper-individualism actually came from. In a world dominated by hyper-individualism the discontent of the masses are muted, absent. In this totalising picture of social atomisation, we miss the story of the re-appearance of the masses on the stage of world history. The Arab Spring, Occupy Wall Street, the Movement of the Squares, Black Lives Matter are mass movements which offer a rebuttal to the idea of total social atomisation and hyper-individualism. These movements offer a counter to Curtis' rather bleak picture of the total impotence of the masses.

There are certainly merits to Curtis' presentation in *CGYOOMH*. Similar to Isabel's comment that Curtis could quite easily have drawn upon critical theory, but refuses to do so, I want to suggest that Curtis' pessimism in 'the people', sheds light on the challenges of political agency in a time that Gilles Deleuze calls 'control societies'. There are a number of overlapping themes of power and control that Curtis naturally shares with Deleuze's account of power, i.e., there is a kernel of truth in Curtis' account of social and political power in the film.

One major theme of *CGYOOMH* is that the masses or the people 'may be stupid' which is in fact the title of Episode 4. But in what way are the people stupid? Curtis does not answer the question outright, nor is Curtis an advocate for any form of individualism. We are presented, rather, with a vague nostalgia for the post-war social democratic period of western capitalism from the 1950s to the mid-1970s. Early into this Golden Age, the fantasies of the collective individual in the communist societies of Russia and China were experimented with but they quickly failed. In China, the project of collective individualism failed even before the Cultural Revolution got off the ground. We already see here a signature move that Curtis makes, to link grand historical moments to the exceptionally talented, but largely unknown shadow figure within a historical sequence: Mao's partner Jiang Qing planted the seeds for hyper-individualism due to her own charismatic presence in the revolutionary leadership in the Chinese Cultural Revolution.

In his discussion of the American invasion of Iraq in 2003, there is no mention or discussion of any influence the anti-war protest movement (which was the largest anti-war movement in U.S. history) may have had on the collective desire of the masses that participated in these protests. It may have been true that the masses were ineffectual in protesting the war, but the total neglect of mentioning the anti-war movement renders his discussion of the historical sequence one-sided. Secondly, Curtis' discussion of the rise of Brexit and Donald Trump locates its emergence in a longer historical origin over growing resentments regarding the deregulation of capitalism as well as the loss of the welfare state, and this is presented as the result of a far more systemic transition from industrial to financially-dominated capitalism in the 1970s. This transition intensified the already precarious conditions for the middle classes and working classes. Curtis furthermore links the rise of these two events to the imposition of austerity policies following the 2008 economic crash. These are by now standard populist accounts of the rise of both Trump and Brexit, and yet Curtis goes further than these accounts by arguing that they are owed to the processes of hyper-individual control mechanisms propelled by the predominance of algorithmic control mechanisms over the lives of everyday citizens. Curtis is certainly correct to point out the nefarious role of Cambridge Analytica on voting patterns in both Brexit and Trump but he again misses the profound resistance to these new forms of power that have occurred, from Wikileaks to Edward Snowden. How can any account of contemporary ideology and power neglect such undercurrents of emancipation, and do these undercurrents not signal the presence of the masses?

Also absent in his re-telling of general powerlessness is the rise of the protest Movement of the Squares in 2010 and 2011 that toppled dictators such as Hosni Mubarak in Egypt, birthed Occupy Wall Street and eventually brought political figures such as Bernie Sanders and Jeremy Corbyn into prominent positions of political power in western parliamentary systems. Where did these protests and left-wing and socialist-oriented political figures come from? In Curtis' view, collective individualism is dead. But there is ample reason to point to the re-birth of democratic socialism and new forms of communist thinking across the world as a sign of a re-awakened masses, a sign of the return of the people to world history.

Although in some ways this missing element of the masses in revolt could also be read as a further proof of Curtis' idea of hyper-atomised individualism. In other words, the fact that the masses revolt but nonetheless experience a total capture and re-routing of their energies for change, offers up a further proof that hyper-individualism is indeed all-enveloping. We saw this in *HyperNormalization* which presented a picture of social and political change that had totally shut down the possibility of collection action. In *CGYOOMH*, Curtis remarks, 'no one has any idea of how to change things', a condition which he links to the absence of the masses in history and our inability to escape hyper individualism.

That the masses no longer speak in the contemporary situation of power is a theme Curtis also tracks in HyperNormalization (2016) where he documents the way that the very radical change agents that sought to revolutionise the system in the 1960s grew to adopt a nihilistic apathy. More generally, Curtis adopts a view of power that is, as Brett (2017) has noted in his prior work on Curtis, indebted to Baudrillard's idea of power as 'hegemony'. For Curtis, power is not situated between the dominated and dominators; it happens behind the scenes and is directed by an elite apolitical consensus and the algorithm has replaced domination. In this dynamic, the people have lost touch with power entirely.

I want to pose four problems and questions that Curtis' framework of power and individualism bring out.

(1) Was there ever a non-hyper individualism?
In *CGYOOMH*, Curtis develops an intricate series of examples centred around the way a new form of insidious individualism grew to dominate the world and reach the point where no one knows how to change the system. Through a narrative of prominent individuals such as Solzhenitsyn and Jiang Qing we are introduced to the idea that the collectivist notions of the individual founded in the communist states of Russia and China were threatened with possessive individualism long before they rose to become the dominant form of individualism globally. But what was individualism before this catastrophe? We aren't presented with a theory of another individualism before these mysterious changes came about. The sense of history on display is an unfolding series of events spurned on by charismatic individual rebels.

How hyper-individualism magically appeared in early communist societies even further reveals Curtis' strange quasi-conspiratorial idea of power and the individual. There is no discussion of the ways socialistic or even communistic forms of the collective individual in communist and Marxist thought was also negotiated and sprouted in these contexts. What precisely does Curtis think of individualism as such? There is no discussion of the positive changes the Chinese Cultural Revolution brought about in Chinese society, the massive levels of education it fostered, to take one example.

(2) What is distinctly modern for Curtis?
A minor point, but one that I think stands out as a bit of an omission in the film is the very meaning of the term 'modern' for Curtis. When does the modern start? We are left to assume that there is no 'post' modern as evidenced by the subtitle of the film. At the same time, because there is only the modern, we have no true historical foothold to interrogate when power was treated differently, or perhaps better, than it is now. This atemporal and ahistorical treatment of the very idea of what constitutes the 'modern' leads Curtis to portray people's relation to the past as a fantasy; a bubble to hide from a dark present.

(3) Does resistance to power also have a genealogy and a logic? Is contestation to power always inefficacious?
Perhaps the best way to encapsulate Curtis' treatment of the contemporary political landscape is by the term 'post-political', a concept which refers to the idea that grand political changes are effectively off the table. The post-political thesis matches well with Curtis' framework of power, a world devoid of collective action. For Curtis, each attempt to challenge power fails and nothing is learned. There is no continuity to revolts or resistance, nothing ties them together. A theme developed in *HyperNormalization* is continued in *CGYOOMY*, for example, is that the very model of individualism in the contemporary period has been weaponised for reactionary ends. Systems of power are beyond the people's control; so complex that they make a mockery of the idea that national governments can even handle the basic management of control. Hyper-individualism affects both the elites and the masses; there's no outside to power.

Curtis' view of power as an overwhelming and all-enveloping trap that encloses all subject positions in modern society should be put into dialogue with the idea of the 'control society' as articulated by Gilles Deleuze in his 'Postscript on the Societies of Control', a short text written in 1992. In this text, Deleuze incorporates Marx's theory of power and he argues that our society has become a control society, wherein power is not to be thought of as 'uni-causal' or only tethered to one causal agent such as the proletariat, or the class struggle, etc. Rather, in control societies, which Deleuze sees arising in rudimentary form in the late 19th century, power moves away from disciplinary or juridical power to a model in which there are many forms of power. Society is an 'archipelago' of different powers. This vision is in concert with Marx's idea of various meshes of power, a structure that we find in post-industrial society and which was brought about due to changes in the division of labour, the rise of salaried workers, insurance, the charity and social work fields, etc.

For Deleuze, 'institutions come before the state' in delegating power in the arrangement of control societies. It is thus important to note that historically, this shift can be understood as centrally housed within a shift in labour regulation techniques, which again means that Deleuze stays very close to Marx in terms of placing labour and labour struggles at the very centre of accounts of social power. The shift in power at the site of labour was a shift in the very psychic mechanism of power; a shift from authority based on the 'you must not' (prohibition) to the need to obtain a better performance and a new division of the monitoring of the division of labour, and hence an internalised prohibition of the superego – characterised by a 'you can' attitude. Thus, power in the control societies takes hold of the individual as social atoms (individuals) wherein individuals become tasked with self-regulating their performance. This is not a theory of the individual that stems from a mad scientist in a lab and a lackadaisical set of technocratic elites that implement this new technology to further social passivity, as Curtis documents. Individual atomisation must be diagnosed as emerging from the processes involved in this specific historical transformation in labour power, not from laboratories of mad scientists and psychologists.

(4) The fate of the revolutionary in the era of 'post-politics'
Curtis argues, echoing the late Baudrillard, that negativity (revolt, contestation etc.) is absent and inefficacious when it does emerge. To the extent that there is negativity, revolt and unrest, this activity is not permitted to take on a collective form of expression. Curtis' rather bleak picture of the world is 'post-political', riddled with deadlocks that prevent collective action that can lead to political transformations. In this context we are led to ask what a revolutionary leader might look like? What fate does the revolutionary individual have in the modern control society? Is there a dialectic internal to the system of total control and hyper-individualism in the context of a social order in which the masses have been pacified? There is no better portrayal of the fate of the revolutionary than we find in Curtis' discussion of Tupac Shakur and Abu Zubaydha. Both Tupac and Zubaydha were heroes of a lost form of collective power, and while they both embodied collective leadership characteristics, the political situation they operated in proved to squash any collective emancipatory end to their projects. They embody the post-political horizon of our time. Tupac was a charismatic hip-hop icon, raised by communist Black Panthers and committed to working class and racial struggle for justice. But he could not forge the collective solidarity he aimed for. Similarly, Abu Zubaydha, a militant Islamist who preached an austere pre-modern form of political theology based in a collectivist end, could not realise these aspirations. Both figures fell sway to hyper-individualism.

The lesson of the film is sent home in the story of these two men; in the post-political cosmos that Curtis presents, the revolutionary figure who aims to restore collective individualism is fated to die a martyr. Although Curtis' pessimist perspective reaches a crescendo in the story of these two figures, it stands out as the most compelling storyline in the entire film. Everything comes full circle in these two martyrs. Their failure to enact the sort of broader collective liberation they longed for is a proof of the overwhelming virus of hyper-individualism. But as we have tried to point out, a history of the modern world which does not make any account of the negativity and contestation *already happening within our present* by mass movements and by the masses makes for a partial and limited portrait of our world.

## "I"-politics and the voice

### Rosemary Overell

I've been circling around writing this up for a while. My contribution to the panel was a bit of a riff – a catchy little performance poem which looped around, and about, this idea of things which persist in our heads; things which push bodies into subjects; move emotions into matters. It's hard to move the voice into words on a screen or a scroll.

But maybe it depends on whose voice is speaking?

My voice is accented Australian. Perhaps that is why my first thought when I saw the title of Curtis' new film was of *our Kylie* (Kylie Minogue for our American friends!), warbling away in her track 'I Can't Get You Out Of My Head' (2002). She's not in the film, but – having made her career back in the metropole – in England; perhaps she's there as an echo. Curtis – surely – knows the hook '*la la la*'?

Here is the chorus:

> [La la la la-la-la-la la]
> I just can't get you out of my head
> Boy, your lovin' is all I think about
> I just can't get you out of my head
> Boy, its more than I dare to think about.

Many cringe at Kylie's pop-songs. Maybe it's her accent? I cringe at my voice, listening back to our recorded zoom discussion.

To say – okay – we don't cringe at Curtis' voice is significant, as Isabel notes above. His voice 'fits' the expository documentary – even in the Griersonian sense which Brett mentions, the patrician voice is, well, *natural* here. Narration anchors montages of images. A lesson. We know that mode and expect *that* voice (Nichols 2001; Chion 1982). Astra Taylor and Tiana Reid (2019) wondered elsewhere – what if that voice-of-God Curtis – was the voice of a Valley Girl? A voice from elsewhere. Isabel addresses the scopic drive above. Here, I want to think about another drive: that of the *voice*.

Mladen Dolar (2006) discusses the voice, via Lacan, as the object of the drive. The voice, then, is always from elsewhere – that little *objet a* that circles, extimate, aphonic – a circuit that speaks a body as a subject supposed to know ... not acousmatic, or always *out there*; but coursing *here* through the body.

A circuit that speaks a *subject*, who is supposed to know ... what? What thing out there? Curtis gives us an *object*-lesson; some know-how on revolutions that missed the mark, as Daniel notes. Dolar writes that the object-voice is a mechanism caught – between meaning and enjoyment. Between language and the body. Revolutions carry the weight of *that* word's meaning – revolt / revolve (recall Lacan's *Seminar XVII*, a revolution is nothing but a circuit, a *turn*; a *re*-turn to the Master [Lacan 1991/2007]). But too, the voice of Revolution (Jiang Qing commanding the crowd in Curtis' film) moves bodies, even more so than writings in *The Little Red Book*. Missed or not, the voice marks out some-thing, and some-bodies.

Meaning and enjoyment. Bodies that enjoy. Dancing bodies! *It's more than I dare to think about.* That move from thinkable thought – a meaningful signification, marked out in a *little ... red* – to something which evades that: the object-voice. *It's more than I dare to think about.* There's this bit that, to riff off another of Curtis' oeuvre, *traps* us in the voice (Curtis 2011). A loving trap? In *Encore* (1998), Lacan notes that *love* is what motors discourse along (p. 16). Back to that little object-voice of the drive; Dolar notes it 'ties language to the body' (Dolar, 2006, p. 59), not quite neatly; nonetheless it sticks around – *can't get you out of ...*

Curtis drops the 'I' of Kylie's song and the common turn of phrase (what is a pop song, if not a turn on the trite? Enjoyable, yes. Catchy? Of course). The subject falls elsewhere – into the 'my head' of whose body? Toscano (2021), most recently, and my colleagues above, note that Curtis is concerned with 'hyper-individualism' as the opposite of collective sociality. As if that thing which gets into our heads works against the kind of discourse required for building social bonds. To move out of one's head, as the slighted 1960s aristocrat Robin Douglas Hulme, says in *CGYOOMH*, requires the 'detonation' of a 'small bomb' inside oneself. A voice explodes outwards from the individual, destroying a fantasy of rapport (*there is no sexual relation*, after his wife leaves him, Hulme suicides).

Curtis mentions in a *New Yorker* article (Knight 2021), aptly titled "Adam Curtis Explains It All" that now we are in 'a moment'. Such 'hyper-individualism ... is a sort of giant baroque thing, which you meet on Instagram and meet on TikTok and you meet in my films'.

A meeting sounds promising – surely social? It depends on who's speaking at the meeting. I note that some voices don't get much air in the film. We see the back cover of Afeni Shakur's LP of revolutionary poetry, but don't hear her. Does this mean her voice is not *there*? A voice can work outside what is heard. Still, it needs a body – this object-voice.

All these bodies, hyped up, and scrolled out on feeds somewhere – looking for 'their people'. I think of some of the social media I teach to second-year university students: TikTok 'Welcomes' scrollers to 'Cottage-Core TikTok'. Other TikTokkers – these timely time-keepers of the present moment declare: 'You've reached Wellness TikTok'.

My students classify TikToks according to Bill Nichols' modes of documentary – does the voice-over make it expository? Wait, it's reflexive though – those hype'beasts' know what they're doing; carving a 'moment'. Not quite a meeting. Not quite social. In this baroque place which, as Brett points out, Curtis' works through, voices clamour. '*Mood*'. '*All the feels*'. '*Today I'm going to tell you about* …'.

Curtis is not so klutzy in *The New Yorker*:

> The mood my films create—and possibly the reason why people like that mood—is because it somehow feels real, even though … odd. It actually gets at what's going on in people's heads, which is sort of what realism always is.
>
> (Knight 2021)

That peopled head again. The voice which might catch on in the body spills out in to what goes on inside 'people's heads'. Talked about to a shrink? To a planner in gentrifying 1970s Notting Hill? Curtis is not a Lacanian. He may not even quite like psychoanalysis (see his 2002 film, *The Century of the Self*). But he's on to something here about mood and what feels real. '*The real feels*' a TikTokker might say. Someone posts on a Discord server under the chan #new-adam-curtis-chat 'Curtis gives me the mood for truth'. The voice – the object-voice – is, in fact, what opens us on to the only affect (or 'feel') which, according to Lacan, does not lie. That affect is *anxiety* (Lacan 2014 [2004]). Anxiety appears when the caught-ness that little object produces comes to the fore. It's when the signifier fails. And we flail. Not paralysed so much – and here I differ from Brett – but as hyper-motile. But maybe tardive dyskinesia (a common side effect of anxiety medication) is a type of paralysis – so much twitching on the spot. *It's more than I dare to think about …*

'Welcome to Wellness TikTok'.
'Today I'm going to tell you about medically diagnosed anxiety'.

What happens when that voice that glitches, misses, drops in, or out (the unheard Shakur; Kylie; or Zubaydah – the terrorist who can't get the voices of Chris de Burgh and Hollywood films out of his head)? Surely the mood – perhaps a structure of feeling as Brett outlines – of which Curtis accounts is anxiety?

Accounts?

Not quite. Anxiety resists a quick counter-attack through neat countables. Diagnosis? No. Words fail to fix. The object-voice then is not the 'meanwhiles …'; 'those in powers …'; 'and thens …' for which Curtis is famed (cf. Toscano 2021). The object-voice is more Kylie's *la la la la*, or the *blah blah* of Lacan's *la-langue*.

Jiang Qing rouses the crowd.

Perhaps we find this in those un-captioned, un-anchored voices in the film. The anxious mood is when Curtis' orienting voice recedes and the object-voice issues forth from frenzied bodies, unsure of where to place ... what? It's often sudden (a cut?); jarring. The screams of The Mekons 'Where were you?' (1978) over footage of a pigeon-fancier; a go-go dancer; parking couples and children running alongside a car. The question of where the 'you' / Other might be – and that they might be nowhere at all – generates anxiety. If the Other cannot be placed, then where, indeed, are *you*? See too, the sequence with a 1970s woman ventriloquist at a holiday camp. Ventriloquism, by its definition (as 'throwing' the voice from a stiff faced puppeteer to the grotesque, mouth-y marionette) is a neat materialisation of the object-voice. In this short scene, the 'dummy' adding to the confusion of whose voice belongs where, speaks in a male voice, to put the (non-white) other (presumably unwelcome at Butlins and elsewhere in postcolonial Britain) quite clearly in their place: 'I do shows in aid of people like *you*'.

So too, might the sequences with non-English language work as indexes of the anxious 'hyper-individual'. We hear the object-voice in Jiang Qing. As Brett discusses, Curtis renders the Russian cover of 'Let It Be' as *'as it was / it will always be'* losing some of the futuristic oomph of *'budet tak'* / 'it will be thus'. The chaotic gurgles of Soviet prisoners singing *Blatnyak* (Блатняк: prison tunes) on the other hand go un-subtitled: the voice works as generalised, hyped up, pacing, and indicative of the destitution of the prisoner who knows he is an object – powerless against state violence. Maybe though, and this will be where I leave off, the 'As It Was' sub-titling (distanced from the literal translation of *budet tak*) is more telling. For the Anglophone viewer the Beatles tune is familiar, but the words are meaningless. The voice though – a sneer – even without the clearly 'reactionary' subtitles, cracks. In these cracks anxiety seethes; the faces of the lip-synching Russian entertainers loom out – are they, or *we*, caught? If it always was and will always be, then Graeber's maxim, which opens the film; that 'we' can make the world differently – seems perilous, at least in Curtis' understanding. That peopled head – 'I' to 'we' – is not quite so simple. In one of the final episodes we hear that Jiang Qing attempts suicide after her arrest as part of the gang-of-four. 'She bashed her head repeatedly against the prison wall'. Without a voice, the head is the first thing to go, the people dissipate; the prison walls, we are told in the steady narrative from Curtis, 'were made of rubber'. A prophylactic prevention of we-ness cut short; another un-subtitled sequence follows – the 'unit of one' (I?), Qing, screams as she is sentenced. Noiseless to the Anglophone but, there, in that shriek there's an appeal to re-build, re-form the social.

## Discussion and Questions

Clint Burnham (Simon Fraser University): *What is Curtis doing formally? The montage and the edits - the perpetual motion reveal – perhaps reveals Curtis' symptom? But in a post-Baudrillardian sense there's a question of the archive and nostalgia - the simulacrum of nostalgia; the machine; the quality of the colour. I mean, I would become a Maoist - even if I had to wear that sign around my neck - if I could just see those colours - those colours of the 1950s and 1960s, of the films and operas! So two questions: one is the question of the archive in your political reading. And the second is the role of Curtis' formal method in your political reading.*

Brett Nicholls (BN): I've tried to grapple with the formal aspects of what Curtis is trying to do. I think his approach to the archive is kind of encyclopaedic really – he has hard drives full of images which he catalogues. They are in *his* head in some ways - perhaps the title of the film is about Curtis' head! He sees the archive as the means for articulating the present (even though this present, given the complexity of the archive, appears to be overdetermined). The present is, in a sense, continuous with the past since we look to the archive to find out how it all went wrong. It is significant, I think, that he doesn't look to the archive for alternative possibilities. Formally – well the issue has to do with the relationship between the narrator's voice – the patrician narrator as Isabel says – and the way he marshals images and sounds to construct statements and moods in the story. But it always comes across as a little bit haphazard.

Isabel Millar (IM): On the question of the narration of Curtis' voice over the images. I always feel really conflicted when watching his films; because, on the one hand, I feel like I'm experiencing something really radical and subversive, but then I hear this *voice* and it just really annoys me! … There's this particular type of *authority* to everything that he does that doesn't seem to let you make up your own mind – and that's paradoxical because what he's doing with his work is that he's *not* telling you what to think and, yet, his voice is *always* telling you what to think. … Maybe that's my own symptom! But I really think that there is something in his method that is deliberately conflictual and obviously he's very aware of that – that there is some sort of *dislocation* going on between what he *appears* to be doing and how he makes you feel – with the way that he constantly undermines himself through his use of music and his humorous takes and so on. It's interesting because, when you listen to Curtis in his interviews, he's very *humourless* – he doesn't come across as a very ironic man. Listening to him talking to Russell Brand the other day – and Russell was taking the piss out of him … but Adam really just could not *bear* Russell teasing him! Russell asked him why can't you laugh at yourself? And Adam was like: 'well I think you're just using humour as a defence'. Russell said 'No! I use it as an attack'. Curtis felt out of control and said 'well I like to be in control and I don't like this feeling of not being in control'. This is why this figure of the Oxbridge man is so important. That voice – it's pervasive across his work – whether we like it or not – there is that *ideology* behind it – that is very comfortable and secure in this world. So however much he might make us feel as though he is having all these radical opinions, there is this really conservative thread that runs through everything he does. I mean he says it himself – that he's more of a neoconservative or a libertarian. Maybe we are all desperately running around trying to find out what he is!

Rosemary Overell (RO): Yes - and I notice Matiss Groskaufmanis's comment in the chat about it resembling 'the endless social media feed of the 2010s; fragments of infotainment with ambiguous dimensions'. It is almost like the older model of a compilation documentary with all these cut ups but it also resembles the scroll feed – with these images and words disconnected.

Jak Ritger (independent scholar): *I want to ask about this thesis that seems to run throughout Curtis' work – that radical movements that are recuperated through 'culture'. Coming at this as an artist and thinking about the aestheticising of politics – what do the panel think of this – can we use these films in a constructive, material way?*

BN: From the perspective of teaching, I find Curtis' films really useful to introduce the ideas we discuss in the classroom. It gives students a sense that these ideas are out there and not this isolated thing. My favourite Curtis film is *The Century of the Self* – this is the most useful in terms of media and communication because it gives us a critique of advertising and so on. His work gives us a good place to start to raise questions.

Daniel Tutt (DT): This links up to Chiapello and Boltanski's idea of 'the new spirit of capitalism' which is this idea that '68 was appropriated as a cultural icon. I mean Curtis doesn't know this idea but if he did – he'd throw it in his film in a heartbeat! The basic argument is that the slogans on the street of '68 in France were quickly incorporated – into business literature – easily incorporated into the corporate sphere in a seamless fashion. One can recoil from this pessimistic *absence* of a dialectic – that there's no negativity in his films – we need to go back and push through this. We need to see these struggles *not* as immanent. But I think there's a Doomsday, almost quasi theological, pessimism in Curtis *apropos* this shift into neoliberalisation. Here, the 'boomer' status works – that he is late Gen X/Boomer – you see this in *HyperNormalisation* as well – with Jane Fonda's disaffection. Is this something only felt *qua* Boomers? There's all these absent collectivities! Any time Curtis refers to the category of the 'all' – I become very suspicious.

RO: I mean he talks about this – he's aware of his own nostalgia or melancholy – as he is someone born in the early 1950s – and has an ambivalent relation –

DT: – he's from a Trotskyist family! There's something there!

IM: Firstly, it goes without saying that he is unparalleled really – nobody else does what he does! His contribution to bringing critical thought and ideas into public discourse is *essential*. The only gripe is *why isn't there more*? And why isn't there different types of people doing this critique? He does have such an important role – because of this we have to hold him to account. But of course – he can't do all that – it's television as well – we can't expect too much from television.

Eugénie Austin (Lacan Circle of Australia): *I want to go over this viewpoint that takes up Curtis from Lacan. I'm struck by some things ... There's such beauty in Curtis' work – and his ability – as Isabel says – to comment on the popular. He's a communicator.... But could somebody put Curtis together with Seminar XVII, the failure of '68 and the 'soundbyte' that revolutionaries will always revolve back to a 'new master'?*

RO: In a way – I *do* think Curtis *is* showing that very circularity of revolution in the 'modern' era. As Brett, Daniel and Isabel also point out – these revolutions fail again and again. A new master is always installed. This is shown with Madame Mao and the Cultural Revolution as well. But I'm also interested in Daniel's point about Curtis' lack of an account for a revolution which does *not* just loop back on itself?

DT: Like all Lacanians, I've bashed my head against a wall about all the aporias and some of the latent pessimism of *Seminar XVII*. The irony – of course – is that Lacan would get a following from Communists, from Anarchists who were attending his seminars! Even after all of that, it's an ambiguity that remains an ambiguity in Lacanian thought. I don't think Lacan is proposing quite what Curtis is proposing [about power] however. I will say this: there is something about the insights that Lacan gives us about politics and *mastery* that we are still trying to tease out. Let's keep in mind, that the Maoists – who saw the necessity for some kind of master figure – became some of the most important Lacanians, for example Badiou. They've all taken the Maoist theses on politics and extended them far into the 'post-political' situation. I think Badiou is a better thinker on the political than Lacan, *and* he still says he is a committed Lacanian. In Badiou's later work we see some of these reformulated Maoist problematics.

IM: In relation to the point about Lacan as a political thinker – it's always that, even in *Seminar XVII*, he's talking as an *analyst*, not as a philosopher or a political theorist. So when he's talking to the revolutionaries and saying 'you will have a new master', he's trying to bring the hysteric's discourse to the fore. He's saying that 'well you're always going to be stuck here, looking for someone else' and in that gesture of rejection you invoke another master to come in and tell you something else. So, he is always trying to bring in, well the analyst's discourse too – there is always going to be a discursive relationship going on and one has to implicate themselves in it. What I think is a really useful way of thinking about it is 'the analyst being a saint' which he talks about in *Television* and in *Seminar XXIII* on Joyce and the 'saint' or the *sinthome*. The analyst has this position as the 'Saint' – the position in the society that tries to take on everybody else's most disgusting, abject outpourings! They do it by trying to consume their own waste – like the Saints who eat the shit of a leper or bathe in the water of a leper or whatever – this gesture of having to be aware of how much you are invested in your own suffering. This is the *use* value of Lacanian psychoanalysis for politics – it's not about bringing a collective together by using psychoanalysis, but you can individually show people how they are always caught in a discourse and caught in a Symbolic suffering. And, under this banner, they are brought together in this collective form of suffering. In a sense, if you want to be corny about it – at least Curtis can be a *Saint* in this sense – he brings to the fore that we are all implicated in suffering and our own suffering.

Cindy Zeiher (The University of Canterbury): *One point has come up again and again – it seems to be underpinning all four presentations – and that is about the* jouissance *of power as a particular kind of structure that can be taken up, imagined, or enacted. ... I struggle with the compatibility between psychoanalysis and politics – it isn't always in sync. For Lacanians, we always come back to Lacan's great claim that we should pay more attention to being more interpellated into the analyst's discourse, in order to interrogate power as a signifier – which brings about a lot of* jouissance *for us. So, for psychoanalysis the question for me in terms of the viability of psychoanalysis in terms of politics is more about the signifier of 'politics' – of politics for the subject – that the subject takes up. That's what we need to grapple with, and handle – how does this work? Because, we could say that, in the unconscious, there isn't any such thing as power. Power is an imaginary form. We can 'think' politics and 'think' power – but for psychoanalysis, which is trying to put the unconscious to work; to put signifiers to work – it really is tricky to put these two forms – which are quite incompatible together.*

BN: I would think about that through Laclau and Mouffe – their social ontology is centred around the entanglement of politics and subjectivity. Their idea of political agency emerging necessarily through dislocation and rupture is, for me at least, really productive. Laclau and Mouffe see politics not for the subject but as a decision in relation to dislocation. As far as Curtis goes, well clearly, he is not a 'poststructuralist'. He seems to hold to a Weberian sense of politics as ideas implemented by institutions on behalf of the people. Isabel makes the excellent point that Curtis seems to think of ideas in idealist terms as socially undetermined. So it is not clear where ideas come from. At any rate, his work tries to map how democratic political institutions came to abandon ideas and the dire consequences that follow.

DT: I think it's interesting. To bring it back to this question of negativity – which a lot of psychoanalysts and Lacanians still have fidelity to – is a limit point, of a liberal democratic conception of politics. That is, that because we have that understanding of 'subjectivity', the 'unconscious' or – like Cindy said – that category of 'power' is maybe not pessimistically discarded but, in a Lacanian sense, is a site of *impossibility*. We can't really think 'politics' *qua* the Imaginary – there has to be a tethering with the Symbolic – and therefore the identifications which compose political formations reside outside of being, or in civic speech. And this actually leads to misunderstandings from Lacanians *a propos* 'identity politics' – a lot of people construe Lacan as arguing that people work through identifications with, say, the 'empty signifier' to use Laclau and Mouffe's term within the context of speech. A lot of psychoanalytic theories will reduce 'identity politics' to *mere* speech which is why Jacques-Alain Miller's school saw the rise of the Front Nationale as primarily an issue about 'free speech'. I think this is a blessing and a curse for Lacanians – because politics is not reducible to discourse. Lacanians need to step out of that fetish of the public sphere as 'politics'... The crisis of liberalism today – its decadence and its stultification of norms is *readily apparent* – and this is one of Curtis' main themes. So, I pose this as a question: how does psychoanalysis think beyond, or confront, this crisis of liberalism? I'm not sure that discourse is the final end.

Anonymous: *I think there's some merit in not having a discussion of 'theory' and 'activism' as apart. We need to think of them together – because if you're not working with people that are also interested in a similar thing that you're interested in, then nothing good or constructive can come from that. ... I'm curious for the panellists – where do you all stand politically?*

RO: That's a really good point about praxis. We don't want to put forward this idea that 'Theory' – with a capital 'T' – is the inverse of 'politics'. I'm an academic in New Zealand, and I do think what I do is some form of praxis. I would go to a recent article written by Anna Kornbluh which is called 'Extinct Critique' (2020) – she talks about the role of the academic and radical politics in the current university system. She has four norms which she puts at the end. One of them is, of course, *teaching* – to build some sort of consciousness within the students – as Brett mentioned – myself too – Curtis' films can help with that. But also, she points out about organising collectively within your workplace. So – being active in a union is a major factor.

BN: I work at the University of Otago in NZ, and I was Branch President of the Tertiary Education Union there for a while! So I have been actively involved in workplace activism and resisting the neoliberalisation of the university. We've been involved in lots of actions to push back against that. I see that sort of activism as really important – it is defending public education.

RO: And also – going back to that question of public intellectualism – I think we have a role as intellectuals to do something with our work that has a public good. I think Adam Curtis functions as a public intellectual too.

DT: Let me say – firstly – I was critical of Curtis in my talk only because I am amongst friends! I am a big fan of Curtis, and I have taught him a lot too. So, props to what he's doing! I think a follow up question would be about the conditions that enable Curtis to occupy this authoritative voice is an interesting thing. Right now, I teach as an adjunct. But, under these pandemic conditions, I've also opened up a free study group in Lacanian psychoanalysis and Marxism: @torsiongroups on Twitter. We've had seminars with a lot of senior Lacanian and Marxism scholars. So it's been good to think with that. I have an article coming out on the *lumpen-proletariat* in contemporary Marxist thought and I'm continuing to work things thinking about psychoanalysis and politics. I do some film-making myself, for PBS, in order to pay the bills! On activism – well it comes in many forms – art is an incredible vehicle. I would also say the very term 'activist' sometimes participates in that false conflation – that there are 'activists' and then there are 'thinkers'. I think that we need to abandon that. Because, say, tonight – all the thinking that is going on here – people are going to walk away thinking about all these ideas and their own work and research and their own politics too. It's all intertwined.

IM: To your first point about theory and practice...how to disseminate theoretical ideas into popular culture and how do you make a bridge between all of these conversations that we have as academics in all these papers and books we write and all these conferences we go to – what difference does it make in the world? And a lot of the time you feel like it doesn't make any difference really, because all we are doing is having conversations between ourselves and only sometimes there's this green shoot that goes through and pokes out into the world ... These things are really rare and very important, and really wonderful when they happen. I think, more cynically, as an academic (when I had) just finished my PhD and published my first book – (I thought) 'oh isn't it exciting?' – but, at the same time for us in academia, our work is not monetarily valued. We don't get paid for anything that we do, unless we are tenured. We talk at places. We write for journals and magazines. We do reviews. We are constantly working, but we can't support ourselves most of the time, unless we are teaching or administrators in universities. That's terrible! We are supposedly creating and contributing to culture and producing knowledge all the time. It's a really important point about theory and practice because how do we continue to have enthusiasm and care about these things...we have to wonder, how does society value that kind of work? If it's not financially viable it will stop. No-one is going to be able to afford to do a PhD. So, it's not just a problem of academics being in their own little world, talking about theory that nobody else understands – it's literally a problem that, people can't make a living (and that's what they've created) – a world where very few people are able to do this. We need to make sure that people like Adam Curtis keep making films, that people can see all these exciting ideas and wonder what books they should go and read – how do I start thinking? And thinking needs to be something which *everybody does*.

RO: Following Isabel's point: Curtis as a Baudrillardian subject himself ... interesting!

BN: I find myself surrounded by Lacanians, which is fine but not really my viewpoint, so I am happy to think about Curtis in relation to Baudrillard (which I admit does bear some affinity to Lacan). I would hazard that in this space, we are all Baudrillardian subjects! There is a sense, though, and here we might draw upon Baudrillard's insights to think about Curtis' paralysis conclusion, that it is all a bit too neat. Isabel points out that Curtis, like Baudrillard's Foucault, is 'talking about a world that is already dead'. In our techno-capitalist world, this is, of course, unavoidable. The real (in

Baudrillard's sense) died a long time ago and carried on only through Zombie-like energy. The death of the real is why critique, speaking truth to power, is pointless and fatal theory vital, and this is why, perhaps, social reality today feels strange. From this viewpoint, however, Curtis is merely working to keep the corpse of the social world alive. There is satisfaction, even solace in this endeavour, this *object*-lesson as Rosie tells us, and for audiences too. As Baudrillard declares, the world is, in fact, a radical and unbearable illusion that we strive to make 'exist and signify at all costs' (2008, 17). Paradoxically, the global North finds solace in the announcement that the world is strange and broken; at least there is a real world, and, even if 'we' are politically paralysed, at least there is something rather than nothing!

Olivier Jutel (The University of Otago): *So is Oxbridge Highbrow conspiracism the ultimate post-politics?*

BN: I don't think Curtis leads to an endorsement of a post-political position, though the point about Oxbridge privilege is well made. I am interested in the question of conspiracism though. You could say on the surface he is arguing the social is overdetermined, though his conclusion – complete political paralysis – would not make much sense with this view. He obviously doesn't develop how his complex histories might lead to more complexity in political formations, and, along with Marxian takes on his films, we would have to note that he doesn't interrogate how paralysis might serve the interests of the ruling classes. He prefers to think of paralysis as a kind of vacuum that is up for grabs. From the Oxbridge viewpoint, maybe the contemporary world looks terrifying. This is surely a drawback. Does this make him a conspiracy theorist or quasi-conspiracist as Daniel puts it? The key question is, I think, is Curtis joining the historical dots, no matter how disparate, in such a way that they end up forming a whole as an epiphenomenon of a sinister underlying cause. This is what conspiracy theorists do with underlying causes such as alien lizards, Jewish bankers, and so on. I would say Curtis doesn't really join the dots; this is why his films are confusing. Audiences don't seem to come away from Curtis thinking it all makes sense. This lack of sense sharply contrasts with conspiracy theory. What I think he is trying to point to is what results from these disparate historical vectors not what causes them. The problem for Curtis, therefore, is that his rather simple conclusion – this all leads to political paralysis – is undermined by his overdetermining histories. This simple conclusion, I would add, tells us as much about the BBC and its documentary tradition as it does about Curtis, as Isabel points out. It is also worth noting that if conspiracism is to emerge, for Curtis, it happens in the context of this paralysis. His take is at odds with figures such as Fred Jameson, who see conspiracy as a kind of poor person's cognitive mapping of the causal underside of the social (1988). Curtis' view, I think, ends up more aligned with Baudrillard's view of the social as an implosive integral reality (but maybe this would be to distort Baudrillard's work).

## References

Baudrillard, Jean. 2007. *Forget Foucault*. Translated by Phil Bietchman, Nicole Dufresne, Lee Hildreth and Mike Polizzotti. Cambridge, MA: MIT Press.

Baudrillard, Jean. 2008. *The Perfect Crime*. London: Verso.

The Beatles. 1970. *Let It Be*. Long Playing Record. London: Apple Records.

Brooker, Charlie. 2009. Adam Curtis – Oh Dearism. *YouTube*, April 14. Available at: https://www.youtube.com/watch?v=8moePxHpvok (Accessed 9 April 2021).

Chion, Michel. 1982. *The Voice in Cinema*. Translated by Claudia Gorbman. New York: Columbia University Press.

Curtis, Adam. 2002. *The Century of the Self*. London: BBC Television.

Curtis, Adam. 2011. *The Trap: What Happened to Our Dream of Freedom*. London: BBC Television.

Curtis, Adam. 2016. *HyperNormalization*. London: BBC Television.

Curtis, Adam. 2021. *Can't Get You Out Of My Head: An Emotional History of the Modern World*. London: BBC Television.

Deleuze, Gilles. 1992. Postscript on the Societies of Control. *October* 59 (Winter): pp. 3–7.

Dolar, Mladen. 2006. *A Voice and Nothing More*. Cambridge, MA: MIT Press.

Hatherley, Owen. 2017. And then the Strangest Thing Happened. *n +1*, 6 March. Available at: https://nplusonemag.com/online-only/online-only/and-then-the-strangest-thing-happened/ (Accessed 9 April 2021).

Hofstader, Richard. 1965. *The Paranoid Style in American Politics, and other Essays*. New York: Knopf.

Jameson, Fredric. 1988. Cognitive Mapping. In *Marxism and the Interpretation of Culture*, edited by Cary Nelson and Lawrence Grossberg, pp. 347–357. London: Macmillan.

Knight, Sam. 2021. Adam Curtis Explains It All. *The New Yorker*, 28 January. Available at: https://www.newyorker.com/news/letter-from-the-uk/adam-curtis-explains-it-all (Accessed 9 April 2021).

Kornbluh, Anna. 2020. Extinct Critique. *South Atlantic Quarterly*, 119 (4): pp. 767–777.

Lacan, Jacques. 2014 (2004). *Seminar X: Anxiety (1962–1963)*. Translated by Adrian Price. Cambridge: Polity.

Lacan, Jacques. 2007 (1991). *Seminar XVII: The Other Side of Psychoanalysis (1969–1970)*. Translated by Russell Grigg. New York: W.W. Norton.

Lacan, Jacques. 1998. *Seminar XX: On Feminine Sexuality, The Limits of Love and Knowledge (Encore 1972–1973)*. Translated by Bruce Fink. New York: W.W. Norton.

MacDonald, Michael (Ed.). Nd. *Adam Curtis Can't get you out of my head soundtrack*. [Spotify playlist]. Available at: https://open.spotify.com/playlist/6PT3N1MFBxAflKAxq1rFFA (Accessed 20 April 2021).

Media, Film and Communications Programme. 2021. CAN'T GET YOU OUT OF MY HEAD: Power and Politics & the Films of Adam Curtis. Otago University Webpage, 19 April. Available at: https://www.otago.ac.nz/cs/groups/public/@mfco/documents/webcontent/otago826777.mp4 (Accessed 23 April 2021).

Minogue, Kylie. 2002. *Fever*. London: Parlophone.

Nichols, Bill. 2001. *Introduction to Documentary*. Bloomington: Indiana University Press.

Nicholls, Brett. 2017. Adam Curtis's compelling logic: the tortuous corridor to the hypernormal. *Borderlands e-journal*, 16 (1): pp. 1–24.

Reid, Tiana. 2019. In Motion. *The New Inquiry*, May 17. Available at: https://thenewinquiry.com/in-motion/ (Accessed 9 April 2021).

Solzhenitsyn, Aleksandr Isaevich. (1974). *The Gulag Archipelago 1918–1956: An Experiment in Literary Investigation.* New York: Harper & Row.

Sugarman, Jacob. 2021. Adam Curtis Wants You To Imagine Another World. *In These Times*, 25 February. Available at: https://inthesetimes.com/article/adam-curtis-cant-get-you-out-of-my-head-bbc-stalker-the-zone (Accessed: 9 April 2021).

The Mekons. 1978. *Where Were You / I'll Have To Dance Then (On My Own)*. Fast Product (Label). 45 RPM 7" single.

Toscano, Alberto. 2021. Dreamworlds of Catastrophe. *Sidecar / New Left Review*, March 31. Available at: https://newleftreview.org/sidecar/posts/dreamworlds-of-catastrophe (Accessed 9 April 2021).

Williams, Raymond. 1972 (1961). *The Long Revolution*. London: Penguin / Pelican.

Woodhams, Ben. 2018. The Loving Trap. *YouTube*, July 26. Available at: https://www.youtube.com/watch?v=x1bX3F7uTrg (Accessed 9 April 2021).

# Afterword

## *Olga Cox Cameron*

Well, as you will have seen if you have read this far, the Irish Psychoanalytic Film Festival was not defeated by the year the cinemas closed. This very wide-ranging collection of papers explores the move from big to small screen, from communal to solitary enjoyment; by no means an unproblematic move, marked as it was by a balking, a pent-upness.[1] Crisis calls for connectedness, for some kind of meaningful action. And we were instead sent home, given coverings with which to protect our own bodies, mandated by the Other to cultivate avoidance, passivity and paranoia. As Don Kunze puts it in his chapter, we contract when we retreat, and Sarah Meehan O'Callaghan in her piece explores this weird pent-upness in cogent detail.

So what was lost, and what if anything was gained?

What was lost was the event.

What does an actual festival do? Of its nature, it is a fragile exercise in connectedness. In an era when perhaps more than ever we have everything to fear from group think, the coming together to celebrate, in its very transience, is important, punctuating as it does the usual rivalries and vague hostilities that fuel the politics of psychoanalysis. From its inception, the festival was the only psychoanalytic event to be co-hosted by the two main psychoanalytic associations in Ireland, the IFPP and APPI, as well as being open to the public and to all other forms of psychotherapy. In re-reading Freud's "Group Psychology" I was interested in a passing footnote commenting on the communal meal as the soldering of a group, and thought of the wonderful suppers largely produced by Liz Monahan on the first night, and by Gerry Murphy's hospitable welcome in DCU in recent years. This was not at all random. Really good food, plentiful wine and a lively buzz were deemed very important components in making a festival.

In writing about collectivity as he did in "Group Psychology," Freud focused on the role of the leader and perhaps did not sufficiently think about the other things at work, including the simple need for group experience at times of major import. Our small screens have recently inducted us into striking instances of this. Crowds gathered spontaneously at Buckingham Palace on the night of the death of Queen Elizabeth, and on daily news bulletins at present we see the women of Iran taking to the streets to publicly cut their hair. We also of course see alarming confirmations of Freud's insight into the brutalising power of leaders stirring up crowds but this is only one instance of collectivity. In his 2016 novel *The Noise of Time*, based on the life of Shostakovich, Julian Barnes refers to an event in Stalinist Russia where the poet Akhmatova came on stage and the entire audience rose instinctively to applaud her, causing Stalin to demand furiously "Who organised the standing up?" (Barnes, 2016, p. 88). Obviously our film festival is not in the same ballpark as this unthought-out move from individual terror into collective courage. But something happens in severality. Barnes' novel is about the catastrophic fall-out for the individual who cannot escape self-betrayal during a reign of terror when; "there were only two types of composer; those who were alive and frightened and those who were dead" (p. 48). And yet as Barnes tells it, the work of art exerts a pull on the collective, not available to the individual. In another anecdote recounted in the same novel;

> when Pasternak who had translated Shakespeare's sonnets, read Sonnet in public, the audience would wait keenly through the first 8 lines, eager for the ninth; And art made tongue-tied by authority. At which point they would join in – some under their breath, some whisperingly, the boldest among them fortissimo, but all giving the lie to that line, all refusing to be tongue-tied.
>
> (p. 87)

It is noteworthy that both these instances of spontaneous collective expression occur in the domain of art, and not politics per se.

So what happens when we are together? Psychoanalysis rightly focusses on the singular, but attending a psychoanalytic film festival involves severality. Coming together to experience an artwork is a particularly interesting venture. We consent to the possibility of being changed by something and this consent is collective. Lacan has written very variously on the relations between psychoanalysis and art, on the modalities by which the unconscious can be caught in the artwork. What he says in Seminar VI – Desire and its Interpretation - is I think particularly interesting in the present context because he is talking about the theatre and therefore something closer to the communal experience of the big screen. The effective work of art he says; "ends up by entering, strictly speaking into our subjectivity and psychology" (Lacan, 2019, p. 248). Lacan is trenchant here; "I maintain, and I will unambiguously maintain - and I believe that I am following in Freud's footsteps, that poetic creations generate psychological creations more than they reflect them." In the Preface to this collection of papers, Ian Parker makes the same point more elegantly when he suggests that the forms of subjectivity that film rolls in front of our eyes quickly spool behind them, inside us, becoming part of our own subjectivity. The papers you have read have very cogently and at times very entertainingly explored the effects of the privatised version of this experience. Now we need to ask what will happen when the festival starts up again? Although not all the films shown in a festival are great art works, there is an immersion in unconscious desire and unconscious fantasy provoked by the unspooling of story in the collective gaze which is different to the singular event. What Lacan says of *Hamlet* can be said of any great film; "it is a composition or structure in which desire can take its place" (Lacan, op.cit., p. 276). In front of the big screen, we are severally engaged in what is for each of us a singular experience since as Lacan also says in Seminar VI, like the actors, we the spectators are "the ones that furnish the material that constitutes our relation to the unconscious …with our imaginary" (ibid.). If this is happening to everyone, or at least to a fair number of people in the audience, is there a discernible fall-out?

The levels at which this immersion in unconscious fantasy occur are of course very variable;

> it is with our own bodily members that we create the alphabet of the discourse that is unconscious – we each do so in different ways, for although we are all caught up in the unconscious, we do not all use the same elements.
>
> (Lacan, ibid.)

The format of the festival gives access to these very varied levels. It also brings together two very different types of gaze which ordinarily are separate.

Unlike a book club where everyone reads the book in private, then comes together to discuss it, thus drawing a strong dividing line between two moments in the experience of an art work, the festival lay-out brings these two moments into the same time zone.

Several of the papers you have read in this volume have spoken of the gaze as o-object. As we know from Lacan's repeated insistence throughout the seminars, the occlusion of this o-object is the condition for the subject to have access to ordinary reality. Lacan says of this o-object that it is "being insofar as it is essentially missing from the text of the world, that which must be renounced in order that the world as world should be delivered to us" (Lacan, 1961–1962, p. 349) If its occultation is what gives us our world when that occultation fails for whatever reason, our foothold in reality also fails, the world as we know it founders; "the emergence of the object of desire…in the phantasy, is correlative to a sort of vanishing, fading of the symbolic" (ibid., p. 252), of the normal supports which maintain self and world in position. The painter Bracha Ettinger expresses this important observation clearly; it is as if the subject and this o-object are like the front and back of the same piece of fabric, the recto and verso of the same sheet of paper. "When the subject appears (as in everyday life) the o-object disappears, and when the o-object finds a way to penetrate to the other side…signifying meaning (symbolic and imaginary, exchangeable through discourse) disappears and goes into hiding" (Ettinger, 2006, p. 41).

Lacan several times suggests that the hit of great art is one of the places where this eruption can be experienced.

If this is true, if the work of art is one of the places where the o-object finds a way to "appear," displacing the big Other and causing a temporary fade out of the subject, what does it mean for this event to be experienced collectively? And what happens when this moment is cut short or encroached on by the fact that a discussion of the film just viewed is immediately embarked on? What occurs then is the adjacency of two quite distinct types of gaze, the gaze as o-object, in which the subject is undone, and the discerning critical gaze which recuperates this object in an imaginary way, through domination and control. Of course most films do not elicit this response, so the adjacency of these two different types of gaze is rare. Nonetheless, it does on occasion occur. And although the gaze as o-object may never be entirely amenable to the appropriative gestures of commentary or criticism, paradoxically its effects are frequently mediated precisely through these appropriative gestures of attempted mastery. So when this adjacency does occur it is not at all without interest. Once the artwork is there as Bracha Ettinger writes,

> it casts some of its shadow on the cultural field, entices it, impels it to expand its frontiers and to absorb some of its traces. It even gives rise to concepts, and once you turn back to the artwork with the concepts aroused by it, it further transforms and works to seduce you from another site.
>
> (op.cit., p. 118)

This may describe what we attempt to do in the festival, knowing that we juggle with certain impossibilities, in particular the private and incommunicable nature of the o-object which in this instance makes itself felt in severality.

In severality and by way of the imaginary.

A huge question for those of us in love with film concerns the role of this imaginary with respect to the o-object which is so central to (Lacanian) psychoanalytic thinking. This question can of course be asked while communing alone with the small screen, but is perhaps more fun in a festival setting.

The later Lacan, in search of a writing capable of indicating the contours of the o-object, expressly favoured mathematics or topology, in order "to rip us away from the imaginary" (1998, p. 43) but years earlier, in his ninth seminar - Identification - he tells us; "there is at the heart of the o object this central point, this whirlwind point through which the object emerges in the beyond of the imaginary knot" (Lacan, 1961–1962, pp. 10–11). Like *Finnegans Wake* Lacan's bulky oeuvre benefits from a reading that is not sequential. The great middle seminars in particular, with theatrical spectacle at their centre, open up very interesting questions about the play of the imaginary as it unspools before us in cinematic performance. And the relation between the specular and the o-object was in fact the central focus of his first incursions into topology; "I(o) and o, their difference, their complementarity, and the mask that one constitutes for the other, this is where I have led you this year." he says at the end of Identification, (op.cit. p. 353) explicitly asking if there a way of accessing the o-object other than via I(o), or if this detour is "the only road that is open to us to discover the incidence of o, one where we first of all encounter the mark of the occultation of the big Other?" (ibid., p. 350).

At the high point of certain dramas, Lacan tells us in his seventh seminar *The Ethics of Psychoanalysis*, we are purged of everything that is of the order of the imaginary. And we are purged of it through the intervention of one image among others (Lacan, 1992, p. 248). Something in us is broken open – a beyond of the imaginary – but it is by way of the imaginary, a particular type of representation, that this is achieved.

To live that moment in the company of each other is not a neutral event. Terry Eagleton captures something of its effect when he describes; it as "a meeting on the ground of what excludes both self and other, of what disrupts our imaginary identities from within while being at the same time, the very matrix of them." And Eagleton very memorably makes the point with which I would like to conclude:

> It is this inhospitable terrain, this kingdom whose citizens share only the fact that they are lost to themselves, which we hold most deeply in common, not a mutual exchange of egos. Certain great works of art can achieve this transformation and disclose this truth.
> (Eagleton, 2003, p. 165)

Time to meet again in festival mode!

## Note

1 I am aware that in what follows I am bypassing the thought-provoking discussions about small screen analysis. The daughter of W.B. Yeats recounts, that when listening to his first radio in 1936, the poet constantly interrupted politely with "I beg your pardon." This exactly encapsulates the inertias of the imaginary-symbolic world of the older analyst – more potent than ideology!

## References

Barnes, J. (2016). *The Noise of Time*. London: Penguin.
Eagleton, T. (2003). *Sweet Violence*. Oxford: Blackwell.
Ettinger, B. (2006). *The Matrixial Borderspace*. Minneapolis: University of Minneapolis Press.
Lacan, J. (2019). *Desire and its Interpretation. The Seminar of Jacques Lacan. Book VI*. Ed. J.-A. Miller. Trans. B. Fink. Cambridge: Polity Press.

Lacan, J. (1992). *The Ethics of Psychoanalysis. 1959–1960. The Seminar of Jacques Lacan. Book VII*. Ed. J.-A. Miller. Trans. D. Porter. London: Routledge.

Lacan, J. (1961–1962). *Seminar IX. Identification*. Trans. C. Gallagher. St. Vincent's University Hospital, Dublin (www.lacaninireland.com).

Lacan, J. (1998). *On Femine Sexuality, The Limits of Love and Knowledge, 1972–1973. Encore. The Seminar of Jacques Lacan. Book XX*. Ed. J.-A. Miller. Trans. B. Fink. New York: W.W. Norton.

# Index

addiction 34–5, 42n10, 43n14, 65, 74, 133–4, 142, 144
Adorno 95–6, 101–3, 107–8, 110
AI/artificial intelligence 8, 113, 115–7, 119, 120–2, 124–9, 170
alethosphere 6, 13, 15, 24n13, 134
algorithm 3, 38, 40, 44n21, 174
anxiety 4, 7, 9, 11–12, 23–5, 29–30, 42, 44n19, 47, 49, 50–52, 55–61, 83, 105, 120, 127, 133–4, 144, 150, 153–4, 160, 157, 159–160, 179–180
artifice 6, 27, 96, 98, 100, 151
artworks 95, 101–2, 106, 108

Baudrillard, J. 164, 168, 174, 176, 181, 186–8
*Black Mirror* 5, 33; *See also* Brooker, C.
Borromean Knot 136, 143
Brexit, 173
Brooker, C. 5, 48, 165

*camera obscura* 8, 96, 107–8, 110–11
capitalism/ist 22, 28, 30, 66, 85, 158, 165, 173, 182, 186
Cartesian cogito 20–1
castration 4, 48, 54, 58, 75, 89, 139
chatbots 8, 112–5, 118- 120, 124–5, 127–8, 129n6; *See also* Sexbot
climate 9, 170–1
*clinamen* 12, 14, 17, 23, 24n12–13
CMA (Computer Mediated Analysis) 9, 150, 153
conspiracy 47, 59–60, 164, 187
contagion 6–7, 11, 29, 34, 44, as Film 52, 61
Corbyn, J. 167, 173
COVID-19 1, 5–7, 11, 28–32, 34, 37–41, 49–50, 78, 105, 112, 126, 150, 163–4

crisis 7, 9, 29–30, 47–9, 52, 60, 61n1, 185, 190
cyborg 133, 135

*das Ding* 144
depression 30, 42n8, 44n19, 48, 115, 120, 127, 133, 156, 159
desire (of the Other) 51, 57, 84
documentary 1, 48, 163–4, 168–9, 177, 179, 182, 187

srives (the) 46–7, 51–2, 56, 124, 156
supes 13–14, 20, 23n8

eating disorders 47, 50
ego-ideal 36, 156
embodiment 30, 58, 67, 70, 143–4
Ernst J. 12, 20–1; *See also* Uncanny (the)

Fink, B. 122, 156–160
Foucault, M. 21, 164, 168, 186
free association 145, 152, 156–8, 160
Freud Museum 152
Freud, S.: *Screen Memories* 1; *A Psycho-Analytical Dialogue: The Letters of Sigmund Freud and Karl Abraham* 151; *Beyond The Pleasure Principle* 49; *Civilisation and Its Discontents* 59, 65; *Group Psychology* 190; *Instincts and their Vicissitudes* 53–5, 61n5; "Parapraxes". *Introductory Lectures on Psycho-Analysis* 150; Introductory Lectures on Psycho-Analysis (Part III) 106; "Letter 52". *The Origins of Psychoanalysis: Letters to Wilhelm Fliess, drafts and notes,* 139; *On Beginning the Treatment (Further*

*Recommendations on the Technique of Psycho-Analysis)* 158; *Project for a Scientific Psychology* 22, 61n2; *Recommendations to Physicians Practising Psycho-Analysis* 156, 157; *Zur Psychopathologie des Alltagslebens* 24n15
fundamental fantasy 40, 56

gadgets 13, 41n2, 132, 134, 140
gaze (the) 3, 7, 36, 40, 47, 51, 54–8, 95, 98, 100–1, 107, 110, 132, 137, 153–5, 158, 192–3

Harold B. 6, 12,
Hitchcock, A. 83
Holbein, H. 54, 56

identification 36–7, 52, 73, 82–3, 120–1, 134, 136–8, 141, 155, 184–5; as *Seminar IX,* 29, 193, 194
identity politics 167, 184–5
ideology 170–1, 173, 181, 194n1
intimacy 7, 27, 40, 65, 79, 80, 84–5, 92, 127, 159
invocatory drive 57, 139, 156
isolation 9, 12, 29, 38, 44n19, 47–8, 51–2, 66, 73, 80, 142–4, 163

jouissance 3, 8, 9, 11, 15, 27, 35, 41n2, 43n14, 43n15, 43n19, 47, 50–2, 58–61, 67–9, 73, 76, 77, 86, 89, 92, 132–5, 139–141, 143, 146, 147, 157–8, 184

Kant 22
katagraph 18–20

Lacan, J.: *Seminar I – Freud's Papers on Technique* 32, 44, 119, 130; *Seminar III - The Psychoses* 136, 147; *Seminar IV– The Object Relation* 147; *Seminar V– Formations of the Unconscious* 25n23, 26; *Seminar VI– Desire and its Interpretation* 55, 62, 191–2, 194, 195; *Seminar VII – The Ethics of Psychoanalysis* 147, 194; *Seminar IX – Identification* 2, 19, 26, 193–5; *Seminar X - Anxiety* 55, 62, 188; *Seminar XI - The Four Fundamental Concepts of Psychoanalysis* 10, 44, 47, 51, 53–4, 57, 62, 84, 98, 147; *Seminar XIV - The Logic of Phantasy* 20, 24n13, 24n14, 118, 130; *Seminar XVII - The Other Side of Psychoanalysis* 10, 92, 133, 178, 183, 188; *Seminar XIX - ...Ou Pire* 136, 147; *Seminar XX - Encore On Feminine Sexuality, The Limits of Love and Knowledge* 88, 188, 195; *Seminar XXI - Les non-dupes errant* 23n8, 136, 147; *Seminar XXII - RSI* 144; *Seminar XXIII - le Sinthome* 183; *Television, A Challenge to the Psychoanalytic Establishment* 149–50, 153–4, 158, 161
Lalangue 133, 139–141
Lang, Fritz 96, 108–9
lathouse 13–14, 74, 132–5, 138–142, 144–5; *See also* gadgets
lockdown 5, 7, 9–10, 29–30, 40, 50, 59–60, 61n4, 62, 63, 85, 133, 158–9, 161

Marxist 132, 166, 174, 185
McGowan, Todd 3, 10, 55–6, 59
mental health 34, 38, 42n7, 42n8, 43n12, 112, 126–8, 128n3, 129, 130, 158
Merleau-Ponty 57, 62, 147
Mirror Stage 23n2, 65, 137–9, 146,
myth 64, 66, 70, 72–3, 75–6, 96, 161, 166

name of the father 20, 134, 142–3
narcissism 58, 66, 75, 135, 138
neoliberal 69, 160, 168,
neuro psychoanalysis 143
neurosis 16, 23n6, 24n11, 134, 148, 150, 155
non-relation 89, 141–2
*Normal People* 5, 7, 9, 10, 40, 78–89, 92–4, 119, 158–9, 161n1, 162

object a 3, 53–5, 56, 58, 61, 134–5, 139, 145, 153–4, 168 *see also objet a,* 35, 40, 58, 107, 177
Odysseus 8, 70–72, 74, 96–101, 104, 106–7, 109–110
Owens 3, 8, 10, 41, 143, 146, 147, 161n1, 161

paranoia 9, 47, 58–60, 62, 145, 170, 171, 190
Parker 27–8, 32, 45, 152, 161, 191
*parlêtre* 139, 141
passivity 7, 46–9, 51–6, 58–61, 156, 176, 190
phone analysis 156

plague 6–7, 21–2, 164
politics 9, 65, 163–5, 167–8, 176–7, 182–7, 190–1
pornography 7–8, 78, 80–2, 84–6, 88, 93, 94, 140, 142
posthuman 133, 141, 146–7
prohibition 7–8, 78, 88, 93, 176
projection 60, 66
psychology 22, 34, 42, 126, 130, 148, 166, 190–1
psychosis 16, 23n6, 134, 144, 147, 155
public health 4, 9, 29, 34, 38, 42n8, 42n9, 46, 48, 50, 60

real, the xviii, xix, 2, 14, 18, 23n5, 41, 44n21, 47, 49, 50–1, 56, 58, 62, 63, 65, 68, 70, 76, 77, 82, 89, 95, 99–101, 108–110, 111, 116, 119, 124, 134–6, 139, 141–2, 144–5, 152–5, 157, 186–7
representation 6, 19, 52, 76, 78, 81, 85, 100, 102, 110, 119, 136–7, 140, 150–3, 160, 194

*The Seminars, see* Lacan, J.
scopic drive 53, 137, 168, 177
scopophilia 51, 53
scoptophilic drive 52, 54
*Screen Memories* 1, 10; *see also* Freud, S.
*Secrets of a Soul* 151, 162
sexbot 135
sexual relation, as impossible (Lacan) 78, 89, 142, 178
simulacrum 1, 181
*Sinthome* 141, 183
social bond 3, 6, 8–9, 31, 37, 43n15, 142–3, 166
social distancing 11, 38, 43n19, 48, 86, 88, 94, 133

speaking being 8, 136,
stain 33, 41, 153, 157, 167, see gaze
substance abuse 34–5; *see* addiction
superego 48, 59–60, 156, 176
surveillance 21, 65, 144–5

*Television* 9, 149, 183; *see* Lacan, J.

*The Four Fundamental Concepts of Psychoanalysis* 53; *see* Lacan, J.

*The Odyssey* 70, 106, 109, 111

*The Truman Show* 14–15, 17–19, 21–2, 24n18, 26
TikTok 29, 178–9
topology 6, 24n18, 28, 193–4
torus 12, 16–17, 19, 21, 23n5, 24n13, 25n20,
transference xviii, 4, 8–9, 92, 113, 116–25, 128, 130, 131, 150, 153, 157–60
trauma 2, 47, 49–51, 54, 56, 62, 67, 91, 148, 156
Trump 37, 48, 50, 173
*tuché* 99, 101–2, 108, 110, 154
Twitter 42n8, 70–1, 102, 159, 164, 185

unary trait, 17, 24n17, 25n18, 136
uncanny (the) 12, 26; *see also* Freud, S.

virtual reality 1, 22, 65–6, 69, 71, 106
visual field 51–6, 58, 151, 155, 157
voice (the), 12, 65, 69, 76, 145, 153–5, 157–8, 177–80

Žižek, Slavoj 2, 4, 10, 22, 26, 27–33, 36–8, 41n3, 45, 48–9, 63, 66, 77, 80–3, 86–8, 94, 109, 111, 146, 158, 161

Printed in the United States
by Baker & Taylor Publisher Services